The Horse-head Fiddle and the Cosmopolitan Reimagination of Tradition in Mongolia

Current Research in Ethnomusicology

JENNIFER C. POST, *General Editor*

**Newly Composed Folk Music
of Yugoslavia**
Ljerka V. Rasmussen

Of Mermaids and Rock Singers
Placing the Self and Constructing
the Nation through Belarusan
Contemporary Music
Maria Paula Survilla

"Maracatu Atômico"
Tradition, Modernity, and
Postmodernity in the Mangue
Movement of Recife, Brazil
Philip Galinsky

Songs and Gifts at the Frontier
Person and Exchange in the Agusan
Manobo Possession Ritual, Philippines
Jose Buenconsejo

**Balinese Discourses on Music
and Modernization**
Village Voices and Urban Views
Brita Renée Heimarck

Song from the Land of Fire
Continuity and Change in
Azerbaijan Mugham
Inna Naroditskaya

The Cantaoras
Music, Gender, and Identity in
Flamenco Song
Loren Chuse

Hanyang Kut
Korean Shaman Ritual Music
from Seoul
Maria K. Seo

Shaped by Japanese Music
Kikuoka Hiroaki and *Nagauta
Shamisen* in Tokyo
Jay Davis Keister

The Gypsy Caravan
From Real Roma to Imaginary
Gypsies in Western Music and Film
David Malvinni

Baakisimba
Gender in the Music and Dance
of the Baganda People of Uganda
Sylvia A. Nannyonga-Tamusuza

**The Horse-head Fiddle and the
Cosmopolitan Reimagination of
Tradition in Mongolia**
Peter K. Marsh

The Horse-head Fiddle and the Cosmopolitan Reimagination of Tradition in Mongolia

Peter K. Marsh

Routledge
Taylor & Francis Group
New York   London

First published 2009
by Routledge
270 Madison Ave, New York, NY 10016

Simultaneously published in the UK
by Routledge
2 Park Square, Milton Park, Abingdon, Oxon OX14 4RN

Routledge is an imprint of the Taylor & Francis Group, an informa business

Library of Congress Cataloging in Publication Data
Marsh, Peter K.
    The horse-head fiddle and the cosmopolitan reimagination of tradition of Mongolia /
by Peter K. Marsh.
        p. cm. -- (Current research in ethnomusicology ; v. 12)
    Includes bibliographical references and index.
    ISBN 978-0-415-97156-0
    1. Music—Mongolia—20th century—History and criticism.   2. Morin huur.
3. Cosmopolitanism—Mongolia.   4. Nationalism in music.   I. Title.
    ML345.M655M37 2009
    780.51'70904—dc22
    2008019941

ISBN10: 0-415-97156-X (hbk)
ISBN10: 0-203-00551-1 (ebk)

ISBN13: 978-0-415-97156-0 (hbk)
ISBN13: 978-0-203-00551-4 (ebk)

Contents

List of Figures   vii
Preface   ix

    Introduction   1

1 Two-Stringed Fiddle Traditions in Pre-Revolutionary
    Mongolian Society   16

2 Building a National Music Culture   47

3 Soviet Modernism and Cosmopolitan Nationalism   73

4 N. Jantsannorow and the Reshaping
    of Mongolian Musical Nationalism   100

5 The Folk "Revival" and the Reimagination
    of the Horse-head Fiddle   121

6 The Persistence of Alternative Music Histories   146

List of Interviews   159
Notes   161
Bibliography   165
Index   173

Figures

1   Map of Mongolia.   xi

2   Fiddles collected by Haslund-Christensen.   27
    a. *khiil khuur* from the Chakar Mongols;
    b. *khiil khuur* from the Manchu Mongols;
    c. *dörwen-chikhe khuur* from the Chakar Mongols;
    d. *khiil khuur* from the Zakhchin Mongols.

3   A Chakar Mongol plays a piece about horses to his horse on
    a *khiil khuur*.   39

4   Amateur performers outside of a rural cultural center.   49

5   Teachers and pupils at the Music & Dance School in
    Ulaanbaatar.   55

6   Jamyan in his office in the Music & Dance College,
    Ulaanbaatar, teaching a lesson.   56

7   The State Academic Theater (formerly the D. Natsagdorj
    State Music & Drama Theater), Ulaanbaatar.   58

8   The Great Ensemble, part of the State Folksong & Dance
    Ensemble. Notice the monastic instruments, such as the *ikh
    büree* (great horn) and *khengereg*, in the rear of the ensemble.   59

9   An instrumental "Quintet" of national musical instruments.   60

10 Dates of premieres of Russian and European operas and
    dance performances in the State Opera and Dance Theater
    (1957–1977).   61

11 Soviet violinmaker Denis Yarovoi teaching his Mongolian
    pupils about the construction of a European violin.   67

12   The front cover to *Ulaan-baataryn Tukhai Duu (Val's)*, by
     S. Gonchigsümlaa (1961).   70

13   The front cover of G. Jamyan's *Atryn öglöö*.   71

14   "Brothers Born from the Breast of Lenin."   76

15   The meeting of the Mongolian and Soviet peoples on Red
     Square, Moscow.   77

16   Inner Mongolian fiddle player Chi. Bulag with an unnamed
     accompanist during a performance at the Horse-head Fiddle
     Naadam, Ulaanbaatar 1989.   116

17   An "orchestra" of horse-head fiddles during the Horse-head
     Fiddle Naadam.   118

18   "*Öwgön khuurch*" (The Old Fiddle Player, 1963) by
     Ü. Yadamsüren.   139

19   G. Jamyan, Ts. Tserendorj and other horse-head fiddle
     players conveying the *Töriin khan khuur*, outside the
     Government Palace in Ulaanbaatar.   141

Preface

Dressed in costumes meant to invoke thirteenth century Mongol soldier uniforms, members of the State Horse-head Fiddle Ensemble, in performances in the concert halls in the Mongolian capital of Ulaanbaatar, perform modern national music that would not sound out of place on the great concert halls of New York City, London, or Tokyo. In terms of the quality of the music and the performers, this ensemble has clearly embraced and mastered the styles of Western-oriented classical music while at the same time appearing and sounding distinctly Mongolian. Such is the mix of "tradition" and "modernity" or the "national" and "international" that one finds upon experiencing Mongolia's contemporary national music. And it is this unique conception of modern culture—simultaneously claiming to be of the ancient Mongolian past and the modern international present—that makes contemporary Mongolian music so fascinating.

A pervasive image of Mongolia found in Western popular culture is of a people living a simple, nomadic pastoral life almost untouched by modern culture. A trip to the nation's bustling cosmopolitan capital will quickly dispel any such notions. And while one may still interpret contemporary scenes of nomads with their herds as dating back centuries, doing so would ignore the fundamental social and cultural transformation that has occurred in Mongolian society in the twentieth century.

This study seeks to bring together the fields of ethnomusicology and Mongolian Studies to investigate the nature of cultural change in Mongolia in the twentieth century through an examination of the *morin khuur* or "horse-head fiddle," a two-stringed bowed lute. Though an organological study, it is less about the instrument itself than about the cultural worlds to which it belongs. The horse-head fiddle is rooted in a largely nomadic, rural, and tradition-oriented society, but it is today a product, and symbol, of a largely urban, cosmopolitan one. This study seeks to tell the story of this transformation that is as of yet untold. In doing so, it also aims to tell a story of Mongolia's transformation, as well.

This study began as part of my dissertation research while a graduate student at Indiana University. A significant part it was made possible by an Individual Advanced Research Opportunities in Mongolia grant awarded by the International Research & Exchanges Board in 1998. I wish to thank the professors who helped me throughout the course of this research project, especially Christopher Atwood, who helped me to conceptualize this project from start to finish. I also wish to thank my committee members, Ruth Stone, György Kara, Sue Tuohy, and Elliot Sperling, for their years of advice and guidance throughout this project and my graduate career at Indiana University.

I have been helped along my journey of understanding the history of Mongolian music and culture by my family, friends, and colleagues, all of whom have given generously of themselves, their time, and resources. Some of the many musicians and scholars I would like to thank especially include B. Bayarsaikhan, L. Erdenechimeg, J. Enebish, N. Jantsannorow, Yo. Batbayar, B. Batjargal, Sh. Bira, S. Merjikhüü, Ts. Batchuluun, S. Dulam, L. Oyunchimeg, R. Enkhnaran, D. Jargalsaikhan, Ts. Pürevkhüü, N. Sengedorj, J. Uugantuyaa, I. Amartuvshin and the Tsetserleg Theater performers, Baljir, Ya. Purevdorj, and Ts. Tserendorj.

I wish to thank those who helped and supported me in the "field," both in Mongolia and in the States, including D. Enkhbaatar, Larry Moses, Bilegsaikhan, M. Mönkhtuya, Heike Michel, Tristra Newyear, P. Narantuya, Brian Baumann, M. Saruul-Erdene, J. Byambaa, B. Suvdaa, Alan Wheeler, Amy Cyr, Paula Haas, Susie Drost, Annette Ehler, Daniel Hruschka, Nick Keelan, Chris Kaplonski, Aleksei Kondrashov, David South, Jill Lawless, Kathy Petrie, Tom Oller, O. Otgonjargal, Morten Pederson, J. Oyuntsetseg, Miki Pohl, Michael Reed, Jessica Woodward, D. Bum-Ochir, Theodore Levin, Gaelle Lacaze, N. Soninkhishig, and D. Tserenpil.

Finally, I wish to thank my wife, Münkhzul Marsh, my parents, Kim and Lil Marsh, and, particularly Beth Marsh and Ralph LeVan and their family, for their many years of support, patience, and encouragement. I could not have completed this work without you all!

Peter K. Marsh

Figure 1. Map of Mongolia.

Introduction

Khoyorkhon chawkhdasny egshigend / Khorwoo yuundaa uyarna we?
(Why is the world moved by the melody of the two strings?)

Mishigiin Tsedendorj

This study revolves around the question of cultural tradition in contemporary Mongolia and its relationship with the past. At its core resides the *morin khuur* or "horse-head fiddle," a two-stringed spike fiddle that became in the 1990s an icon of national identity and a symbol of the nation's ancient cultural heritage. While pointing to the deep past, this instrument-as-symbol also represents a very modern cultural tradition, and changes in its construction and the meanings associated with it reflect many of the tumultuous changes that have taken place within Mongolia itself in the twentieth century.

Mongolian society at the end of the twentieth century bore little in common with itself at the turn of that century. In many ways they represent two fundamentally different societies, one largely rural, nomadic, and tradition-oriented; the other largely urban, industrial or post-industrial, and cosmopolitan. The adoption of Western-inspired modernity in the decades following the Soviet-backed Peoples Revolution of 1921 initiated the growth of a "new society" in Mongolia, one based on the principles of progress, science, and rationality. Many Mongolians eagerly adopted the new ways of living, working, and being in the world. But the passing over time of those who had experienced life in the so-called "old society" accelerated the rupture between these two worlds. By the end of the twentieth century, Mongolians nostalgic for the past and fearing the loss of their unique cultural identity, sought to reconnect with the "ancient" or pre-Revolutionary past. Such motivations helped to shape the environment that led to the so-called Democratic Revolution of 1990, during which the Mongolians broke away and attained complete political, economic, and cultural independence from a then-crumbling Soviet Union.

The nature of this relationship between contemporary Mongolia and its pre-Revolutionary past, however, remains complex and poorly understood. In defining itself as an independent nation, the Mongolian government asserts clear and unambiguous links with the past as a means of legitimating its authority to rule in the present. This legitimacy has been claimed literally with the construction of the Chinggis Khan Mausoleum in front of the State Parliament Building in the nation's capital,

Ulaanbaatar, in the early 2000s. Built of massive sections of iron and stone, the structure features statues of Chinggis Khan and other Great Khans of the thirteenth and fourteenth centuries whom the modern state recognizes as founders of the Mongolian nation. Nationalism has replaced socialism as the dominant system of social organization in the country, and art, in this case sculpture, and architecture demonstrates this break with the immediate past.

Perhaps in reaction to the incessantly forward-looking ideology of socialism, Mongolian nationalism of this period looked backwards, over and beyond socialism, and into the Mongolian *deer üyed* or "deep past," a vague concept that has come to refer to the time in Mongolia before socialism (Humphrey 1992: 375). The "revival" or "awakening" of traditions from this deep past has led some Mongolians to describe the early 1990s as a period of *ündestnii sergen mandal* or "national renaissance" (*ibid.*). And indeed, Mongolians were encouraged to learn to read and write the ancient Uighur (or vertical) script, wear the traditional Mongolian *deel* or gown in public, and teach their children to use wise Mongolian sayings and proverbs.

Music also played an important role in defining this new era. Musical anthropologist Carole Pegg describes the 1990 Revolution as bringing to an end a communist regime that for nearly seven decades "repressed, assimilated, and refashioned performance traditions" in Mongolia to suit political ends (Pegg 2001: 284). The period of national renaissance or "revival," by comparison, would see a renewed interested in the so-called national musical traditions, which were dominated by the professional musical institutions. The State Folksong & Dance Ensemble, for instance, began to include in its shows excerpts from the traditional Buddhist *tsam* dance, long banned during the Socialist period, and the State Philharmonic began to feature concertos composed by Mongolian composers for national instruments and orchestra.

But of all the musical events that marked this revival, perhaps none were more evident than those involving the horse-head fiddle. Almost immediately following the 1990 Revolution, the instrument became increasingly visible in political rituals at the highest levels. In 1992 the Mongolian President ordered the creation and installation of a horse-head fiddle called the *Töriin khan khuur* or "State Sovereign Fiddle" in the nation's Parliamentary Building, where it is kept along with other official symbols of state. In the same year, a small "orchestra" of horse-head fiddles called the Horse-head Fiddle Ensemble was established and it has become the most popular state-sponsored musical ensemble in the country. It often plays for formal state events and rituals, such as concerts honoring visiting dignitaries. Since the early 1990s, the Mongolian President's annual address to the nation on the first day of the Lunar New Year festival, called *Tsagaan sar*, has been paired with a formal performance of a horse-head fiddle. And in the same period, the instrument has come to be a permanent part of the opening ceremonies of the State Naadam, an annual festival of traditional sports held each year in Ulaanbaatar and attended by the national political leadership and international dignitaries. Each of these new uses of the horse-head fiddle was rhetorically tied to specific events or stories set in the distant past, making its "revival" in the 1990s clear evidence of a nation and people in touch with its past and once again in charge of its own destiny.

At the same time, however, many Mongolians also described this emergence of the horse-head fiddle in the post-Socialist period not in terms of a sudden break with the immediate past, but rather as part of a long-term process of cultural development. In an article written in 1987 and published in 1991, musicologist Jambalyn Enebish described the origins, development, and use of the horse-head fiddle within traditional nomadic pastoral societies. But he ends his article by describing the instrument's contemporary situation, saying that into the 1980s, the horse-head fiddle "continues to play an expanding role in the Mongolian musical culture" (Enebish 1991: 80). Horse-head fiddle players, he says, were being professionally trained, and as a result, their new musical abilities were allowing them to perform the growing repertoire of both national and world classical musical compositions (*ibid.*). Writings by Enebish and other Mongolian scholars often draw upon such metaphors as *tsetseglüülekh* ("blossoming"), *khögjüülekh* ("developing"), and *bayajuulakh* ("becoming enriched") to describe not just these instrumental traditions but also the overall growth of a national musical culture throughout the twentieth century.

For many scholars, musicians, and instrument makers associated with the horse-head fiddle, the Socialist period in Mongolia was not one of repression and the forced assimilation of European culture. On the contrary, it was a period when the horse-head fiddle traditions "flowered" to a degree never before seen. Its emergence as a national symbol in 1990 was just the end of a long process of linear development that, while rooted in the distant past, received new impetus and direction after the Peoples Revolution of 1921. The Russian and European influence that resulted from Mongolia's inclusion into the Soviet sphere of influence was seen by many in the musical arts as an opportunity to develop their traditions rather than as a threat to their survival. In the 1960s, a group of young Mongolian instrument makers worked with a Russian violin maker to "improve" the construction of the horse-head fiddle by borrowing ideas from the construction of the European violoncello. As we will see, this group continued its work throughout the 1970s and 1980s, long after the violin maker had left, and by the 1990s, says a student of one of these fiddle makers, they were close to creating the "perfect" horse-head fiddle. Going back further, to the late 1940s and the 1950s, we will see how the famous horse-head fiddle performer and teacher G. Jamyan revolutionized the teaching of the horse-head fiddle by borrowing from the methodology of the European violoncello to create his own unique method. These were clearly not people forced to modernize ancient traditions to fit the political needs of a brutal communist regime.

There was undoubtedly much more going on in the musical worlds of Mongolia in the twentieth century than can be accounted for with revival narratives, despite their pervasiveness in the discourse of the 1990s. The evidence does not support a common historical perception that the ruling Mongolian Peoples Revolutionary Party (MPRP) followed in lock-step with the Soviet leadership, or even that the Party leadership itself shared the Soviet Union's communistic goals. Nor do such narratives account for the critical role played by the Mongolians themselves in bringing about and implementing the processes of cultural modernization in their country throughout the Socialist period.

What contemporary scholars of Mongolian music and culture need is a way of looking at tradition and cultural change that can account for the complex nature of these concepts in twentieth and twenty-first century Mongolia. As music is bound to politics and society, so must contemporary scholarship critically investigate the role of political and social change on the nature and meaning of musical expression in the country. In writing about twentieth century cultural history, in particular, scholars must understand that the two political systems that brought Western-inspired modernity to Mongolia, namely socialism and nationalism, are not mutually exclusive. They must also account for differences between the Mongolian and Soviet leadership as well as for differences within the Mongolian political and intellectual elite itself. Music scholars must examine twentieth century music using a broad historical frame that can account for the profound influence of the condition of modernity on the country, its people, and traditions.

Unfortunately, contemporary scholarship on Mongolian music is lacking in such complexity and breadth. Literature by Mongolian scholars about the horse-head fiddle specifically, and musical traditions in general, tends to be written from perspectives that are strongly influenced by socialist or nationalist ideologies, and most fail to critically address the role that Western-inspired modernity has played in twentieth century Mongolian conceptions of music and art. Musical scholarship by non-Mongolian scholars is little more helpful. With the exception of *The Music of the Mongols* (1971/1943), early to mid-twentieth century scholarship[1] tended to focus on the traditional musical arts in Mongolia. When the twentieth century is addressed, few undertake a critical look at these arts in the context of broader cultural change. This situation was likely due to the relative lack of access that non-Mongolian and non-Soviet researchers had to the Mongolian Peoples Republic (MPR) or to academic materials related to it during the Socialist period, given the poor state of foreign relations between the MPR and many Western nations. As a result, many European and North American scholars had to rely heavily upon secondary sources.

In 1960 Jean Lynn Jenkins wrote about the "morienhur" on display in the Cambridge University Museum of Archaeology. Drawing her primary information about the fiddle from the work of Emsheimer (1971), she failed to recognize that she was writing about a fiddle tradition that, by the early 1960s, had been largely by-passed by contemporary cultural developments in the MPR.[2] In her entry on "Mongol Music" in the *New Grove Dictionary of Music and Musicians* (1980), Roberte Hamayon also draws upon secondary sources (again, Emsheimer 1971) to write an account of essentially pre-modern fiddle traditions.

British anthropologist Carole Pegg is likely the first professionally trained, non-Mongolian scholar from Europe or North America to conduct research in Mongolia for nearly half a century. She had the great luck of being in Mongolia just before and after 1990, and thus was able to investigate the musical life of the country under two very different political systems. Her most recent work (2001), like the articles she has published (1991, 1992a, 1992b, 1995), offer a wealth of information about traditional musical practices in Mongolia, particularly of the far western *aimag's* (provinces) of Khowd and Uws, where she spent considerable time. Pegg's work is enriched with data drawn from the interviews and recording sessions that she conducted with Mongolian traditional musicians, singers, and dancers. It thus provides us with a richness of detail about performance contexts that earlier scholars, and even Mongolian musicologists, have generally failed to produce.

In contrast to her work on the traditional musical practices, however, her analysis of the professional musical traditions is relatively less developed. As I did at first, she tends to characterize the professional folk arts as being something imposed upon the Mongolians by a Soviet-backed socialist regime. In her view, this regime disrupted and appropriated the local music traditions that thrived in the pre-Socialist period, turned them into modernist forms that it then used to promote a "centrally invented and repressively administered 'socialist national identity'" (Pegg 2001: 250). This repression, she says, only really ended with the regime's demise in 1990, which opened the door for the revival of musical practices and traditions long kept "underground" and out of sight of the regime. These are traditions that "endured in opposition to state versions of history and identity" (*ibid.*, 284).

What I found in my research does not support her findings that traditional folk culture was necessarily in opposition to the policies of the Soviet-backed ruling Party and government. While there are many instances of outright suppression of traditional musical arts, especially in the early years after the Peoples Revolution, cooperation between artists and the national leadership seems to have been more prevalent. What suppression there was appears more often to have been an attitude of disinterest on the part of cultural officials in the local or past-oriented musical traditions, which in the long-term likely had just as profound an effect on the survival of these traditions as outright suppression would have had. Another important element missing from her analysis is a critical examination of just who made up the national leadership during the Socialist period. While there were some hard-line socialists within this national leadership, it may be more accurate to characterize this leadership as consisting of many different levels of educated Mongolians, many of whom were strongly nationalist and intent on promoting the development of the Mongolian nation and its musical culture. Furthermore, while I agree with her that the Mongolian performing arts "have entered the arena of global discourses and practices" (*ibid.*, 285), I disagree with her on the timing. My research suggests that this process began decades before the 1990 Revolution and that it was critical to the formation of the national musical culture in Mongolia rather than being a late addition to it.

Scholars from other countries within the Soviet bloc have written about similar cultural continuities that connected the Soviet and post-Soviet periods. Ethnolinguist Valery Tishkov, for instance, writes about the nationalist governments that took over control of many Soviet republics as the USSR crumbled in the early 1990s.

> Generated by primordialistic visions of ethnicity and by historical-materialistic mentality of social engineering in accordance with unilinear realization of 'historical law,' Soviet political and academic rhetoric did not change much after the collapse of the Union and its ideology. A belief in Lenin's principles and 'theory' as a reference of authority was easily replaced by arguments of sacral and providentialistic character (Tishkov 1992: 52–53).

Tishkov characterizes such rhetorical continuities as being supported, on one level, by the populations of the new nations themselves who "need to explore ethno-nationalism in public Soviet discourse as a form of poetic therapy, as a form of healing for the deep trauma experienced by the Soviet people on individual and collective levels" (*ibid.*, 52). But he also characterizes it, on another level, as being directed by a national leadership that was loathe to give up its "ethno-political privileges" in the new democratic era (*ibid.*, 60).

Ethnomusicologist Ted Levin also looks to the needs of the political and intellectual elite to account for the distinct cultural continuities that he found existing between the Soviet and post-Soviet professional musical institutions in Uzbekistan. The nationalistic leadership, which he says was essentially the same as that which served in the Soviet era, "has adapted the cultural strategies of Soviet nationalities policies to serve its own ideological aims," the most important of which is "arguably the abiding struggle to consolidate national consciousness" (Levin 1996: 49). A form of classical music known as *Shash maqâm*, which was promoted as a national musical symbol of the Soviet era, was immediately remade into a national musical symbol of the "independent" era.

Soviet era Uzbek cultural institutions used performances of the *Shash maqâm* as evidence of an Uzbek "great tradition," a rhetorical device that effectively reimagined Uzbek cultural history as linear, progressive, and exclusively "Uzbek." As a "great tradition" that rhetorically connected the present to the ancient past, this musical form helped to promote the idea of Uzbekistan as an historically stable entity. At the same time, Levin says, it also "produced notable distortions in the way that both cultural boundaries and cultural commonalities were perceived and reified" (*ibid*., 46). He finds that such strategies as the creation of a "great tradition" typically reflect political needs rather than social realities. When faced with the task of nation building, the national leadership returned to Soviet concepts of culture and tradition. Despite its efforts to distance itself from the legacies of Soviet colonialism, Levin says, "the *Shash maqâm* ensemble, like the Uzbek National Chorus, has remained an *idée fixe* of both musicians and the cultural *apparat*" (*ibid*., 49).

Like the *Shash maqâm* in Uzbekistan, the horse-head fiddle in Mongolia was a symbol of cultural identity, and specifically cultural modernity, both during and after the Socialist period. It was also promoted by a cultural leadership that, by and large, did not change from one period to the next. What made the situation in Mongolia different from those described by Tishkov and Levin was that in Mongolia, the process of cultural modernization was not directed solely from the nation's leadership. It was an idea that was picked up and adapted by Mongolians of many levels of society, from the political and intellectual elite down to individual musicians, fiddle makers, and music lovers. While the modernity that was introduced into Mongolia came through the Soviet Union, it was a part of a much broader idea.

COSMOPOLITANISM

I argue that the musical and conceptual continuities that connect the Socialist and post-Socialist periods in Mongolia are rooted in a fundamental social transformation of the twentieth century that I am calling cosmopolitanism. By this I am referring to the imagined connection that people sense they have with a broader translocal or international community, but which is manifest in distinctly local ways. Mongolian cosmopolitans are those who, often by virtue of their training, education, or experience, identify with a broader international culture or way of life, and who seek to bring a uniquely Mongolian version of this to their homeland.

Ginsburg (1999) defines Mongolian cosmopolitanism in terms of their education, experience, and general outlook. Early generations of Mongolians were sent by the Party to study abroad in Russia and other parts of the Soviet Empire. In these places they were socialized into the Russian and Soviet ways of life, in ways that gave them a broader worldview and an affiliation with Russian culture not generally shared by those in their homeland who did not have these opportunities. Many of these Mongolians took Russian spouses, became fluent in the Russian language, and generally felt at ease in Russian culture. In the process, Ginsburg says, they came to view the world through Russian lenses (Ginsburg 1999: 260). They developed an affiliation or connection with a broader international community, which in this case was largely circumscribed by the Soviet world. When we speak about Mongolian cosmopolitanism of the Socialist period, we are speaking about these Mongolians' openness to a distinctly Soviet form of internationalism. The Communist Party of the Soviet Union (CPSU) considered "cosmopolitanism" per se to be a phenomenon of capitalist nations and was thus taboo. The preferred term for this worldlier outlook was "internationalism." Given the associations of this term with communism, however, we will use the term cosmopolitan, keeping in mind these qualifications.

Accustomed to the Soviet ways of life, these cosmopolitans achieved upward mobility within Soviet-backed Party and government institutions. Most were placed in positions within the intellectual class, such as the intellectual and technical elite, which included teachers, engineers, and doctors, as well as university professors and diplomats. One's position within the broader intellectual hierarchy largely depended upon one's level and status of education.

In his examination of middle class cosmopolitanism in twentieth century China, Richard Kraus (1989) defines the cosmopolitans as not only the intellectual and technical elites, but also the political elites, particularly members of the Socialist Party. For Kraus these twentieth century Chinese cosmopolitans together formed what he calls a composite social identity, which he defines as an "urban middle class" (Kraus 1989: 25). It was less of an actual class than a status group, as the members shared cultural symbols and experience. Grouping these urban-oriented elites together, he says, places emphasis on the cultural elements that they collectively shared, rather than upon the conflicts between them that were often highlighted (*ibid.*).

Given their European-styled education and experiences, Chinese cosmopolitans generally adopted the view that China's feudalist past hindered its economic and social progress. They tended to view Western cultural achievements as superior to those of their own nation, which many viewed not just as an alternative but also backward and undeveloped (*ibid.*, 27). This view further directed their attention to Europe and Japan.[3] For many of these cosmopolitans, the adoption of the piano was a step in the direction of bringing about the modernization of Chinese culture. Constructed in factories and designed to sit in living rooms in urban homes and apartments, the piano was a part of this new industrializing and urbanizing sphere of social life of twentieth century China. In the process of adopting the piano, these Chinese also adopted the worldview associated with its European traditions. As Kraus says, "Not only did Balzac, Chopin, and Dickens provide fine entertainment, but they also spread middle-class values. The piano thus preceded its 'natural' social basis to China, but was quickly taken up as soon as a modern middle class began to appear" (*ibid.*, 28). As a status symbol, the instrument expressed cosmopolitan values of modernity and sophistication even when it sat idly in the living room of a home. For these cosmopolitans, cultural modernity was defined in Western cultural terms and in ways that rejected the more traditional elements of Chinese culture.

Like their Chinese counterparts, many of the early Mongolian cosmopolitans also viewed Mongolian cultural development as having been long hindered by unprogressive traditions and a self-serving aristocracy. As they rose to positions of power within the Party and government, they saw themselves less as protectors of the ancient cultural heritage than as agents of cultural modernization and change in Mongolian society. As we will see in Chapter 3, many of these cosmopolitans placed emphasis on the development of a "new culture" (*shine soyol*) in Mongolia, including the arts, literature, theater, and so on, that would be brought about through both "reviving" (*sergeen yawuulakh*) the essential Mongolian cultural traditions lost as a result of centuries of feudalism and aristocracy (Tsendorj 1983: 29) and then "developing" (*khögjüülekh*) them in accordance with the contemporary examples of socialist "Elder and Younger brother" nations (Tsendorj 1983: 63). This is the process by which these Mongolians constructed a distinctly cosmopolitan national culture. The "new culture" would ideally exist at an international level of cultural development, while also being marked as uniquely Mongolian.

Furthermore, these cosmopolitans were no mere stooges of Soviet political aims in Mongolia; instead of merely imitating Soviet norms, they adapted them to the Mongolian contexts. Their roles were to act as intermediaries between Soviet internationalism and the Mongolian people (Ginsburg 1999: 260). But Ginsburg argues that the sentiments of most Mongolian cosmopolitan elites in the Socialist era were directed more toward nationalism than communism, and their goals more often sought the survival of Mongolian national independence than the advancement of Soviet power (*ibid.*, 248).

They likely picked up some of these ideas of national sovereignty from their experience with European nationalism (much of which was embedded within Soviet nationalities policies). But the motivation to enact them may have come in part as a reaction to what many cosmopolitans perceived as Russian racism. Russian relations with Mongolia have long been shaped by perceptions about the backwardness of the "Asiatic" peoples of Russia's "East" in general, including those of the former Soviet republics (cf. Becker 1986a, 1986b, 1991; Karpat 1986). Russian Tsarist expansion into Central Asia, Siberia, and to some extent Mongolia, throughout the nineteenth century was directed toward territorial expansion, economic exploitation, and the development of international trade routes. But these moves were often legitimated by arguments that the peoples of these regions were backward and in need of the civilizing efforts of Russia and the West. These efforts included settling the nomadic herders and hunters into towns and villages, introducing them to Orthodox Christianity and encouraging Russification of their indigenous culture. The Russian attitudes of "manifest destiny" over the "little peoples" of the East were not unlike those of the American government towards the American Indians in the nineteenth century (cf. Grant 1995).

The logic of cosmopolitanism provided these Mongolians with a way of rhetorically connecting Mongolia, and by extension the Mongolian people, with the contemporary world community, while also allowing it to express a national essence or distinctiveness. We find few figures in twentieth century Mongolia who struggled outright against any efforts to modernize Mongolian culture or to stop any connections it made with the outside world. And we find even fewer who appeared bent on abandoning Mongolian culture in exchange for a Soviet or "international" culture. Mongolians, by and large, appear to have occupied a middle ground between these two extremes, at some points demanding the nation undertake a faster program of cultural modernization and at others calling for this work to be slowed down. These two sides of the cosmopolitan continuum were often played out in Mongolia through the rhetoric of the "modern" (*orchim üyein*) and "traditional" (*ulamjlal* or *ugsaatny*) and the "new" (*shine*) and "old" (*khuuchin* or *deer üyein*).

These arguments resonate with Clifford Geertz's concept of epochalism and essentialism (1973). New states are often confronted with the daunting and difficult task of constructing a collective subject, a "we," to which "the state can be internally connected." The process of constructing this new national identity is often marked by pressures to conserve or protect essential identities on the one hand, and to link or integrate with broader international identities on the other. Geertz labels these two pressures or tensions, "'The Indigenous Way of Life' and 'The Spirit of the Age,'" or more succinctly, "essentialism" and "epochalism" (Geertz 1973: 240–241). The first looks to "local mores, established institutions, and the unities of common experience—to 'tradition,' 'culture,' national character,' or even 'race'—for the roots of a new identity," while the second looks to "the general outlines of the history of our time, and in particular to what one takes to be the overall direction and significance of that history" (*ibid.*, 240). What makes Geertz's approach to this phenomenon so useful in examining cultural trends within nation-states is his idea that these two sides are essentially complementary aspects of a single process. They are even bound together within individuals. Few actors entirely reject either of the two poles, unless they move to the extremes, and the very process of nationalism involves movement along this continuum.

Thomas Turino compares this fundamental ambiguity in national identity to the processes inherent in cosmopolitanism (2000). At the same time that people of a nation are internalizing and mastering the cultural traits of Europe, the Soviet world, or some other realm of the cosmopolitan, they are also fashioning their own versions of them. In such ways, Turino says, these practices become realized in specific locations and actual lives. "Cosmopolitan cultural formations," he says, "are . . . simultaneously local and translocal" (Turino 2000: 7). He calls this insoluble dilemma between the two the "paradox" of the cosmopolitan: "nation-states are dependent on cosmopolitanism, but are simultaneously threatened by it; unless nation-states maintain their unique identity, they will disappear as distinct, and thus operative, units on the international scene" (*ibid.*, 15).

MODERNITY AND NATIONALISM

At the core of this cosmopolitan paradox between the modern and the traditional, or the translocal and the local, is the concept of modernity. Modernity is the basis upon which these discussions and debates are taking place. It is a long-standing and pervasive idea that was formed so powerfully during Enlightenment Europe. Modernity is a European myth, say Jean and John Comaroff, "a narrative that replaces the uneven, protean relations among 'ourselves' and 'others' in world history with a simple, epic story about the passage from savagery to civilization, from the mystical to the mundane" (Comaroff and Comaroff 1993: xii). It is essentially the story of Progress. "It tells of the inexorable, if always incomplete, advancement of the primitive: of his conversion to a world religion, of his gradual incorporation into civil society, of improvement in his material circumstances, of the rationalization of his beliefs and practices" (Comaroff and Comaroff 1993: xii).

In accepting the basic tenants of modernity, the Mongolian cosmopolitans shared in the Soviet discourse of nation, but largely to the end of promoting cultural and national identity, as well as cultural pride. Partha Chatterjee finds very similar processes at work throughout the twentieth century among colonial subjects in other parts of the world. For many of them, expressing nationalism in the same terms of their colonial masters was a way of counteracting the colonial discourse of power and reasserting their own legitimacy.

> Nationalism sought to demonstrate the falsity of the colonial claim that the backward peoples were culturally incapable of ruling themselves n the conditions of the modern world. Nationalism denied the alleged inferiority of the colonized people; it also asserted that a backward nation could 'modernize' itself while retaining its cultural identity. It thus produced a discourse in which, even as it challenged the colonial claim to political domination, it also accepted the very intellectual premises of 'modernity' on which colonial domination was based (Chatterjee 1986: 30).

Though rooted in Modernity, Progress and the other Great Ideas of European history, Mongolian cosmopolitans were able to create a space for the formation and expression of distinctly national identities, similar to what Turino found in Zimbabawe, where, he says, "cosmopolitanism became a central basis for a corporate, black, middle-class identity and for nationalism itself" (Turino 2000: 11). In Socialist period Mongolia, of course, we cannot speak about a middle-class identity. But we can speak about Mongolians who shared common experiences and world-views, and were elevated to positions of relative power and privilege in this society.

TRADITION AS OTHER, TRADITION AS SELF

Another characteristic common of modernism is its tendency to define itself in opposition to the "traditional." It becomes the universal against which everything else is judged, and given the logic of modernism, implies that the non-modern must stand counter to the very ideas upon which it is founded, such as "objectivity, rationalism, and progress" (*ibid.*, 7). The "traditional" in any society, however, is less often an existing entity and more often a rhetorical construction. But in Mongolia, the "traditional" ways of being and of making music survived throughout the Socialist period, in spite of often being ignored, suppressed, or forced into hiding (cf. Pegg 2001). These traditional ways, representing pre-Revolutionary cultural traditions, were not necessarily governed by the same logic of "objectivity, rational-ism, and progress" that the cosmopolitan nationalists held up as the beacon of civilization. Modernism militates against such alternatives, Turino says, "precisely by redundantly projecting [them] as a primitive past" (*ibid.*).

At the same time, modernism needs such alternative traditions and ways of life in order to define itself. One common strategy cosmopolitans use to define the local from the translocal is through adapting those very tradi-tions that stand in opposition to modernism. This may account for why modern national cultures tend to draw from the traditional arts and cul-tures in order to construct a unique national identity. This gives the national cultures a clear "national" identity that contrasts well in an international context. During the opening ceremonies of the Olympics, for instance, the displays of national difference are typically played out upon a basis cosmo-politan sameness (*ibid.*, 16).

CONSTRUCTING TRADITION, IMAGINING TRADITION

The theory that traditions and identities can be constructed usually stand in opposition to theories that posits tradition as a homogeneous and static entity, which was typical of early anthropological work in Europe and America and has long since been discounted in the Western social sci-ences. In the 1980s Hobsbawm and Ranger popularized the concept of invented traditions to account for traditions purposefully and consciously constructed, usually by national governments and colonial regimes, to serve largely national and political ends (Hobsbawm and Ranger 1983). Both considered such modern and often national traditions to stand in contrast to authentic traditions, which Hobsbawm described as those traditions based on "what has actually been preserved in popular memory" (Hobsbawm 1983: 13).

Later works questioned the very concept of authenticity. Indeed, this concept implies the existence of traditions that are conscious and those that are unconscious, or those that are "invented" and those that are "natural." Such a division is strikingly similar to the rhetorical differences that many make between the "modern" and "traditional." Many scholars have sought to break these dichotomies by stating that all tradition could have at one time or another been made-up or invented.

Sue Tuohy suggests that human beings constantly "select and invent ideas poems, rituals, and so on to create . . . an image of a coherent and vital tradition" (Tuohy 1988: 47). Traditions are pieced together, not unlike bricolage. People gather together bits and pieces of available material to create the whole, which is then soon broken apart and recreated in new ways. There is a great fluidity in the processes of creating traditions. It is a "creative activity that utilizes selection and invention of materials to create the image that a tradition, something that is tied to the past but also has meaning and force to people today, exists" (*ibid.*, 48). It is this sense of an imagined tradition that will be used in this study.

In the twentieth century, the construction of national traditions in many nations has most often been the realm of the national cultural institutions, and they are usually used to convey images of the nation that fit with political needs. The "great traditions" typical among the Soviet (and former Soviet) nationalities that Ted Levin writes about is a good example of how national institutions can dominate the construction and promotion of national traditions. William Noll (1993) writes about the similar importance of national institutions in Poland in the early to mid-twentieth century. Even before the establishment of the Soviet Union, he writes, the Polish urban intellectuals and activists (read cosmopolitan nationalists) realized that national political entities could only emerge with rural participation. Through newly established cultural centers around the country, as well as through the newspapers, schools, churches, and the media, these intellectuals sought to propagate a sense of national identity among the rural populations. They introduced new national and international forms of music, instruments, and dances, and encouraged popular participation in these centers and new national arts. These new arts helped to link the rural and urban populations, and the joint participation of people in these standardized arts led to an imagined sense of belonging to the nation (Noll 1993: 150).

This sense of imagination is drawn from Anderson's concept of the imagined community, in which people who do not know each other still feel a sense of connection with one another, and thus also with an imagined sense of the community as a whole. The community is imagined, Anderson says, "both as inherently limited and sovereign. It is *imagined* because the members of even the smallest nation will never know most of their fellow-members, meet them, or even hear of them, yet in the minds of each lives the image of their communion" (Anderson 1991: 6; italics in the original). The nation "is imagined as a *community* because, regardless of the actual inequality . . . the nation is always conceived as a deep, horizontal comradeship" (*ibid.*, 7).

THE HORSE-HEAD FIDDLE AS A GREAT TRADITION

One of the most important musical developments in Mongolia in the Socialist period was the construction of the national musical institutions, such as the nation-wide system of cultural centers, modern musical ensembles, schools, and research institutions, which employed cadres of professionally trained composers and performers. With them came an entirely new national form of musical tradition. Modern folk music in Mongolia, which is known as *ardyn khögjim* (literally, "music of the people") stands in contrast to the folk music of pre-Socialist Mongolia, which is known as *ugsaatny khögjim* (or "music of the roots"), and the distinction between these two is important to the thesis of this study.

Ugsaatny folk music refers to the musical practices and instruments identified with particular regions or ethnic groups in Mongolia. It is music suited to the traditional contexts in which music was long performed prior to—and since—the beginning of the twentieth century. This typically means music performed in the small spaces of the Mongolian round "tents" called *gers* or in small *ger* encampments called *ails*. The music was often performed by amateurs, was participatory in nature, and had meanings that connected it to the natural and spiritual worlds that surrounded the people living on the Mongolian steppe.

Ardyn folk music, in contrast, developed as part of the new national musical culture (*ündestnii khögmjiim soyol*) in the twentieth century, particularly in the growing urban areas. Mongolian national music draws inspiration and ideas from a vast body of *ugsaatny* folk music that music researchers collected throughout the Socialist period. These local musical ideas were then arranged and mixed with ideas from international sources, such as European and Russian classical music, creating a unique mixture or syncretism of these two sources. National music consists of both local and international musical styles, and thus can be identified with both, but in a generalized way. Much of this music, while being unmistakably "Mongolian" in sound, is not meant to be linked with any particular place, people, or region in the way *ugsaatny* folk music typically is. It is instead meant to represent Mongolia as a nation. As a modern syncretism, national *ardyn* folk music is also well suited to the new "Europeanized" instruments, ensembles, and performance spaces that were created as part of the new national musical culture in the country.

As an explicitly modernized form of music, *ardyn* folk music is typically viewed within this national musical culture as being more progressive, and thus more highly valued, than the *ugsaatny* folk music. This style is assumed by many to reflect the overall evolutionary development of the Mongolian culture itself, particularly in its consolidation of ancient local or regional identities into a new a national consciousness, something of a national "horizontal comradeship" within a broader Soviet "internationalism" (Levin 1996:49). The fiddle's modern development as part of the national *ardyn* folk music tradition in Mongolia is likewise evidence of a linear and progressive cultural history that links contemporary Mongolia with both the essence of its past and the spirit of its present. With the decline and collapse of Soviet influence in the 1980s and 1990s, the horse-head fiddle was "reimagined" by these institutions in order to aid in the consolidation of this new national consciousness. In this way, the horse-head fiddle served important political goals, even if doing so required significant distortions in the narratives of Mongolian cultural history.

That the horse-head fiddle was reimagined in nearly identical ways in the post-Socialist period as it was in the Socialist period was not merely the result of political or bureaucratic inertia, but rather that of the fundamental cosmopolitan transformation of Mongolian society that began in the decades following the 1921 Peoples Revolution. While introduced through Soviet cultural policies, this transformation has brought about a conceptual change that runs much deeper within Mongolian society than lingering "Soviet" legacies.

This study seeks to unpack the pervasive influence of the cosmopolitan on contemporary cultural tradition in Mongolia by focusing upon its representation in and through the horse-head fiddle. Chapter One highlights the evidence for the horse-head fiddle in its pre-revolutionary context in order to provide a contrast with how the fiddle was transformed in the decades following the 1921 Peoples Revolution. Chapter Two examines the fiddle within the context of the newly established professional musical arts of the mid- to late twentieth century, paying particular attention to the final decades of the Socialist era. Chapter Three explores the development of cosmopolitan nationalism in Mongolia during Socialist period, seeking to convey something of the degree to which it altered the rhetorical concepts of modernism and tradition. Chapter Four examines the role of the composer N. Jantsannorow in reimagining the horse-head fiddle in the 1970s and 1980s and repositioning it to become an important symbol of nationalist ideology in the post-Socialist era. Chapter Five examines the fiddle in the context of the post-Socialist era, highlighting ways in which it was reimagined into a national symbol during a period of folk "renaissance" or "revival." And Chapter Six examines several alternative histories of the fiddle in order to point out those Mongolians who do not accept, and even resist, the ideological underpinnings of cosmopolitanism in Mongolia.

1 Two-Stringed Fiddle Traditions in Pre-Revolutionary Mongolian Society

With professional horse-head fiddle performers wearing costumes fashioned after thirteenth century military uniforms and television advertisements showing Chinggis Khan being serenaded by horse-head fiddle players in his palace, it is clear that one of the most important claims to the status of this instrument in contemporary Mongolia is its supposed connection to the nation's deep past. The belief that this instrument is indeed ancient, and specifically that Mongols played it in the thirteenth century in the period of Chinggis Khan and the Mongol Empire, is widespread in Mongolia. Some music researchers have even popularized the view that the instrument has autochthonous or indigenous origins in Mongolia, with roots that extend back in time for thousands of years.

The physical evidence to support such claims about the ancient origins of the horse-head fiddle in Mongolia is thin. The organic nature of traditional fiddles, which are made from wood, animal skins, and hair, means that practically no fiddles older than the nineteenth century have survived in museums, private collections, or archeological sites. Researchers have instead turned to other forms of evidence to learn about the musical practices of the ancient Mongols. Literary sources, many of which date back to the twelfth and thirteenth centuries, have proved to be especially useful. These include diaries and reports from missionaries, travelers, and researchers; official histories written by Chinese and other non-Mongol historians; and literature written by the Mongols themselves. In recent decades, work on the oral histories of the Mongolians has contributed new perspectives to our knowledge of their cultural life.

Taken together, however, the extant physical and literary evidence for the horse-head fiddle prior to the early nineteenth century is weak. In fact, it is difficult to say that there was even an instrument known as the horse-head fiddle prior to the late nineteenth century. When speaking of ancient history, it is better to speak instead of a two-stringed bowed lute, as this is, in essence, what a horse-head fiddle is. This term also distinguishes between a bowed and a plucked lute, which is also mentioned in the literary sources. The evidence for two-stringed bowed lutes from the nineteenth century on is clear and well documented. It tells us that the instrument is most clearly associated with the two main ethnic groupings in Mongolia: the Khalkha Mongols of the central, eastern, and southern regions of the country, including the Govi (or Gobi) Desert; and the Oirat Mongols, an ancient confederation of smaller Mongolian ethnic groups in the far western region.

This chapter seeks to tell the story of the two-stringed bowed lute from the period of the Mongol Empire to the eve of the Peoples Revolution in 1921 primarily drawing upon literary and oral historical sources. We begin by testing the strength of the data supporting the claim that the two-stringed bowed lute can be placed in medieval Mongolia. We will then build a picture of the cultural life of the Gobi Khalkha and western Oriats in the pre-Revolutionary period, stretching from the mid-nineteenth century to the early decades of the twentieth, and then sketch the important roles that the two-stringed bowed lute played in the leisure, work, and spiritual lives of the Mongols. We end with an examination of how this pre-Revolutionary, tradition-oriented world began to disintegrate under pressure from outside forces, particularly civil war in China and the beginning of World War II, and what this meant to traditional musical practice. Revolution in Mongolia proper in 1921 would set the stage for the arrival of a very different kind of social and cultural order at the hands of Mongolian socialists.

THE LUTE IN THE PERIOD OF EMPIRE

The earliest evidence of stringed musical instruments among the Mongols comes from the period of the Mongol Empire of the twelfth through fourteenth centuries. The most significant indigenous historical work from this period is the *Secret History of the Mongols*, which is believed to have been written in the fourteenth century. It aims principally to tell the story of the boy named Temüjin and his rise to power and elevation to the rank of Chinggis Khan. Mongolists interpret this work more as a hagiography than a biography given its rather idealized depiction of his life and its use as a political tool to promote the political fortunes of one ruling clan, the Chinggisid Borjigit clan, over others. In spite of any exaggerations, however, the work does provide fascinating insights into the cultural world of the medieval Mongols. But it provides no direct reference to the playing of any bowed string instruments.

Such evidence is found elsewhere, mostly as hints and fragments of information found in the letters and diaries from travelers and historical records. The social stability that the Mongol Empire brought to parts of Europe and Asia in the thirteenth and fourteenth centuries contributed to the revitalization of trade and commerce throughout the Eurasian continent and led to the final resurgence of the international network of trade routes known today as the Silk Roads. These routes facilitated not only the trade in silks, spices, and other trade goods but also the exchange in cultural ideas and products, including art, music, and religious and political ideas.

Christian missionaries, among them Franciscan and Dominican monks, were among the first Europeans to make the long and treacherous journey to the various courts of the Mongolian khans. There they met with relatives of Chinggis Khan, all members of his Borjigit clan, and recorded much of what they encountered in letters and diaries. Some of the first descriptions of music among the Mongols are found in the accounts written by the Franciscan William of Rubruck, who traveled to the courts of two of Chinggis Khan's sons, the Khans Batu and Möngke, between the years 1253 and 1255. His descriptions include fascinating details about daily life among the people he encountered—as well as of his own, often disparaging attitudes toward them. In one passage, Rubruck describes an evening of music making, dancing, and drinking in tents at the palace of the Great Khan Möngke, doing his best to describe the unfamiliar objects and behaviors around him.

> In summer *cosmos*[1] is all they care about. There is always some *cosmos* standing lower down the dwelling, in front of the doorway, and close to it stands a minstrel with his guitar [*citarista cum citharula sua*]. (I did not see our sort of lute or guitar [*citaras et viellas nostras*] there, but I did see many other instruments which are not used in our part of the world.) At the point when the master begins to drink, one of the stewards calls out in a loud voice, 'Ha!,' and the minstrel strikes his guitar. On an occasion when they are holding a great feast, they all clap their hands and dance to the tune of the guitar, the men in front of the master and the women in front of the mistresses. And after the master has drunk, the steward gives the same shout as before and the minstrel stops. Then they all drink round in turn, men and women alike, and at times compete with one another in quaffing in a thoroughly distasteful and greedy fashion (Jackson 1990: 76–77).

The term *citharula* is related to *cithara*, which in southern and eastern Europe of this time referred to a number of different a pear-shaped[2] plucked lutes. Rubruck did not record the names that his hosts used for these instruments or the kinds of music they played, seeking instead to relate the instruments he encountered with those with which his readers would have been familiar.

Such ambiguity and inexact terminology is unfortunately common in writings of early travelers. The Franciscan missionary John of Plano Carpini, who visited Batu, Chinggis Khan's third son and Khan of the Golden Horde,[3] in Russia in 1246, was equally vague in describing the musical behaviors he encountered. He described him as a man who never drinks, "especially in public, without there being singing and guitar-playing for them" (Dawson 1980: 57). Writing some four or five decades later, Marco

Polo, who lived among the Mongols in China from 1275 to 1295, alludes in a bit more detail to a stringed musical instrument in his description of how the Mongols, or "Tartars," prepared for a battle in his book *Description of the World*:

> Soon both armies were drawn up in battle array and only waiting for the sound of the kettle-drums. For the Tartars [*sic*] do not dare to start a battle till their lord's drums begin to beat; and while they are waiting it is their custom to sing and to play very sweetly on their two-stringed instruments and to make very merry in expectation of battle (Polo 1958: 315; see also 117, n. 1).

Accompanying singing with "two-stringed instruments" sounds intriguingly like musical customs that have long been a part of Mongol society. Polo's use of this phrase supports the speculation that the Mongols had some kind of two-stringed and likely pear-shaped lute. What is not clear is whether or not this lute was bowed or simply plucked. The distinction is important because, so far, there is little evidence of that Mongol lutes were bowed at all.

Chinese dynastic records offer a bit more information about the musical instruments of the Mongols of this era. The historical annals of the Yüan dynasty, founded by Kubilai Khan, grandson of Chinggis Khan and the fifth supreme khan, in the thirteenth century, give special attention to the musical arts of the dynastic palace and provide some of the first information about the actual terms the Mongols used for their musical instruments. According to the annals, Kubilai ordered the establishment of a music and song ensemble to be used for state and political ceremonies and private festivals (Dashdorj and Tsoodol 1971: 17; Khüükhenbaatar and Tömörtogoo 1968: 68–69). They report that the palace employed one hundred and forty-nine musicians and singers, but give little information about what their duties were. The Inner Mongolian musicologist Börön cites a related historical document that provides more detail about the musicians in the palace, stating that Kubilai employed a *khuurch*, *tsuurch*, and *büreechin* (Börön 1982: 3), which can be roughly translated as a "player of a lute or fiddle" (*quɣurči*), a "player of the end-blown flute" *(č'ōrči)*, and a "player of a wind instrument" (*büriyeči*). Some scholars (Dashdorj and Tsoodol 1971, Badraa 1998, Erdenechimeg 1993, among others) suggest that this *quɣurči* must have referred to a player of a two-stringed bowed lute, such as a horse-head fiddle. But it is unclear how many strings this instrument had or if it was bowed or plucked. In addition, given that the root word *khuur* (or *quɣur*) also referred to stringed musical instruments in general, it is difficult to be any more specific than to say that this was some kind of bowed or plucked lute.

Other historical sources provide more detail of the kinds of stringed instruments the Mongols used at courts throughout the Empire. A historian of the court of Timur in Samarkand, in present day Uzbekistan, wrote a treatise in Persian in 1413 that listed the names of Mongolian instruments present in the court orchestra, including the *yatuyan*, a plucked harp or zither (in modern Mongolian, *yatga*);[4] *šiduryu*, a long-necked plucked lute with a small body (Modern Mongolian, *shudraga*); and *tš'ōr*, an end-blown flute (Modern Mongolian, *tsuur* or *tsoor*, but often also used to refer to a "musical instrument" in general) (Nixon 1985: 1). The German linguist Doerfer notes that the names *shudraga* and the *yatugan* had both entered the Persian and Chagaadai languages by the fifteenth century (Doerfer 1963: 365 [vol.4]), suggesting that these were terms—and instruments—that were introduced to these regions during the period of the Mongol Empire. A Persian-style painting from the court of the Mongol Ghazan Khan (1295–1304) shows him and his queen seated on a throne surrounded by princes and courtiers being entertained by three musicians, one of whom is holding a harp and another playing a pear-shaped lute-like instrument which resembles the *biiwaa*, which is related to the modern Japanese *biwa* and the Chinese *pipa* (Phillips 1969: 196, pl. 32). Though not a bowed fiddle, it had the same rounded body that we would find Mongolians using with their plucked and bowed lutes centuries later.

THE LUTE IN THE SEVENTEENTH TO NINETEENTH CENTURIES

After the collapse of the Mongol Empire in China in the mid-fourteenth century, many Mongols returned to their homeland where they resumed their nomadic ways of life. This was also a period of major civil unrest in the country. A series of wars broke out that eventually pitted the majority Khalkha Mongols of the central and eastern regions against the Oirat Mongols, a confederation of smaller Mongolian ethnic groups the far west. Fighting continued until the beginning of the sixteenth century when the Khalkha Altan Khan (1507–1583) led his armies against the Oirat confederation and defeated it, bringing most of Mongolia under his, and Khalkha Mongol, control. While consolidating his power, Altan Khan signed a treaty of alliance with the Buddhist lamas of Tibet that initiated a period of rapid and widespread conversion to Tibetan forms of Buddhism within Mongolia. After the Khan's death, however, fighting among the Mongols restarted and political unities once again frayed. It was in this period that Altan Khan's homeland, which bordered northern China, came under the rule of the Manchu Qing dynasty, beginning what has become a long process of political, economic, and cultural integration of southern Mongolia into a Greater China.

At the beginning of the eighteenth century, the far-western Zungar Khanate of the Oirat Mongols organized a successful military campaign against the Khalkha, driving them eastward from the central Mongol steppelands. Fearing defeat, the Khalkha leadership formed an alliance with the Manchu Qing dynastic rulers. The Manchus seized the opportunity to enter Mongolia, contributing soldiers armed with muskets and canons. Primarily armed with compound bows and arrows, the Zungars were eventually defeated by the combined Khalkha and Manchu forces. This victory allowed the Khalkha to return to their homeland, but at the cost of their independence. The Manchu armies stayed on in Mongolia, forcing it to become a vassal state within the vast Qing dynasty. Renamed Outer Mongolia, the country would remain in this position until the collapse of Qing rule in 1911.

Through their efforts of divide and rule, the Qing brought relative peace and stability to the Mongol nation. It also encouraged the nascent Buddhist faith among the population. This was also the period when some of the most important works of Classical Mongolian[5] one of these works, Luwsandanzan's *Altan Tobch* (Golden Summary), makes reference to a *quyur* (*khuur*) in a story describing the time when Chinggis Khan sent his son Jochi to "vanquish the Kipchak [Turkic] nation." Lord Borchi, an aide to the Khan, instructed Jochi, saying:

> Son Jochi, listen, your imperial father sends you to widen the earth to oppress [govern] foreign people. Be firm. There is a pass that cannot be passed, it is said that there are passes not to be [passed]. Do not think how you can climb those passes. If you think you can climb those passes then do so without complaints. Then on the other side of the pass these is a song and a fiddle in front of you (Vietze 1992: 84).

While the meaning of Borchi's command is not clear, there is no doubt in the text that he is referring to some kind of stringed musical instrument. What's not clear is what kind of instrument it was—whether it was plucked or bowed, or how many strings it had.

Greater clarity is found in historical sources dated to the early eighteenth century. In decades proceeding then, Khalkha and Oirats continued to skirmish, despite overall Qing control. In the beginning of the eighteenth century, a contingent of the defeated Zungars chose to leave their homeland and migrate west across Central Asia and into southern Russia, where they finally settled on the banks of the Caspian Sea. Over time this large group of Oirat Mongols came to be widely known as the Kalmyks.

In the early decades of the eighteenth century, German scientists, working on behalf of the newly founded Russian Academy, carried out ethnographic work in this southern region of Russia, including among the Kalmyks. Founded in 1724 by Peter the Great on the model of the Berlin Academy of Sciences, the Russian Academy supported a number of ambitious and expensive explorations to different parts of what the Russians called the "vast and mysterious" expanses of southern and eastern Russia and Siberia. The natural scientist Peter Simon Pallas was a member of this expedition and kept detailed notes of his travels, which he published in his two enormous works, *Reise durch verschiedene Provinzen des Russischen*

Reiches (1771–1776) and *Sammlungen historischer Nachrichten über die mongolischen Völkerschaften* (1779). Among his observations were descriptions and even illustrations of the music and musical instruments he encountered.

Pallas's first visit to the Kalmyks, in 1769, came at a time when they were still able to maintain direct contact with their co-tribesmen in Zungaria, their homeland in present-day western Mongolia and north-west China. Pallas described Kalmyk instruments and musical practices that were both Mongol and Central Asian. He wrote of attending performances of song and dance accompanied by two *quγurs* (*khuurs*), among other instruments, which become clear in his description and illustrations were bowed lutes. Pallas described one of the two lutes as corresponding "to the *kobys* of the Kirgiz" (Emsheimer 1991b: 247). Until the beginning of the twentieth century, the Russians regularly referred to modern day Kazakhs as Kirgiz, and the Kirgiz as Kara-Kirgiz. So Pallas was in all likelihood referring to the *kobys* of the Kazakhs, a Turkic people similar to the Kirgiz, from whom the Kalmyks likely borrowed this instrument. The other lute Pallas described was a traditional Mongol bowed lute known variously as the *khuuchir* or the *dörwön chikhtei khuur*, or the "four-eared bowed lute."[6] Though a Mongolian bowed lute, musicologists do not consider the *khuurchir* to be an ancestor of the modern two-stringed bowed lute. For the first time, however, Pallas's report does present clear evidence that the Mongols associated the term *khuur* (or *quγur*) with a bowed lute. Previously, this connection was not clear.

The Swedish anthropologist Ernst Emsheimer cites another account of a Kalmyk bowed lute, one by the Swedish military officer Christopher Schnitscher, who was working for the Russian government in 1714 as an escort for a Chinese delegation traveling over the Russian territory. In his description of his travels, Schnitscher gives a detailed account of a concert the delegation was treated to by their Kalmyk hosts:

> After the meal the oboists and violinists, who also came from Astrakhan [the political center of the Kalmyk Khanate], had to play some music. . . . After the musicians had played for an hour, a harp, which was more than one 'Faden' long and had 5 gut strings, was brought into the tent; and two singers also came. Two fellows played on the harp. Besides this harp they also had two violins with strings of horse gut, which had such a soft sound that they could hardly be heard. They stuck a knife, instead of a bridge, under the strings when they played. Likewise they had a humming-iron [jew's harp] that was one and a quarter of a cubit long, which produced the best sound of all the other instruments (Müller 1760: 344–345, quoted in Emsheimer 1991b: 249).

The "harp" to which Schnitscher was referring was likely the Mongolian *yatuγan* (or *yatga*). While the word "violin" suggests he was referring to a bowed lute of some sort, we can only guess at what it looked like. That it used "horse gut" (probably horsehair) strings is intriguing since Mongolian two-stringed bowed lutes traditionally used horsehair strings.

In their account of their travels through parts of southern Mongolia in the mid-nineteenth century, Frenchmen Évariste Régis Huc and Joseph Gabet wrote about attending a Lunar New Year celebration with a Mongol noble and his retinue. They write that after their dinner they were entertained by a "*toolholos*" (*tuulič*, or epic singer) who performed upon a "rude three-stringed violin" (Huc and Gabet 1928: 73). They give no further description of this instrument, but they could have been referring to a *khuuchir* with three strings instead of four. Again, however, though intriguing, the evidence is too vague to be very useful in tracing the development of the two-stringed bowed lute.

The earliest and clearest description of this instrument comes from the pen of the Scottish missionary, Rev. James Gilmour, who worked in Outer Mongolia between 1870 and 1882[7]. In his book *Among the Mongols* (1883/1970), Gilmour describes an evening in which he visited a rural encampment of a group of Buddhist lamas. While sharing a meal with them, he noticed a strange looking stringed instrument near the walls of the lamas' *ger*. So detailed is his description of this instrument, this passage will be quoted in its entirety.

Then followed conversation about the texture and make of foreign clothes, about foreign customs, and about the distance from Peking to foreign countries. When these subjects were exhausted, a curious-looking instrument lying on the top of one of the boxes attracted notice, and one of the lamas volunteered to extract music from it. It was a fiddle, but *such* a fiddle! The main part of it was a hollow box about a foot square and two or three inches deep, covered with sheep skin, and a stick about three feet long stuck through the sides of the box. It had only two strings, and these consisted of a few hairs pulled from a horse's tail and lengthened at both ends by pieces of common string. The fiddle itself was uncouth enough, but the bow beat it hollow. This last was a bent and whittled branch of some shrub fitted with a few horse-hairs tied on quite loosely. The necessary tension was produced by the hand of the performer as he grasped it to play.

Fiddles are not uncommon in Mongolia, but this one seemed so rude and primitive, that, even though we were the guests of the maker and owner, it was utterly impossible to refrain from laughter on beholding it. The lama to whom it belonged was not in the least annoyed or disconcerted at our mirth, but, smiling quietly, took his bow, set the box on his knee, went through the preliminaries of tuning with all the gravity of an accomplished musician, produced from his purse a small paper of resin, applied the minutest quantity to the hairs of the bow, and, subsiding into a permanent attitude, proceeded to entertain his guests with the Mongol air of 'Pinglang yeh.' The strains of the fiddle were soft and low, and pleasing in the extreme. Compared with the high 'skirling' tones of many Chinese and Mongol instruments, the sound of this one was more like that of some good piano touched by a skilful hand. The lama was a skilful player, as a few seconds sufficed to show. He had made the fiddle himself, and knew how to use it, and he soon showed that highly artistic effects could be produced from a very clownish-looking instrument. The lama played a few more verses, and it was then evident that it was time to stop him (Gilmour 1970: 266–267).

As a traveler's account, Gilmour's description of his encounter with a two-stringed bowed Mongolian lute is unusually detailed and reveals many clues about the construction, design, and use of such an instrument in rural Mongolia at the end of the nineteenth century. Had earlier writers been even half as descriptive as Gilmour was, we would have a much better idea about the instrument's origins and development. The evidence we have examined so far suggests that the Mongols have a long tradition of plucked, "guitar"-like lutes and at a certain point bowed lutes emerged into common practice. What is not clear is when this occurred or what they looked like. The four-stringed *khuuchir* can be dated back to the Kalmyk Mongols of the eighteenth century, and we can assume that it is likely much older. But the historical literature cannot confirm the existence of the two-stringed bowed lute or fiddle in Mongolia earlier than the Gilmour's account in the 1880s. Earlier references to "fiddles" and "two-stringed instruments" are intriguing, but not conclusive. There are, however, other clues to assess the age and development of this instrument, including characteristics of its construction, dispersion, and use.

CONSTRUCTION OF THE PRE-REVOLUTIONARY TWO-STRINGED FIDDLE

Gilmour's description of the two-stringed fiddle he saw as "not uncommon" is a valuable clue to the age and development of this instrumental tradition in Mongolia in the late nineteenth century. It is well established by oral histories and observations from later decades that on the eve of the Peoples Revolution, roughly the three decades prior to 1921, the two-stringed fiddle tradition was practiced in nearly every part of the country. That it was stronger and deeper in some regions more than others, has led musicologists to identify three broad regional traditions: the Oirat, central Khalkha, and Inner Mongolian. The Oirat traditions include those of the many small ethnic Mongol subcultures of the western *aimag*s, particularly Khowd and Uws *aimag*s; the Khalkha traditions include those of the Khalkha Mongols of the central, southern, and eastern *aimag*s, particularly those of the central steppelands and the Gowi (or Gobi) desert regions. The Inner or "southern" Mongolian traditions are those of the Mongol ethnic subcultures that occupy the province of Inner Mongolia in the Peoples' Republic of China.

Though this study is limited to the fiddle traditions of Mongolia proper, those of the Khalkha and Oirat Mongolians, we can learn much about pre-Revolutionary fiddles through the work that the Danish explorer and ethnographer Henny Haslund-Christensen did in Inner Mongolia in the early twentieth century. Haslund-Christensen participated in a number of scientific expeditions to central, eastern and southern Mongolia in the 1920s and 1930s. The Danish Expedition of 1938–1939, sponsored by the Danish National Museum and under the direction of Sven Hedin, was the most productive for Haslund-Christensen. Before he left, the Swedish Broadcasting Corporation gave him an unwieldy apparatus that recorded sounds directly onto gramophone disks. In spite of its size and weight, Haslund-Christensen says he was able to make one hundred and twenty-four recordings of the music he encountered. He also took photographs and collected songs texts and actual musical instruments, including fiddles.[8] Upon his return to Denmark, he turned most of his data over to his colleague, the Swedish musicologist Ernst Emsheimer, to be classified, catalogued, and analyzed. The results of this work appeared in his publication, *The Music of the Mongols, Part I: Eastern Mongolia* from 1943 (republished in 1971), the first book in the English language about the music of the Mongols.

Emsheimer focused his analysis on six fiddles, each of which was from a Mongol subculture of Inner Mongolia, including the Edsen-gol Mongols, Zakhchin Mongols, Khorchin Mongols and Chakhar Mongols (Emsheimer 1971). Aside from photographs, song texts, and some notes, Emsheimer had little contextual data about these instruments to work with and his text makes it clear that he was often hard-pressed to make sense of what he found. But his detailed descriptions do provide a good basis for understanding broader fiddle traditions of the time, especially the degree of variation that existed among those from different regions and ethnic groups.

There were some basic elements that were common to all two-stringed fiddles. They were all of a relatively simple design and constructed using materials common to most herders' immediate environments. They consisted of a wooden neck (*esh*)[9] and body or "box" (*khairtsag*), two wooden bridges (*maar* or *tewkh/tebke*), and tuning pegs or "ears" (*chikh*). The body was typically covered with a piece of dried skin or hide, often from a goat or sheep (Enebish 1991), and the neck fit down through the center of the frame, sticking out at the bottom. The fiddle was strung with two bundles of horsehair strings (*chawkhdas*), one thicker than the other, which were held in place at the base of the instrument with some combination of string, small wooden pegs, or even iron nails, and at the top with the tuning pegs. The bow (*num* or *tatuur/tata ur*), as described in Gilmour's story, could be fashioned from something as simple as a branch strung with horsehair. The bowed lutes of this time in Mongolia were most commonly hand-made by the very people who performed on them. Such self-sufficiency was—and remains—one of the requirements of surviving as nomadic herders in this part of the world.

As we see in Figure 2, the two-stringed fiddle that Emsheimer examined came in a variety of shapes and sizes. While he classified them in terms of ethnic subcultures, there is not enough information to speak about any of them as being representative of any particular ethnic group. Emsheimer was frustrated by degree of variation among the fiddles he examined. In regards to the shape and size of the sound boxes, he determined that "no definite rules seem to exist for the proportions of the frame. These vary, at all events, not inconsiderably" (Haslund-Christensen 1971: 83). While all of the fiddles were "spike fiddles," that is, fiddles with necks thrust through the center of the sound box, the length of each neck, he laments, "seems to be as little laid down in any definite rule as the proportions of the sound-box" (*ibid.*, 84–85), varying in length from the shortest (83.8 cm) to the longest (113.4 cm). And while most of the fiddles were covered with skin on the front and back sides of the wooden body, one of them had a wooden face. Making fiddles with a wooden face would not become a common practice until the late twentieth century.

Furthermore, though the fiddles Haslund-Christensen brought back all had box-shaped bodies, it was apparently just as common in the period for the fiddles to have ladle- or spoon-shaped bodies. Some Mongolian musicologists, such as Badraa and Enebish, suggest that the earliest two-stringed fiddles were created when herders attached horsehairs to a ladle they commonly used to scoop *airag* (fermented mare's milk) (Badrakh 1960: 57; Badraa 1998d: 98; Enebish 1991: 78). Badraa contends that this ladle-shaped design developed over the centuries into two main types of musical instruments: the plucked lute, or *towshuur* (*tobšiγur*), which came to be widely used among the western Mongols, and the bowed fiddle, or *shanagan khuur* (*šinaγ-a quγur*, literally "ladle fiddle"), which came to be widely used among the central Khalkha. Badraa (1998a: 91) says that *shanagan khuurs* were common among the Mongolians and sur-vived as late as the 1980s in various parts of central Mongolia, including Arkhangai, Zawkhan, Öwörhangai, Khöwsgöl and Dornogowi *aimag*s. Badraa, Enebish, and other scholars believe that the ladle-shaped fiddle developed into the box-shaped fiddles, like those Haslund-Christensen found in Inner Mongolia.

The sound boxes were commonly painted and often "richly ornamented" (Emsheimer 1971: 84). The sides and wooden back of the Chakhar-Mongol instrument (Figure 2a) have even been ornamented with elaborate carved ornaments that represent animals. Sound holes were carved into the sides or backs of each of the fiddles that Emsheimer examined. Each was circular in form, "and by means of segment-like formations they are shaped into an artistic ornament" (*ibid.*, 84). The other fiddles, in contrast, have little or no ornamentation (Figures 2b & 2d).

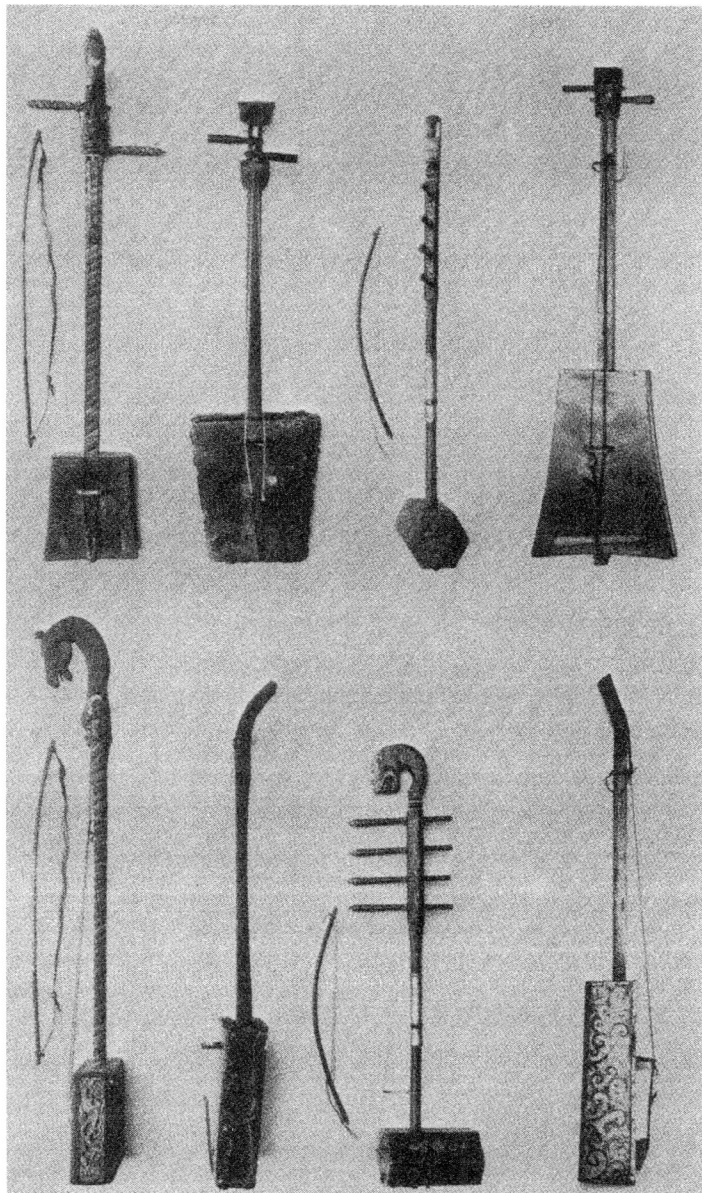

Figure 2.   Fiddles collected by Haslund-Christensen.
a. *khiil khuur* from the Chakar Mongols;
b. *khiil khuur* from the Manchu Mongols;
c. *dörwen-chikhe khuur* from the Chakar Mongols;
d. *khiil khuur* from the Zakhchin Mongols.
   (Haslund-Christensen 1971)]

The ornamentation at the crown of each fiddle, along with its name, also varied considerably. Of the four fiddles that Emsheimer studied, only one of the Chakhar fiddles (Figure 2a) has a horse's head. The other Chakar fiddle has the head of some unknown mythical creature. Badraa says that in this period the types of fiddle heads ranged from 'sea monsters' and dragons to lions and horses, and they were, in turn, named after the beast they represented. A fiddle with a sea monster (or serpent) head was called a *matar khuur* ("crocodile," or more likely, "serpent")[10]; a dragon headed fiddle was a *luu khuur*; a tiger headed fiddle, an *arslan khuur*; and a horse headed fiddle, a *morin khuur* (Badraa 1998a: 91). Each of these creatures is a staple of Mongolian folklore.[11] Japanese musicologist Haruo Hasumi (1997: 4) suggests that a dragon's head was likely reserved for use on the fiddles of the aristocracy, while common herders most likely used the horse's head. Badraa cites a particular prince, the Ilden Beile of Sain Khan *aimag*, as owning a *shanagan khuur* with a *matar* head. He says the prince named it the "black fiddle" (*khar khuur*) and could trace its lineage back five generations within his family. In the 1940s, the *matar* head was replaced with a horse's head (Badraa 1998a: 91), an act that makes sense in light of Hasumi's suggestion about the *matar* head's association with the Mongolian aristocracy. As will become clear below, this was a period when it was particularly dangerous for Mongolians to express any association with the Mongolian aristocracy.

At the same time, many Mongolian fiddles appeared to have had no head at all (e.g., Figures 2b & 2d). Indeed, the Oirat fiddle, called the *ikel* (*ekil, igil*), is commonly crowned not with the head of an animal but with a *gurwan erdene* ("three jewels") symbol. It may be significant that Gilmour made no mention of whether or not the fiddle he saw had any kind of a head. Likewise, many fiddles were given names that did not correspond to any carved heads. A common name for a two-stringed fiddle was, simply, "bowed fiddle" (*khiil khuur*)[12] (Emsheimer 1971: 82). Many Mongol subcultures, including the Buriat, Khorchin and Ööld Torgut, used the term "fiddle" (*khuur*) (Emsheimer 1971: 82, Börön 1982: 2). Others, including the Chakhar and Üzemchin,[13] used "shovel fiddle" (*khürz-n quγur*) or "stringed fiddle" (*kilγasu-n quγur*) (*ibid.*). Börön says that the Khorchin Mongols of Inner Mongolia commonly called their ladle-shaped fiddles *tsuur*, a name that has appeared in other works to refer to a musical instrument in general (*ibid.*).

Common among nearly all two-stringed fiddles was their use of horsehair. Emsheimer says that the strings of Mongolian fiddles were commonly black, "though apparently more seldom, white horse-hair" (Emsheimer 1971: 85). Berlinskii quotes the early twentieth century fiddler, Luwsan *khuurch*, as telling him that these hairs should preferably come from the tail of an exhausted horse. In this way, he says, "the bow would be able to express all of the fiddler's sorrow and joy" (Berlinskii 1933: 15). Enebish says that the hairs must come from a fast horse (Enebish 1991: 79). To prepare the strings, the Mongols would first soak the horse-hair in warm soapy water in order to purge them of their oils. They were then hung to dry and stretch, and then grouped together into loose bundles, one of which had more hairs than the other (*ibid.*). Musicologist Maya Matthea van Staden writes that the loose bundling of horsehairs allows each hair to vibrate independently, producing a diffuse sound rich in overtones, which she says is widely admired by the Mongolians (van Staden 1999: 11). Among the Khalkha Mongols, the "thick string" (*budun utas*) tradition-ally would be placed on the left-hand side as seen from the perspective of the performer and the "thin string" (*naryn utas*) on the right. The strings of the western Mongol *ikel*, to the contrary, are reversed; the thin string on the left and the thick on the right. This and a general lack of a "head" on the *ikel*'s crown are two of the most characteristic differences between the traditional Oirat and Khalkha fiddles.

At least one of the fiddles that Haslund-Christensen brought back had a "small bridge" (*baga tebke*), placed near where the strings come off of the ears, which could be used to make fine adjustments to the pitch. The "great bridge" (*yeke tebke*) was placed in the middle of the sound box, and marked the lowest point at which the strings will vibrate. The bridges of all these six fiddles were made of wood, but Berlinskii quotes a fiddler named Luwsan as saying that the bridge of the Khalkha *khuuchir* should be made from a human jawbone. Luwsan explained that because the jaw is an important part of the vocal apparatus, its bone will "make [the fiddle] sing particularly well" (Berlinskii 1933: 15).[14] Haslund-Christensen observed a fiddler among the Sönid Mongols who could change the timbre of his fiddle by inserting the blade of a knife under the great bridge (compare with Schnitscher's account of a fiddle using a knife bridge among the Kalmyk Mongols above). As a result, the vibration of the tones was considerably intensified and, according to him, produced a sound that was extremely popular among the Sönid Mongols (Haslund-Christensen 1971: 87).

The "bow" of pre-Revolutionary two-stringed fiddles appeared to con-sist of a curved piece of wood that was loosely strung with horsehair. The performer held the bow with one hand, pressing down on bow hairs with the fingers to produce the tension necessary to make the main fiddle strings vibrate. Rosin is also necessary to make the string vibrate. Emsheimer observed that among the Sönid Mongols of the Shili-yin Gol league in Inner Mongolia, the bowstring was rubbed with pulverized rosin bought from Chinese merchants (*ibid.*, 86–87). The lama fiddler that Gilmour observed appeared to use pulverized rosin. Mongolian fiddlers also traditionally used lumps of dried pinesap.

The large degree of variation in the construction of the two-stringed fid-dles of the pre-Revolutionary period, even within particular regions, sug-gests that these traditions were broadly dispersed and very local. The idea of the two-stringed fiddle had spread widely, but it had also been reinvented as it spread depending upon local customs or even the whims of particular fiddle makers. The ability of these fiddles to express local identity was further enhanced when the fiddle maker made use of materials in his immediate surroundings, such as wood from local trees or skins and hairs from local animals, or when he ornamented his fiddles with locally meaningful symbols. Yet, in spite of their many variations, the two-stringed fiddles shared much in terms of performance contexts and cultural meanings. An examination of these cultural aspects of the two-stringed fiddle will help us to further deeper our understanding of the age, development, and importance of this instrument in pre-Revolutionary Mongolia.

CULTURAL ATTRIBUTES OF THE
PRE-REVOLUTIONARY TWO-STRINGED FIDDLE

Gilmour's account of the lama and his fiddle demonstrates the commonness of the two-stringed fiddle among the Mongols. This was not an instrument that was restricted to the aristocratic palaces or Buddhist monasteries, but was performed by Mongols in all sectors of pre-Revolutionary society. Among the herders, the fiddle was most commonly used in the context of the *ail* or home-encampment. The Mongolians of this era had such sayings as "a *ger* with a horse-head fiddle was a complete (*büren*) *ger*," while one without a fiddle was a "widow (*belewsen*) *ger*" (MIAT 1999: 13). Van Staden (1999: 5) suggests that as well as owning a fiddle, most families "had a player in their midst." These sayings are often repeated today in reference to all Mongolians. But since the two-stringed fiddle with the horse's head, or the "horse-head fiddle," was principally a Khalkha and Inner Mongolian instrument, these sayings were likely most common in central and southern Mongolia.

In the lives of the nomadic herders, music and song, and to a limited degree dance[15], were a part of everyday life, accompanying nearly every type of activity. It is not difficult to imagine a scene in which a herder returns home in the evening from herding and, after an evening meal, picks up his fiddle and performs melodies or accompanies members of his family or visiting friends in singing and dancing. Everyone would be expected to participate in some way, and the context of performance could be almost anywhere. Musician M. Ganbold from Uws *aimag* remembers when, as a youth, he and his friends would ride out to their favorite spots near the mountains and streams of their homeland to play their fiddles and sing (*ibid.*). Other musicians have spoken about taking their fiddle with them to the pastures and playing on them while watching their herds. Kler noticed that any gathering for Mongols of Inner Mongolia was a chance to share jokes, tell stories, and sing songs, often on topics they cherished. For men, this typically meant songs about beautiful women and fast horses. Kler writes that among the Ordos Mongols of the early twentieth century, when several friends meet either on the grass of the plains or at home they start telling tales. At such a time one will hear an incredible number of legends about extraordinary fast horses, beautiful horses, or brown geldings killed in battle (Kler 1947: 24).

While Mongolians have likely always admired those with musical talent, one's participation in musical activities at whatever level has been more highly valued than one's technical abilities. It was common for men, in particular, to have had the ability to play a few tunes passably well on a two-stringed fiddle, even though few likely had the talent, time, or training necessary to excel on the instrument. This general willingness to play and participate in communal activities was considered important to the primarily nomadic way of life of pre-Revolutionary Mongolia. Playing the fiddle was also used to build or maintain social relations. A musician in Arkhangai *aimag* told me that when a visitor entered an *ail*, he would be expected to sit down and play something on the *ail*'s two-stringed fiddle as a greeting. Those who could not play the instrument were asked to bow even a single note on it or to touch it as a sign of respect (Enebish 1991: 77, n. 2; cf. Nansalmaa 1987: 350). In a similar way, it was apparently common during festivities then, as today, to encourage everyone present to sing a song or play something on a fiddle. Those who could not or refused were often publicly, if playfully, chastised. This description of such an occasion was included in an article written for foreign tourists in a Mongolian magazine.

> During festivals among the Khalkha Mongols, everybody would be expected to sing. If somebody cannot sing or play the horse fiddle he will be told, 'Learn later! Learn to play the horse-head fiddle!' If he does not do this, then they [*sic*] will be reminded that they must be able to play the fiddle while singing, 'I know no songs. But let me play the hundred and eight *zee*.'[16] The person would then be made to drink a bowl of *airag*. This one hundred and eight *zee* is the first step to learning to play the horse-head fiddle (MIAT 1999: 13).

Not only were all expected to participate in music making when it occurred in social settings, but, as van Staden writes, among the Oirat Mongols in particular, "honesty" of expression was more important than talent:

> Everyone can join the circle of *tatlaga* [a fiddle genre of songs, instrumental pieces and dances] dance and music, and one may be a dancer, musician, singer and listener all in the same evening. At the end of the evening everybody is supposed to feel better thanks to the divergent range of emotions that have been celebrated, both happy and sad. And some will say with a wink, 'without the horse-head fiddle the evening wouldn't have been as good' (van Staden 1999: 10).

Fiddle playing was a common part of family and communal rituals, including such life-cycle rituals as celebrating the raising of a new *ger* or the first cutting of a young child's hair. It was also a part of important calendrical rituals such as marking the beginning of the Lunar New Year or the opening and closing of the official "seal," a political ritual during the Manchu Qing dynasty. Communal festivals, called *nairs*, could range in size from a few people meeting in someone's *ger* to large gatherings with hundreds or thousands of people, such as the annual *naadam* festivals that would draw people from many miles away. There are many variations of the Mongolian saying, "a festival without songs to sing or fiddle players to play is not a festival" (Dashdorj and Tsoodol 1971: 15).

But there were also professional and semi-professional fiddle players, those who made or supplemented their living with fiddle playing. Berlinskii writes about storytellers who would wander from *ail* to *ail*, playing their fiddle and telling stories, and "receiving in return a pittance or small hospitality" (Berlinskii 1933: 11). In towns and villages, one could meet such people in places of trade or near Buddhist temples, "usually on the day of a religious festival where people came to pray" (*ibid.*). These storytellers, or *ülgerchid*,[17] often adapted their stories to comment upon their hosts and audience, mocking the rich "if they did not throw enough copper coins to satisfy the musician's needs" and praising the common people "if they showed him attention and affection" (*ibid.*).

Not all storytellers lived so precarious an existence. While the teller of stories might be treated like a paid servant, the teller of epic tales or *tuulič* was usually accorded great respect in Mongolian society. Mongolist Boris Vladimirtsov writes that among the Oirats of Khowd *aimag* in the early twentieth century,[18] while the telling (*khaila-*) of heroic stories was common, the telling of epic tales was often limited to particular contexts.

> The [heroic stories] are sung both at public and private parties, at holidays, even at chance banquets; they are performed under favorable circumstances, at any gathering or assembly, at the time of a trip which is either long or with a lot of people, at watchposts and in military camps. But more often than not, the Oirat heroic epics are performed in the camps of princes (Vladimirtsov 1983: 24).

Princes were often connoisseurs of epics and many acted as patrons of talented singers (*ibid.*). Anthropologist Carole Pegg writes of the great respect that common citizens customarily accorded to *tuuličid* in this period (Pegg 1995: 90). While the singers would receive gifts from their hosts, these traditionally were not understood as payment, but rather a duty. The singers bestowed prosperity upon those homes they performed in and thus they must be honored (Vladimirtsov 1983: 25).

Luwsan *khuurch*, or Luwsan the Fiddler, was a talented musician of the early twentieth century who rose from being a common storyteller to a respected *tuulič*.[19] He was born into a poor herding family in Tsetsen Khan *aimag* in Mongolia in 1888. His grandfather, father and mother all were well-known fiddle players, and as a youth he took a special interest in his mother's fiddle, an interest she encouraged by teaching him how to play. His mother died when he was twelve years old and his father remarried two years later. But then, he too died. His stepmother then took all of the family's possessions and moved away. She left her stepson with only "his mother's fiddle, a silver cup, a lame horse, and two sheep"—both of which were soon eaten by a wolf (Berlinskii 1933: 13)!

Luwsan went to work for other herders as a hired hand, playing his fiddle while with the herds and hiding it from his masters while at home. By his teens, however, his skill and talent had spread widely throughout the region and he was often invited to perform as *nairs* (feasts or banquets), *ger*-raisings and other celebrations, while also continuing to herd. At the age of 17, Luwsan left his homeland and traveled with a camel caravan to the city of Urga (present-day Ulaanbaatar), where he worked as a caravan driver while continuing to perform. His luck changed when his reputation as a musician and singer reached the Jebdzundamba Khutugtu, "The Living Buddha" and the theocratic head of the Mongolian government, who invited him to perform for him in his court. Luwsan told Berlinskii that he received "50 *lan* [of silver], silk for making a *deel*, and a *khadag*" in payment (*ibid.*, 14). He then began to work at and around the court of the Jebdzundamba Khutugtu, over time attaining a high status as a court musician that he maintained for the rest of his life. Vladimirtsov relates a similar story about the storyteller named Parchen who also rose from common beginnings to become a respected *tuulič* for the princes of Khowd (Vladimirtsov 1983).

The *tuuličid* were highly respected, even feared, in Mongolian society in large part because of their association with spirits and the spirit world. Vladimirtsov writes that a *tuulič* can enter into "a state of aroused inspiration, when the words of the epic are deposited quite by themselves in regular measure"; and when the conditions are just right, he says,

> the Oirat singer is quite overcome, forgetting everything around him and everything is given over to the process of creation. The Oirats of [northwest] Mongolia thus regard their singers; they acknowledge that different supernatural forces, spirits inspire the singer at the moment of ecstasy in forms of images (Vladimirtsov 1983: 39–40).

In a series of interviews with well-known epic singers of Khowd, Carole Pegg was able to get more specific information about the roles and abilities of epic singers and the worlds in which they can enter or influence.

> In 'old' Mongolia, it was thought that the act of [epic] performance could please the shamanist spirits of nature (*baigalyn ongod*) and also ritually

exorcises evil spirits (*chötgör*) and demons (*zetger*) (Avirmed IN). Epic performance was considered especially important when settling into a winter place. The benevolence of the ancestral spirits would guard against a harsh winter of a sudden bad fall of snow (*zud*), which might kill men and animals (Bayad Jamyan IN). Similarly epics were performed before a hunting expedition, since it was believed that if pleased, the spirits of nature would 'give' game to the hunters (Enhbalsan IN). When the performance had been particularly well executed, there would be no chase: the animal would simply wait for the hunters. In cases of infertility or illness in people or animals, epic performance was used for exorcising rather than pleasing spirits (Avirmed IN) (Pegg 1995: 84).

The *tuulič* played such important roles in nomadic society as clearing communal spaces of malevolent spirits, encouraging ancestral spirits to help guard the family and its animals, and helping hunters to locate and kill game. The *towshuur* lute, common among the Oirat, was critical to this work, since it was the instrument most often favored by the *tuulič* of the west (Vladimirtsov 1983: 41). Pegg reports that the singer's *towshuur* itself was considered to have spiritual powers, its presence "within the *ger* was thought to be able to push away or elude danger" (Pegg 1995: 87).

The Khalkha Mongols shared a similar understanding of the two-stringed fiddle, considering it to be one of the traditionally sacred objects within an *ail*. It was hung on a wall or placed on a table in the most respected part of the *ger*, the *khoimor*, located in the "rear" (*ar tal*) or north side of the *ger*, which is opposite the front door, located in the "front" (*üüden tal*) or south side. This is a part of the *ger* in which the other valued objects a herder's family might own are placed, including its Buddha and Buddhist scriptures, jewelry, and family photographs. In the highly structured sphere of the Mongol *ger*, the *khoimor* is also the part of the home where the eldest or most senior males of the *ail* would sit, further suggesting the traditional association of the fiddle, like the horse, with the male gender. In addition, the fiddle was also customarily positioned to face towards the fireplace (*golomt*), which is located in the very center of the *ger*, and never to the "east" (*züün tal*), which is the "women's side" of the *ger* (Nansalmaa 1987: 350). As we have already seen, however, women have long played fiddles in Mongolian society, despite these traditional associations of the fiddle with men. When fiddles are not used, they are often covered with a *khatga*, a silk sash that is used to show respect. Enebish writes that when Mongols nomadize "they load the fiddle on the leading camel (resting on soft luggage) and face it forward" (Enebish 1991: 77, n. 2). All of these practices and customs indicate the respect Mongolians throughout the country traditionally have shown to the two-stringed fiddle, a respect that associates this instrument with sacred objects.

The two-stringed fiddle traditionally was often perceived of as an object that could protect an *ail* from misfortune of all types. With a fiddle hung in a *ger*'s *khoimor*, an *ail* was shielded from evil spirits, which were believed to come from out of the north or northwest. A fiddle maker named Enkhjargal told me that in the pre-Revolutionary period the Mongols believed that every *ger* should have three objects: a fiddle, an Altangerel sutra (a Buddhist scripture), and a *mona* (or cudgel), adding that each helped to protect the *ail* from misfortune (Enkhjargal 1998.12.05). A "fiddle-less" *ail* (*khuurgui ail*), in contrast, was vulnerable to all sorts of evil influences: "'a family should not be without a *morin khuur*, without it the family is cursed'" (van Staden 1999: 5) and "an *ail* without a fiddle and song is one with strife, noisy quarrels, and great anxiety, and where the children are constantly frightened and crying" (Jambaldorj 1996: 104).

While owning and showing respect to a fiddle was a way of utilizing its power of protection, the Mongols also believed that the sound of the fiddle is also powerful. The folklorist Dulam writes about a Zakhchin painter from Khowd, M. Amgalan, who told him that if a herder loses his favorite horse, "the herder begins to play the fiddle to chase away bad influences" (Dulam 1987:41). The historian Jambaldorj writes that "in times of great death and loss of his beloved horses and animals, a herder can push aside evil obstacles [*gai tüitger*] by playing the horse-head fiddle in a ceremony called 'opening the door to the sky'" (Jambaldorj 1996: 104). Just what this ceremony was is unclear, though intriguing.

The power of the fiddle to push aside malevolent influences and purify a space or time is evident in rituals associated with *Tsagaan sar*, the Lunar New Year. Some western Mongols traditionally play the *tsuur*, a vertical flute, during this time as a means of separating "all that could have come from the past year" (Dulam 1987:41). The Khalkha Mongols traditionally play fiddles during the New Year ceremonies to ensure happiness to all who hear its sound. With the resurgence of these traditions in recent years, fiddlers say they are in great demand by families and friends during this time of the year.

The power of the fiddle's sound extends to animals, as well. Some families play for their horses and camels so that they will "be beautiful and productive" (*ibid.*). Enebish writes that

> A horse-head fiddle is also considered to be a good fortune to one's horse or herd of horses. Therefore, there is a custom where the male horse herder, after putting his horses out to pasture in the evening, will come to his *ger* and make music with his horse-head fiddle (Enebish 1991: 77, n. 2).

In similar fashion, many Mongolians traditionally drew upon the power of the fiddle's sound in the course of herding their animals. One of the most important uses of the fiddle among the nomads has been its use to encourage female animals, particularly camels, to adopt an orphaned newborn. When a baby camel loses its mother, herders often try to encourage one of the adult female camels to adopt it as one of its own. But adult camels are notoriously reticent to do this, and often push away the orphan camel that is not its own. The Mongols believe that they can facilitate this adoption by playing the fiddle and singing or chanting a special song for the mother camel. As it was explained to me, a woman would approach the mother camel with the new-born in her arms, softly chanting "*khöös, khöös,*" while a man sits nearby playing a special tune on his two-stringed fiddle. There is something about the sound of this chant and the timbre of the fiddle, some say, that "softens" the mother camel's reticence. Herders say that when the mother camel begins to "cry," when tears begin to fall from her eyes, her heart has been moved by the sound of the fiddle. After this the mother camel then accepts the new-born as one of her own and allows it to nurse. Dulam says this technique was also used to calm a camel or horse that had lost a newborn (Dulam 1987: 41). Such techniques are still employed by herders today.

The close association between the fiddle and animals is perhaps best reflected in the origin legend of the two-stringed fiddle, the story of Khökhöö Namjil. One of the most popular versions of this legend describes Khökhöö Namjil as a soldier who is sent far into the countryside to work guarding the border or herding animals. His loneliness and longing to be with his beloved in his distant homeland moves Khökhöö Namjil to sing songs of love and longing. So beautifully does he sing that one day the *ezen*, or spirit-master, of a nearby mountain appears before him and, in honor of his talent, gives him a magical winged horse called Jonon Khar. Every evening, Jonon Khar whisks Khökhöö Namjil to the distant home of his beloved, and every morning the horse brings him back to his work. One day, however, the horse is killed; in some versions its wings are cut by a jealous woman, in others it is shot from the sky by hunters or killed by thieves. Another version has his beloved cutting the wings in order to keep Khökhöö Namjil from leaving. In grief over the loss of his companion horse and any means of returning to his beloved, Khökhöö Namjil begins to create a fiddle from the various parts of his magical horse. Its skull, bones, hide and horsehairs are all used to construct a "horse fiddle," or *morin khuur.* Khökhöö Namjil then travels around the countryside with his fiddle, moving from *ail* to *ail*, and telling the tale of his beloved horse while imitating its gallops and neighs. Local people then copied Namjil's fiddle and, in so doing, so the story goes, spread the idea of the horse-head fiddle throughout Mongolia.

In this story, the fiddle is used to bring back to life an essential aspect of Khökhöö Namjil's beloved horse. It is almost as if the fiddle becomes a medium through which the horse's spirit can communicate with its earthly owner and his audiences. This resembles the traditional role of the *tuulič*, who was also considered by Mongolians to be in touch with the spiritual world. It also demonstrates what we might call the liminality of the two-stringed fiddle in tradition-oriented pre-Revolutionary Mongolia. The instrument appears to reside at the edge or threshold of not only the human world, but also the animal or natural and spiritual worlds. The instrument is a part of each: it is human-made, largely from animal parts, and can embody or communicate with some aspect of the spirit world. In this way, the two-stringed fiddle reflects the complex environment of the pre-Revolutionary nomadic pastoralists in which humans needed to maintain a sense of balance with their natural environment, their own animals and those that lived around them, and the many different kinds of spirits that existed and interacted with the natural and human worlds.

Furthermore, the close connection of the fiddle with the horse in this legend is especially intriguing. In creating his unique instrument from Jonon Khar's body, Khökhöö Namjil is able to, in effect, bring his horse back to life and play, or "ride," it as he did when it was alive. This dedication to his horse reflected the traditionally close relationships that existed between Mongolians and their horses, as well as the powerful role that horse spirits played in the Mongolian spiritual cosmology. In Mongolian folklore, the powerful heroes always rode powerful horses. Sometimes the horses could speak with their masters and offer wise advice about how to get out of difficult situations. Similarly, Mongolian shamans would call upon horse spirits, whom they considered to be wise and courageous, to come and guide them through the spirit world. Mongolian shamans sometimes referred to the drums they beat to set them into a trance as their "horse," which they would "ride" in the spirit world. This close relationship between the horse and master reflected the relationships that developed between herders and their horses, which are still found today. As we see in Figure 3, the respect that Mongolian herders show towards their horses is often extended to the respect they show towards their horse-head fiddles.

The "Khökhöö Namjil" origin legend of the horse-head fiddle has become very popular in Mongolia in the late twentieth century and it is generally considered to be an ancient tale. But it may not be that old. There is evidence that some of the most common contemporary versions of this legend were pieced together only in the twentieth century from a number of other versions of stories told among the Khalkha and western Mongols (Gyorgy Kara, personal correspondence; cf. Erdenechimeg 1994).

This again raises the central question of this chapter: how old is the horse-head fiddle? As our evidence shows, the two-stringed fiddle with a horse's head was just one of many different kinds of two-stringed fiddles and lutes that were common in pre-Revolutionary Mongolia. While the Mongolians cherished the horse above all of their other animals, there is little evidence to suggest that this resulted in a preponderance of horse-headed fiddles prior to, if not even within, the nineteenth century. More likely, horse heads were just one of several types of heads and other ornaments that adorned the crowns of Mongolian stringed instruments—many of which likely had no heads at all.

What makes two-stringed fiddles so beloved in Mongolian society may have less to do with the animal carved into its crown than with the instrument's sound. As von Staden points out, the two-stringed fiddle has a unique timbre which results from its strings, which are actually two bundles of horsehairs. This loose bundling of the strings, and also of the bow-strings, allows each of the hairs to vibrate individually, creating a diffuse or "thick" sound that is rich in overtones. This timbre contrasts sharply with that of the plucked string instruments, such as the various lutes, and even the other popular Mongolian fiddle, the *khuuchir*, all of which use strings that are either pulled taut or made from metal or other materials. They do not have the same "thick" timbre as the two-stringed fiddle.

The research by ethnomusicologist Ted Levin on the traditional music-cultures of Tuva and Mongolia supports van Staden's observation that Mongolians tend to admire this particular kind of timbre. Levin (2006) investigated why Mongolia and Tuva have such deep and lively traditions of overtone singing or *khöömii*, a style of singing whereby a singer articulates naturally occurring overtones in the human voice. Overtone singing in these countries is a tradition rooted in the lives of nomadic herders, and in asking them where the tradition originated, these herders often pointed to the sounds of their natural environment. Levin found that herders of this region are able to hear subtle distinctions in the ambient sounds of their environment, such as the complex of sounds that the wind makes when blowing over rocks on a mountain top or those that water makes when flowing over stones in a creek. Singing using overtones is a way in which herder can imitate these sounds and even "talk back" to the spirits of the land that make them. Levin calls this process a "sound mimesis." Using it, both the Mongolians and Tuvans have developed what is essentially a tool of survival, i.e. an ability to hear sounds that portend approaching danger, into a distinctive form of art in which musical sounds reflect or evoke those of their ambient environment. Levin links this preference that Mongolians and Tuvans have for these "thick" or overtone-rich timbres in the voice to the widespread and lasting popularity of the traditional two-stringed fiddles among both peoples. This idea could offer powerful insight into reasons for the popularity of the horse-head fiddle in Mongolia to the present day.

What becomes clear in examining the cultural attributes of the traditional two-stringed fiddle is how closely tied the instrument is with the ways of life of the pre-Revolutionary Mongolians. In its construction, performance, and sound, the instrument was closely identified with the people, customs, and even spirits of particular areas or regions. But at the same time, it reflected a single specific idea—a spike fiddle strung with two loose bundles of horsehair strings—that spread widely throughout Mongolia, from the far west to the central and southern regions. Levin's theory of sound mimesis may even offer clues as to why Mongolians link this instrument so closely to their traditional nomadic ways of life. This is a link that could not then be shared with the largely agricultural Chinese to the south or Russians to the north. Though we are unable to prove the existence of

Figure 3. A Chakar Mongol plays a piece about horses to his horse on a *khiil khuur* (Haslund-Christensen 1971).

the two-stringed fiddle prior to the nineteenth century, the deep roots this instrument has in Mongolian society and culture strongly suggests that its origins extend back much further in time.

REVOLUTION AND MUSICAL CHANGE

Pre-Revolutionary Mongolian society can be fairly characterized as being relatively conservative. Much of everyday life in this period was guided by tradition and custom. Most Mongolians practiced forms of pastoral nomadism that had remained relatively unchanged for many centuries. But change was occurring, and particularly at the end of the nineteenth and early twentieth centuries. The Mongolians were not untouched by the outside world, even in this era. Changes in the policies of the Manchu Qing dynasty, for instance, allowed an ever increasing number of Chinese merchants to move into Mongolia in the last decades of the nineteenth century. Mongolians had increasingly frequent contact with the Chinese and Chinese goods, and their money lending practices saddled an increasing number of them with crushing levels of debt. The impoverishment of Mongolian society by the beginning of the twentieth century had put enormous stress on traditional nomadic ways of life. At the same time, the Chinese were introducing new, urban ways of life to the country, particularly in the centers of Chinese commerce, such as in the town of Urga (present-day Ulaanbaatar), where Chinese forms of popular literature, theatre, and music were popular among both Chinese and Mongolians.

Two major events in the beginning of the twentieth century, the collapse of the Qing dynasty in 1911 and the Russian Revolution in 1917, would set forces into motion throughout Inner Asia that would soon severely disrupt the Mongolian's tradition-oriented ways of life. Though the Mongolians declared their independence from the Qing dynasty upon its collapse, the decades of the 1910s and 1920s saw their vast lands being fought over by Chinese warlords and Russian revolutionaries. The social and economic disruptions of war not only disrupted traditional society, but also made new cultural ways available to the Mongolian people.

In the late 1930s, Henny Haslund-Christensen returned to eastern and southern parts of Mongolia (his previous visit had been in the late 1920s) to find that many of the pre-Revolutionary musical traditions that he had earlier encountered and written about were being put aside, or altogether dropped, by Mongolians in favor of what he termed foreign traditions. When he arrived in Inner Mongolia, for instance, Japanese troops were developing their state of Manchukuo, in the province of Manchuria, and seeking Inner Mongolian assistance and support in return for promises of protection and autonomy. The dispirited youth that Haslund-Christensen had met in the previous decade were now "marching towards a brighter future" in which they believed they would become wealthy by providing the raw materials for Japanese industries. He also found that they were embracing new cultural ideologies that originated "outside the frontiers of their country" (Haslund-Christensen 1971: 26). In the south and east parts of Inner Mongolia, he says, "the occupying powers had begun to enrol [*sic*] Mongol youth in their respective schools and armies, and the whole population was now being exposed to the effective batteries of modern propagandistic technique" (*ibid.*, 22)

Haslund-Christensen found a society transformed. In the city, "one saw only few horsemen, and none of the younger town-dwellers was clad in the colorful garments of the old days" (*ibid.*, 27). When he enquired about the whereabouts of the "representatives of the older time," whom he had known among the Khorchin Mongols of Inner Mongolia, he was told that "with some exceptions, the singers and musicians of the old era had long since fled to remote valleys where they were now endeavoring to spend the rest of their lives in conformity with the traditions of the past" (*ibid.*, 22, 28). And those who had not fled were incarcerated in the town prison "for having been too deeply rooted in the past to be able to understand the message of the new era" (*ibid.*, 28).

Everywhere he went, he found the old traditions that the Mongols had practiced for centuries as part of their pastoral nomadic lifestyles were being abandoned:

> Chieftains who had formerly guided the destinies of proud tribes were now losing their authority over the youth of their own clan; trou-badours who had themselves spent their youth at the feet of the old

masters to learn the chants and folk-songs of the past were now without a single disciple to whom they could pass on their precious inheritance; and story-tellers who had once been honoured guests in every camp had now to yield the place of honour at the hearth-fire to the young men who could bring news from one of the propaganda-centres of the great powers (*ibid.*, 22)

The ways in which tradition, and particularly musical tradition, had been transmitted from one generation to the next were being disrupted by the social change. For him, the abandonment of this "precious inheritance" of music and song meant the loss of those core characteristics that defined the most essential elements of the old society, a process that could only lead to the loss of all cultural uniqueness and difference:

> Neither the printed word nor pictures can reproduce that which more than anything else reflects the soul of the country and the most intimate cultural inheritance of the nomad tribes that are gradually dying out. One must become attuned to the proud and melancholy tones of the Mongol melodies in order rightly to feel the magnificent and impressive beauty of the mighty deserts and steppes; one must listen to the words in the old folk-songs to realize that these isolated and frugal herdsmen are descendants of the men who seven centuries ago were the most powerful people in the world.—The power and magnificence of their period of greatness has long since vanished, but the memory of the past has been confided from father to son generation after generation, right up to the threshold of our own culture-leveling times (*ibid.*, 16)

Haslund-Christensen paints a rather romantic picture of the old musical world. But he describes its destruction in terms of an assault by the powers of the modern industrial world upon the weak and tradition-bound societies, and frames his descriptions in terms of modernist dichotomies of "old-new," "youth-elders," and "tradition-modernity." While he understood the complex internal and domestic political changes taking place within Mongol society, he preferred to look at the old society as an essentialized whole that had value to the world precisely because of its apparent difference from Western or European ways. "An understanding study of the nomads' special gift," he writes, "would undoubtedly be a source of healthy renewal for the nervous life of this over-industrialized and intellectualized world" (*ibid.*, 21).

Haslund-Christensen felt that scientists like him should go out and collect samples of the traditional Mongolian musical culture for preservation and storage. He took it upon himself to set down the most important aspects of Mongolian music and song before they disappeared, much like a botanist might seek to collect species of plants threatened with extinction before their proper scientific classification. "It was on this journey," he writes, "that I realized with terrible clearness that the age-old Mongol nomad-culture was being completely effaced, before science had managed to record even its most important feature" (*ibid.*, 19). While he clearly overstated the demise of traditional Mongolian society, he was one of the first to articulate the threat that these modern cultural ways posed to the continuity of Mongolian cultural traditions.

Haslund-Christensen's view of modernity as an unstoppable march towards cultural homogeneity and the control of the poor and weak nations by the rich and powerful was almost exactly opposite the view of modernity being promoted by the Japanese and their supporters. While the Mongolian youths he encountered in his journeys through the region welcomed their efforts to bring the fruits of modernity to their people through the destruction of burdensome social traditions, Haslund-Christensen viewed their work as destroying the very foundations of a great society. The very nature of Western-oriented modernity as it spread into Central Asia in the early twentieth century, often on the wings of revolution and war, demanded that people make choices about the value of tradition and progress.

AN ETHNOGRAPHY OF THE MONGOL FIDDLER SANGRUP

Haslund-Christensen's brief ethnography of the Khorchin fiddle player Sangrup documents how this modernity likely affected individuals in premodern Mongolian societies in the early decades of the twentieth century. He met Sangrup *khuurch* while recording the songs of elderly prisoners of the Khorchin Mongols of Southern Mongolia and describes him as having been famous before the social unrest that accompanied the collapse of the Qing dynasty. The Japanese had imprisoned the fiddler for working as a musician in the palace of the Mongol prince Otai, who had participated in the resistance of Mongols against the Chinese. Haslund-Christensen won Sangrup's release and together they set off for remote parts of the Khorchin territory which, he reported, "had not yet been reached by the new epoch" (*ibid.*, 28). Through the course of the following weeks together, Sangrup provided his new European friend with interesting insights into the place of the fiddle and fiddle players in traditional Mongol society.

Sangrup's talents as a musician and epic singer were recognized and nurtured while he was still young, and at a certain age his skills were tested by an older epic singer or *tuulič*. The tests included attempting "to imitate the clear gurglings of streams, the gentle soughing of the wind in the rushes of the river-bank and the mystic echoes of eternity issuing from the invisible interior of the conch [shell]" (*ibid.*, 29). When the *tuulič* felt assured of Sangrup's abilities, he began to teach him the texts and melodies of the "old songs," including those that sing "the praises of high gods, proud heroes and famous horses" (*ibid.*, 30). He was taught what songs were appropriate for which contexts, as well as the "mysteries of acoustics," which was achieved "by studying the sound effects that the wind could coax from the hollow interiors of human and animal skulls" (*ibid.*).[20] He also learned how to construct two string instruments, the four-stringed *khuuchir* and the two-stringed fiddle (*ibid.* 1971: 30).

Sangrup eventually became the favorite troubadour of Prince Otai, with whom he traveled to Peking during the last decades of the Qing dynasty and performed for its "proud princes and romantic princesses" in the Forbidden City. When he returned to his homeland he was in demand by the common people who wanted him to perform in their *ger*s. "No festival was in those times regarded as complete by the Khorchin tribe," says Haslund-Christensen, "unless Sangrup Khurchi was present" (*ibid.*, 31).

During the battles between the Mongols and Chinese that accompanied the end of Qing dynastic rule from 1911 to 1913, he lost everything that he owned, including his instruments. He constructed a new fiddle and then set about "consoling and inspiriting the survivors with the mighty songs of the past" (*ibid.* 1971: 31). But as the older generations one-by-one passed on, the younger generations quickly adapted to the new era, turning away from the generations of their parents. The youth, he said, "had become tired of listening to the songs and epics glorifying the past, and [they] turned their faces resolutely away from the dispirited old men to join their voices enthusiastically in the new marching songs, that were full of golden promises about the splendid future they themselves would build up" (*ibid.*, 29). Sangrup *khuurch* spent the years after the civil war in relative obscurity, often being "abused by the younger members of his tribe" for not joining with "the singers and expounders of the new songs" of the Mongol people. His loyalty to the old songs of his tribe finally landed him in prison, where he sat until Haslund-Christensen found him.

He had hoped to find a young and talented Mongol youth to whom he could transmit the songs and music of the Khorchin people as his master had done to him. He saw himself as a carrier of tradition who was chosen by his tribe to carry their musical heritage. In Haslund-Christensen's words, "Sangrup regarded his singing as a sacred calling, and the old songs as a sacred treasure for which he must find an heir, before he could go to his fathers with peace in his heart" (*ibid.*, 29). He turned his attention to Haslund-Christensen and his recording device as the best hope for preserving the musical tradition. He believed that it was only a matter of time before the youth of his tribe would remember their roots and again seek out the musical treasury that he was carrying. But lacking a pupil to teach, he agreed to set down this tradition into Haslund-Christensen's recording device.

> Sangrup had never doubted that a coming generation would seek its way back to the old song-treasury of the people, and now it began to dawn upon him that with the aid of my mystical machinery he would be able to preserve the precious heritage in safety through an evil time, until Mongols should once again have an ear and a feeling for the tones

that were of the same origin as themselves. At last he had found the solution he had so long sought, that would enable him to return to his fathers without the heritage that had been entrusted to him being irrevocably lost (*ibid.*, 30).

Haslund-Christensen's account of Sangrup provides us with information about the life and work of a pre-Revolutionary fiddle player and *tuulič*, with which we can compare with others, including Berlinskii's account of Luwsan *khuurch* and Vladimirtsov's account of Parchen *khuurch*. But the story of Sangrup also provides us with a good example of how the turmoil that accompanied the coming of the Revolutionary period disrupted musical traditions. Haslund-Christensen's portrayal of this collapse resonates with romantic conceptions of tradition that would become popular again in Mongolia in the 1980s and 1990s. These included the view that traditional musical culture embodied a primordial identity of the Mongol people, a key to the "soul of the people"; that this culture was a material substance that could be set down and stored onto phonograph records, separated from the lived contexts in which it had meaning; and the view that this culture will inevitably disappear as a result of the cold logic of modernity.

THE SUPPRESSION OF MUSICAL TRADITION IN MONGOLIA

The destruction of the pre-Revolutionary musical traditions and customs in Inner Mongolia at the hands of the Japanese occurred in similar fashion in Mongolia in the early decades of the Peoples' Revolution at the hands of troops from the Soviet Red Army and Soviet-backed Mongolian army. In order to consolidate its power in the late 1920s and early 1930s, the leadership of the Mongolian Peoples Revolutionary Party (MPRP), backed by General Secretary of the Communist Party Joseph Stalin, ordered that the waning, if still considerable, authority held by the Chinggisid aristocracy and Tibetan Buddhist religious institutions be completely overturned. MPRP chairman Marshall Choibalsang set the army and secret police against all those in the country that were deemed opposed to the Peoples Revolution. Many thousands of lamas and monks were expelled from their monasteries and many others were killed. Nearly every monastery in the nation was destroyed or converted into warehouses. Members of the old aristocracy were imprisoned or killed, as were many of the nationalists and intellectuals who helped found the nation in the 1910s and 1920s (cf. Sandag and Kendall 2000).

These Party efforts were accompanied by civil strife that disrupted all aspects of the tradition-oriented ways of life of the pre-Revolutionary period, especially the musical traditions. Members of the Mongolian and Soviet secret police went out into the countryside in this period, entering the homes of herders and arresting those they believed to be associated with the former aristocracy or Buddhists leadership. Their search for those working "against the revolution" also often led them to target those objects and beliefs associated with pre-Revolutionary society. A musician from Arkhangai says that he has heard stories about folk fiddles being destroyed in the province during this period: "The soldiers seized the fiddles from their *ger*, took them outside and burned them along with the Buddhist scriptures" (Amartuvshin 1998.09.30). Enebish agrees that this was possible, adding that in these early years of the Revolution, the Party was "intent on destroying all parts of the old order, including anything of great value within it" (Enebish 1998.10.25).

With the system of traditional patronage destroyed, the professional and semi-professional fiddle players and story-tellers were left with little to do. Pegg tells us that some of them suffered persecution, while others "were reduced to living in holes in the ground" (Pegg 1995: 78). This was all a part of what she calls "the brutal demise of heroic epic performance under the Soviet regime" (*ibid.*, 77).

But not all talented artists were suppressed in this period. Clearly, those who could adapt or even reinvent themselves in ways suitable to the new regime had a better chance of survival. Around the time of the Revolution, for instance, Luwsan *khuurch*, as Berlinskii says, "actively rose up on the side of the Revolution." He became a member of the Mongolian People's Party and "helped to propagandize the idea of the Mongolian revolution" (Berlinskii 1933: 14). Luwsan sang songs in support of the Party and the Revolution in "traditional" ways, i.e., singing with his fiddle. From Berlinskii's point of view, the old fiddler was still "infected with elements of the pre-Revolutionary ideology of the ruling class of feudals and theocrats," elements from which he "had yet to free himself" (*ibid.*). But in working with the Party, Luwsan actively brought together the "old" and the "progressive" in new ways.

> He continuously unites in his performances the democratic elements, which have been ripened in the depths of feudal structure, with the repertoire and traditions of court musicians. . . . [In doing so,] he demonstrates the complex dialectic of the contemporary era in Mongolia, that is, the dialectic of collision between old Mongolia and the Mongolian People's Republic (*ibid.*).

The Russian composer and musicologist Boris Smirnov tells a similar story about another old Mongolian folksinger named Jigmed *khuurch*, who also chose to work with the Party in this period. He says he met Jigmed at the radio center in Ulaanbaatar in 1958, where he was making recordings of songs that asked people "to build a new life"; he also recorded songs about the "motherland and heroes of labor" (Smirnov 1975: 74). He says that when he asked him for his opinion of the new musical culture in Mongolia, Jigmed *khuurch* replied by playing his fiddle and improvising "a song devoted to the great new musical culture that made life more beautiful" (*ibid.*).

The shifting international situation in the first decades of the twentieth century, particularly the collapse of Qing dynastic rule and the success of the Russian Bolshevik Revolution, initiated processes that would severely disrupt the continuities that defined pre-Revolutionary Mongolian society. In particular, Western-inspired modernist ideologies that were brought to Mongolia through Russia and Russian-educated Mongolians introduced new terms and ideas about what constituted a people, culture, and nation. New modernist concepts of time and history meant that societies would from this time forward be defined in terms that contrasted "modern" with "traditional" and "new" with "old." People were forced to decide if they were going to accept the perceived inevitability of progress and modernity or resist and fight against it. The destruction of two-stringed fiddles and repression of fiddlers in this period shows how closely such musical instruments were associated with tradition-oriented or "old" Mongolia. To the Revolutionaries, the fiddles were as much a symbol of the past as the Buddhist sutras and idols of Chinggis Khan. The act of destroying them was symbolic as well as practical.

At the same time, officials in the new Revolutionary government understood that building a new musical culture (*shine khögjmiin soyol*) did not have to mean the utter obliteration of the old. Instead, in the words of a popular revolutionary song, this new culture could be "founded upon the ruins of the old." Older traditions, cleansed of their association with "the ideology of the ruling class of feudals and theocrats," could provide a basis upon which to build a new musical culture that was unmistakably more modern and international in form and content. In the following chapter, we will trace the role that traditional instruments, like the horse-head fiddle, played in founding a modern and cosmopolitan national musical culture.

2   Building a National Music Culture

As we saw in the previous chapter, the success of the Peoples Revolution of 1921 in Mongolia came at the expense of many of the traditional ways of life of the preceding era. Unlike the turmoil in Inner Mongolia, however, the full destructive force of the Revolution did not come about until nearly a decade later when the ruling Mongolian Peoples Revolutionary Party (MPRP) became radicalized under the influence of the Soviet Communist Party and its General Secretary, Joseph Stalin. Under the direction of its own strong-man, Marshall Choibalsang, who was closely allied with Stalin, the MPRP went after the so-called enemies of the people, aggressively, many say ruthlessly, targeting the Tibetan Buddhist institutions and the surviving elements of the Chinggisid aristocracy. On the eve of World War II, after years of suppression and purges, Choibalsang and the MPRP held a position of unrivaled political authority in the country.

While raids and arrests were effective in bringing about immediate changes in peoples' behavior, the Party leadership understood that transforming peoples' consciousness required more long-term and subtle methods. From the mid-1940s on, it began increasingly to turn its attention to bringing about a "cultural revolution" (*soyoliin khuwisgol*) among the Mongolian people. This new effort would not only protect the gains of the Revolution from its enemies, but would also return the Mongolian people to the path towards national development and the eventual the attainment of Communism. The link that the leadership made between development and cultural uplift is clear in the introduction to a book for young cultural workers published by the Party several decades later. "Raising the level of cultural and intellectual knowledge of the workers," it says,

> will not only help direct the work at improving Communist education and raising the workers' aesthetics and knowledge, but it will also renew their knowledge of theory and politics, enrich their forms of work, and strengthen the growth of the material base of socialist culture (Chuluunbat 1972: 12).

For the MPRP, the institutionalization of culture and the arts was as vital to the development of the nation as was expanding the economy and reforming the political structure. From the end of World War II onwards, building a new culture in Mongolia involved the processes of centralization and nationalization. Largely regional and fragmented music-cultures were absorbed into an expanding system of schools, theaters, and other cultural institutions, each of which was linked to central Party institutions in the nation's capital. At the same time, so-called characteristic elements representing each of the many Mongolian music-cultures were selected and cleansed of any association they may have had with "the ideology of the ruling class of feudals and theocrats." They were then remodeled after the "best" elements of international socialist culture to create a new syncretic cultural form that appeared to be distinctly Mongolian but which shared a clear affinity to the musical styles of other socialist "brother" nations. This new syncretism was often glossed as "national in form, socialist in content."

This chapter will trace the institutionalization of the musical arts in the MPR and the development of a distinctly Mongolian national musical culture. The process of centralizing control over the cultural activities throughout the country began in earnest in the early decades after the Revolution, but reached its peak from the mid-1950s to the 1970s, when the Party turned its attention to building up the leading cultural institutions in the capital city, Ulaanbaatar, and developing new, syncretic musical styles that reflected both national and international musical elements. As we will see, this spirit of fusing the Mongolian with the European will extend to those who build the horse-head fiddle, leading to the development of the "modern" horse-head fiddle that would, in its sound and form, reflect the musical and cultural ideals of the era.

THE FIRST CULTURAL CENTERS

The seeds of this new musical culture were sewn soon after the Peoples Revolution. In the early 1920s, the revolution was still largely centered in the nation's capital, Urga.[1] This changed over the next two decades as the Party worked to reach out to Mongolians in the countryside and to reorganize their cultural activities within Party-sanctioned institutions. The earliest of these efforts were those by national cadres (*ündesnii kadr*), groups of Party activists, cultural workers, teachers, musicians and others that were sent out to rural villages and encampments to play music, sing Revolutionary songs, and spread the word about Lenin and Marx (Tsendorj 1983: 11). Before long the Party also turned its attention to opening cultural centers. The first structures were called *ulaan ger* or "red gers," which were essentially *ger*s transformed into public meeting places. Later, more permanent wooden structures were built that came to be known as *ulaan bulgan* or "red corners," referring to the squared nature of these buildings.

Most of these centers disseminated news and Party information. They also organized educational and cultural activities like the teaching of literacy and hygiene, concert performances, theater productions, and film screenings (Natsagdorj 1981: 260). Concerts were typically organized by local people, playing instruments they or the centers owned. Figure 4 shows performers of a small ensemble organized outside a cultural center, likely located in central Mongolia. There is a wide variety of instruments, some of which, like the *limbe*[2] and *khuuchir*, are Mongolian, others of which, like the guitar and mandolin, were imports from Russia.

Despite their small size, these cultural centers became vitally important in organizing and implementing the Party's "cultural-enlightenment work" (*soyol gegeerliin ajil*). At a general meeting in 1924, the Peoples' Revolutionary Party passed a resolution that describes the opening of these centers across the country "as vital to the teaching and enlightening [of] the people" and "to spreading the Party's ideology" (Tsendorj 1983: 11). The Party viewed activities that drew people from communities together as opportunities to engage in political work. Performers in one rural cultural center remember how Party officials often came onto the stage after concert performances to give political speeches, convey recent information about the Party, or offer criticism about some individual's behavior (Gankhuyag, et. al, 1998.11.13). In this new era, the arts and politics were explicitly bound together.

Figure 4.   Amateur performers outside of a rural cultural center (Natsagdorj 1981).

While the opening of new performance spaces may have appeared inno-cent enough, their cultural implications were profound. Often located in the middle of towns and villages, cultural centers aimed to redefine the center of communal cultural activities from the family *ail* to the public stage. Once in public view, these activities could be much more easily monitored and controlled by local Party officials, who could ensure that what appeared on the communal stages fit with the ideology of the Party. The strict hierarchi-cal nature of this control, furthermore, meant that the activities in even the most remote *ulaan ger* could fall within the gaze of officials up the chain of command to the highest levels of the Party leadership. These efforts were part of the broader process of centralizing the control of cultural activities in the country.

Another important part of building the new national musical culture was integrating new Russian or European cultural practices into local custom. Setting a concert performance on the stage of a cultural center, for exam-ple, involved a distinct break with many of the pre-Revolutionary musical values and traditions and mandated new forms of behavior. Instead of the inclusive setting of the home or *ail*, in which everyone was encouraged to participate, the stage physically separated the performers (*jüjigchid*) from the audience members (*üzegchid*). On stage, the performer received all of the attention, while the audience sat quietly and watched. This separation was, over time, further emphasized with the use of stage lighting, sound amplification, and special costumes. This is just one example of how the Party, by enforcing new performance etiquette in the cultural centers and concert halls, promoted a subtle transformation in people's behavior, which also advanced the cultural revolution it sought to achieve.

NATIONALIZING THE MUSICAL ARTS

The most significant investment in the nation's cultural institutions occurred in the post-War era, particularly from the mid-1950s to the early 1970s, a period that paralleled important changes in the nation's economy. The Party believed that a key task in "building socialism" in Mongolia was the completion of the process of nationalizing private property and the means of production. The Party organized massive campaigns in the mid-1950s that aimed to reorganize herders from private rural encampments into state-run *negdel*s or agricultural and herding collectives. They began in earnest around 1957 and were largely completed—dramatically—by the early 1960s. Mongolist Charles Bawden reports that the number of Mon-golian herders not collectivized dropped from 62% in 1956 to less than 1% in 1963 (Bawden 1989: 394). One reason for this drop may have been the large number of people the Party sent from the countryside to the newly developed and massive industrial complexes in the equally newly developed cities of Erdenet and Darkhan in the north-central part of the country.

In the same period, the Party organized cultural campaigns aimed at consolidating its nationwide efforts at cultural uplift. One of the most ambitious initiatives was the campaign called the Cultural Leap Forward, which was initiated by the Fourteenth Congress of the MPRP in 1959.[3] The Congress defined the goals of this campaign as "raising the cultural level of the working people, indoctrinating them in the spirit of communism, and fighting against the vestiges of old thinking" (Magban 1964: 46). These new collectives and complexes were considered ideal locations for cultural centers. As part of this campaign, the Party worked to "place a cultural organization in each county (*sumu* or *sum*), industrial complex, and agricultural collective (*negdel*) and brigades (sub-units of *negdels*) in the country" with the result that, as collectivization and industrialization increased, so too did the number of cultural organizations (Dashdondog 1965: 26).

Producing results in the campaign to raise the cultural level of the working masses, however, proved to be an enormous and often frustrating undertaking for the Party leadership, which invested heavily in terms of time, capital, and people. The plans called for the expansion of existing cultural institutions and the building of new ones, as well as for increased Party supervision and control over how they were operated. Furthermore, the Party's broad definition of culture extended beyond institutions of music and art to include those of education and health care, as well. One of the new programs, for example, called for expanding the number of libraries and reading rooms, raising the number of radios and record players in the homes of herders, and increasing people's participation in the activities at the cultural centers. In the bureaucratic optimism of the period, orders were also made to increase the consumption of vegetables and even improve the extermination of roaches (cf. Magban 1964)!

However successful the campaign was at exterminating roaches, Party statistics did show broader cultural advancements. In his speech to the Central Committee during the Fifteenth Congress of the MPRP in 1966, Party Secretary Y. Tsedenbal announced that since the late 1950s, "more than 300 clubs, over 1,000 clubrooms, 312 libraries, 7 cinemas and more than 70 mobile and stationary cinema projectors have been put into operation in the centres of agricultural co-operatives and other localities" across Mongolia (Tsedenbal 1966: 85–86). These numbers are almost double those from before this period (Chuluunbat 1972: 12).[4]

Arkhangai *aimag*, a rural province located in the center of Mongolia, provides a more focused example of this increase in the number and size of rural or province-level cultural institutions. The Party's "Cultural Leap Forward" campaign came to be known in this province as the "Years of Cultural Offensive" (*Soyolyn dowtolgoony jilüüd*), and its goals were incorporated into the local Party's three- and five-year plans (Regsüren 1973: 300). In 1941 Arkhangai had two *klubs*, two *ulaan gers*, and five *ulaan bulgan*. By the early 1970s, this number had increased to one *soyolyn töv* or "Cultural Palace,"[5] eighteen *klubs*, and ninety-four *ulaan bulgan* (*ibid.*, 299). This enormous increase in the number of *ulaan ger* was likely due to the increase in the number of *negdel*s and brigades in the province during the period of collectivization in the late 1950s. Just as importantly, cultural organizations also were being opened or expanded in increasingly remote parts of the province.

The Party's sustained attention in this period to the development of the cultural institutions in both urban and rural areas helped to transform the musical arts in Mongolia. These cultural centers, from tiny "red gers" to massive "cultural palaces," became increasingly popular centers for cultural activities. By offering a variety of activities, such as song competitions, concerts by visiting artists, and film screenings, the centers increasingly began to compete with traditional home or *ail*-centered cultural activities. In the newly developed urban areas in Mongolia, where most people lived in high-rise apartment blocks, cultural centers and theaters provided natural meeting places for people, especially for the younger generations. At the same time, many Mongolians have also commented on how participation in events at cultural centers was at times mandated by local Party officials, showing the importance the Party placed on making these centers a part of the lives of all citizens of the state.

The new urban lifestyle experienced by many Mongolians in this period also worked against efforts to maintain many older musical traditions. Working full-time in an office or factory made maintaining one's skills on a musical instrument much more difficult. Long work-weeks also tended to push social activities, such as collective music-making, to the days off from work. In addition, new urban forms of entertainment were gaining popularity in the cities and spreading to the countryside. These included the rise of new song forms, such as *niitiin duu* or "common song" and *zoxiolyn duu* or "composed songs," both of which featured a soloist accompanied by a small ensemble. The songs have folk-like melodies and are often set to pastoral themes, such as the beauty of a countryside girl or the splendor of the steppe. But these are songs written to be performed by professional performers in the new medium of the concert stage. Their short length (typically around 3–4 minutes) and evocative and varied themes made them ideal for concerts, as well as for the new broadcast media of radio, phonographs, and film.

The centralization of cultural centers in Mongolia paralleled the building of infrastructure that brought electricity, radio broadcasts, telephone connections, and newspapers from the capital to nearly all parts of the nation. By the mid-1960s all of the nation's *negdel*s and provincial centers had been connected with Ulaanbaatar through radio and telephone communication links (Tsedenbal 1966: 75). At the same time, an increasing number of people, even in distant rural areas, had access to inexpensive radios,[6] allowing them to tune-in to broadcasts from the capital city. Such broadcasts, along with the print media, films, and later television, helped to establish a truly national popular culture. The ability for Mongolians in almost all parts of the country to access this popular culture simultaneously must certainly have affected each individual's perception of him- or herself as a citizen of a sovereign nation. One of the key goals of the Party's campaigns of "cultural uplift" was to encourage individuals to see their identity as citizens of a modern and sovereign nation as more important than their identities as individuals from a particular region, clan, or ethnic group.

The nature of the broadcast network developed in the 1960s facilitated this goal. Broadcasts originated only in the Party-run studios in Ulaanbaatar. Mongolians could receive them, but could not create their own. This spoke-like, one-way broadcast system added to the Party's centralized control over information and entertainment in the country. But it also meant that people throughout the country knew what was going on in the popular culture of the capital city, and it was no coincidence that new urban song forms, like the *niitiin duu* and *zokhiolyn duu*, became popular across the nation in the same period as the growth of these broadcast networks. As has happened in many other parts of the world, mass-mediated popular culture developed hand-in-hand with advances in electronic technologies and communications. In Mongolia of the 1960s and 1970s, these advances were accompanied by the expansion of cultural contacts between Mongolia and Russia and other parts of the Soviet world, which had a profound influence on the shape of the new national musical culture.

DEVELOPING A NATIONAL MUSICAL CULTURE

The nation's most important musical institutions, including key schools and musical ensembles, were based in Ulaanbaatar. The Party charged them with setting the standard for cultural activities pursued everywhere else in Mongolia. They were to create art, in the words of Party Secretary Tsedenbal, that reflected "the inspired labour and heroic feats of the builders of socialism" (Tsedenbal 1966: 82). They were also to guide and oversee these nationwide cultural activities, making sure that they "promote the ideological and political development of workers" (*ibid*.).

Many of the most promising and gifted music students from the countryside were sent up the chain of rural cultural centers to study in the leading colleges and music schools in Ulaanbaatar. Most would be returned a few years later to work as performers and teachers in their respective homelands. The most gifted, however, might be selected to stay in the capital city to perform in the leading orchestras and folk ensembles, or even sent abroad for advanced training in schools in Russia and other parts of the Soviet Union.

Throughout the Socialist period, the relationships between Mongolian and Soviet international cultural institutions were especially close. This was reflected in exchanges not only of music students, but also of music teachers, coaches, conductors, administrators and others. Mongolian music schools adopted Soviet educational curriculum, methodologies, and organizational structures. While courses and lessons were taught in the Mongolian language, Russian became a necessary second language for all students, faculty and scholars, as this was the *lingua franca* of the Soviet world. Russian musical terminology even formed the basis of the musical language in Mongolia until Mongolian musical dictionaries were developed. As in most colonial nations, Mongolians during this period needed to speak the language of the dominant power in order to get ahead in the new system. But rather than being resentful of this power dynamic, most Mongolians appeared to have accepted or even embraced it. Many Mongolian musical performers, faculty, and scholars from this period speak of willingly learning the Russian language and of developing close personal relationships with their Russian and Soviet colleagues, many of which remain strong today (Figure 5).

The leadership of the MPRP and the Soviet Communist Party welcomed such close working relationships as part of their broader strategy of emphasizing the alliance of the Mongolian and Soviet peoples. This idea was a common trope in the propaganda of the day, which described the "Elder brother-Younger brother" relationship and the "Eternal friendship" between the Mongolian and Soviet peoples.[7] As a "younger brother" nation, the MPR needed to develop its own unique identity while also being a part of the broader Soviet "family" of nations. Developing a national musical culture was an important part of this overall strategy. The national musical ensembles, compositional styles, instrumental designs and so on, that emerged in this period typically fused the "best" elements from European classical music with "selected" elements from Mongolian folk music, resulting in a style that was, by and large, a syncretism of European and Mongolian musical elements. And while most of these developments were mandated from the highest levels of the Party leadership, many of the most important were also made at the level of the teachers and performers themselves.

MUSIC EDUCATION

Beginning in the late 1950s, the Party significantly increased the number and size of music schools in the country. The most important of these was the transformation of the Art High School (*Urlagiin dund surguuli*) of Ulaanbaatar into the Music & Dance College (*Khögjim büjgiin dund surguuli*) in 1957 and 1958. In this process, new departments were created, such as the department of instrument making and repair, and existing ones expanded, such as the departments of classical opera and dance. It also allowed the school to considerably boost its enrollments. By the 1960s, the Music & Dance College became the largest and most important institution for the training of the national cadre, who were still being prepared and sent to work in schools and cultural centers throughout the country (Tsendorj 1983: 30; Enebish 1982: 30).

Figure 5.   Teachers and pupils at the Music & Dance School in Ulaanbaatar (Tüdew 1986)

The Music & Dance College, along with all of the other music schools, primarily trained students for careers as performers in the musical genres of classical (*songodog*) and folk (*ardyn*) music. These were the genres performed by the largest and most prestigious opera, symphonic, and folklore ensembles in Ulaanbaatar. While the performance styles of the two genres were very different, it was commonly expected that both students and teachers, especially in the 1950s and 1960s, be able to perform equally well in both domains. For example, G. Jamyan both taught and played on the horse-head fiddle and the European violoncello. Performers of the European flute would also play the *limbe*, opera singers would sing national folk songs, and ballet dancers would dance folk dances. Jamyan described how the paucity of professional players in this period often required him to perform the horse-head fiddle on some days and the violoncello on others (Jamyan 1999.10.12). This was also a period when the distinctions between the professional and amateur, as well as the national and classical, were neither clearly drawn nor strictly maintained.

By the mid- to late-1950s, however, the increased attention to professionalism within the new musical culture accelerated the assimilation of European classical performing traditions. Surprisingly, this was a process often undertaken by the artists themselves, rather than from instructions from Party officials. As the dominant teacher and performer of the European violoncello, Jamyan incorporated elements of its performance methodology into his teaching and playing of the horse-head fiddle. These included developing ways of holding the horse-head fiddle and its bow, of fingering the notes on the strings, and of moving the bow over the strings all of which resembled those of the violoncello. These changes helped horse-head fiddle players to perform European and European-styled classical music. Jamyan also developed a series of fundamental exercises that he used in teaching the instrument to his students and that he later published in what has become the standard method book for the instrument, *Morin khuur surakh garyn awlaga* (Handbook for the Study of the Horse-head Fiddle, 1978).

His ideas about playing and teaching methodologies contributed to the modernization of the horse-head fiddle tradition. In insisting that fiddle players learn to play the instrument by first mastering a series of abstract exercises, such as arpeggio and scalar exercises, Jamyan broke with the more traditional methods of teaching the fiddle based on watching and imitating other fiddle players and by learning from playing actual musical works. His approach assumed that students could read musical notation and understand a composition's "musical grammar," such as its pitch, rhythm, timbre, and so on. Jamyan also demanded that his students play with clear and precise tuning, and had a piano in his office that he would use in his lessons to check students' intonation (Figure 6). Each was a new development in the methodology of playing and teaching a folk instrument.

Figure 6.   G. Jamyan teaching a lesson to a pupil in his office in the Music & Dance College, Ulaanbaatar. Notice the piano in the background (Chagnaa 1987)

In the 1950s and 1960s, it was much easier for individual teachers like Jamyan to establish their own particular methodologies or performance styles given the relatively small size of the professional music community. This is one reason why Jamyan's ideas and methods have become so well established in the country. Not only was he the first to address issues of methodology seriously, but he had many students. It can be argued that he and his disciples have established something resembling a fiddle-playing guild that works to both disseminate and protect the musical standards Jamyan initiated. Patronized by the state musical institutions from their beginnings, such guilds arose throughout the professional musical world and often set the national standards for the performance of folk musical instruments.

MUSICAL ENSEMBLES AND INSTITUTIONS

Expanding the number and training of performers in these educational institutions was directly related to the increase in the number and size of both classical and national music ensembles in the country. The State Music and Drama Theater (renamed the State Academic Theater in 1981, Figure 7) was opened in 1963. An enormous, columned building erected near Sükhbaatar Square in downtown Ulaanbaatar, it offered a stage larger than the Opera and Dance Theater, which was built in the 1940s, and it was the only building with the capacity to present large-scale productions of theater, music and opera in the capital city. The Theater became the home for several state theatrical and musical ensembles, including the State Folksong & Dance Ensemble.

By the 1960s there was a host of major classical music ensembles active in Ulaanbaatar, including the Opera Theater Symphony Orchestra (*Duuriin teatryn simfoni khamtlag*), established in 1951. In the early 1960s, this ensemble began to premiere and perform many large-scale works of Mongolian and international composers. The State Drama Theater Symphony Orchestra (*Ulsyn dramyn teatryn simfoni khögjmiin khamtlag*) was established in the same year as another ensemble, the Radio Committee Symphony Orchestra (*Radio khoroony simfoni orkestr*), and it consisted of forty-five musicians drawn from the orchestras of the Folksong & Dance Ensemble, State Circus, and the Children's Theater (Tsendorj 1983: 42).

The "Great Ensemble" (*Ikh chuulga*, Figure 8),[8] is one of the ensembles that make up the State Folksong & Dance Ensemble (*Ulsyn ardyn duu büjgiin chuulag*). It premiered on the thirty-fifth anniversary of the People's Revolution in 1956. As the name implies, it was then, as it remains today, a large "orchestra" consisting of forty to fifty musicians who are grouped and arranged on stage in ways that were meant to resemble a symphony orchestra. Each section of the ensemble consists of a group of like-instruments that roughly correspond to European symphonic

Figure 7. The State Academic Theater (formerly the D. Natsagdorj State Music & Drama Theater), Ulaanbaatar (MPRP 1971).

instruments. The horse-head fiddles, for instance, symbolically play the role of the European violoncelli; the *khuuchir*, the role of the violins or violas; the *limbe*, the modern flutes, and so on. Common national instruments, including the *yoochin* and *shudarga* were also grouped in the ensemble and, depending on the music being performed, typically provided harmonic or melodic counterpoint to the primary melody instruments, such as the horse-head fiddles and the *khuurchirs*. As with a European orchestra, the ensemble is led by a conductor who stands on a podium in the front of the ensemble. A chorus or solo vocalists would join the ensemble as needed. By the early 1960s, under the direction of the composer, L. Mördorj, the Great Ensemble had become established as one of the major music ensembles in Ulaanbaatar.

The most widespread form of the national musical ensemble, however, was the small ensemble consisting of five core instruments, including the horse-head fiddle, *khuuchir, shanz, yoochin,* and *limbe* (Figure 9). Music historian G. Tsendorj described such ensembles as the "classical grouping of Mongolian national instruments" (*Mongol ündesnii tsöökhüül khögjmiin songodog bütets*). It was not uncommon for these groups to expand to include other instruments, including the *yatga* and *shudarga*, as well as contemporary instruments like the *ewer büree* (bull's horn), *ikh khuur* (great

Figure 8. The Great Ensemble, part of the State Folksong & Dance Ensemble. Notice the monastic instruments, such as the *ikh büree* (great horn) and *khengereg*, in the rear of the ensemble (MPRP 1971).

fiddle), and snare drum (more on these instruments below). These origins of these small modern folk ensembles, organized in cultural centers around the country, is something of a mystery. While they appear to be fashioned after European chamber ensembles, they also appear close in design to the small Chinese musical ensembles that were common among the Chinese satellite settlements in pre-Revolutionary Ikh Khüree (present-day Ulaanbaatar) and Kiakhta, among others (Gyorgy Kara, personal communication).

The repertoire available to these ensembles expanded and became much more challenging from the 1960s on. The building of large performance spaces, along with the expansion of the size of the ensembles and higher-level training of performers, facilitated the performance of large-scale symphonic and operatic works. Figure 10 lists the dates of premieres of Russian and European operas and ballets beginning in the late 1950s. It shows a sharp increase in the number of premieres in the late 1960s and early 1970s. The new repertoire included some of the most challenging operas, ballets, and symphonic works by European (Beethoven, Mozart and Schubert) and Russian composers (Tchaikovsky, Borodin, Rachmaninov, and Prokofiev). For the Party, the ability of State ensembles to perform such music was a sign of success of the nation's campaigns of cultural uplift. The two hundredth anniversary of Beethoven's birth in 1970, for instance, was celebrated by a gala concert that included a performance of his Fifth Symphony (Tsendorj 1983: 45). The one hundredth anniversary of the V. I. Lenin's birth, in the same year, was marked with a performance of Shostakovich's Twelfth Symphony (*ibid.*).

Figure 9.   An instrumental "Quintet" of national musical instruments (Smirnov 1963).

COMPOSERS, ARRANGERS, & CHOREOGRAPHERS

Just as new generations of professionally trained performers allowed the new and newly expanded ensembles to perform major classical music compositions, so too did a new generation of professionally trained Mongolian composers and choreographers make their presence known in the concert halls of Ulaanbaatar. Some of the most respected of this new generation included D. Luwsansharaw, E. Choidog, and Ts. Namsraijaw, while the older, more established composers, arrangers, and choreographers included B. Damdinsüren, L. Mördorj, and S. Gonchigsümlaa.

Like their colleagues in other Soviet republics, Mongolian composers struggled to define a distinctly Mongolian sound within the late-Romantic European classical style of composition popular among Soviet musical institutions. Following the nationalist models of musical composition popularized by such Russian composers as Rheinhold Gliere, Mongolian composers drew upon as the so-called national cultural heritage (*ündesnii soyoliin tow*) for material and inspiration. L. Mördorj, for instance, uses arrangements of Mongolian folk and revolutionary song melodies in his First Symphony, subtitled "My Motherland" (*Minii ekh oron*, 1955). Mördorj described his work as depicting "through its four movements the Mongolian nation's ancient past and future" (Chagnaa 1987: 57). The

A. FOREIGN OPERAS

1.	P.I. Tchaikovsky	*"Eugene Onegin"*	1963 (June 8)
2.	A Dorgomiicheskii	*"Lusyn dagina"* (Dragon Fairy)	1964 (June 8)
3.	Puccini	*"Chio chio san"* (Madama Butterfly)	1967 (April 14)
4.	V. Muradeli	*"Oktyabr'"* (October)	1969 (March 1)
5.	Ch. Gounod	*"Faust"*	1969 (March 1)
6.	S. Rachmaninov	*"Aleko"*	1969 (July 13)
7.	A. Borodin	*"Igor van"* (Prince Igor)	1972 (May 4)
8.	B. Smetana	*"Khudaldagdsan ber"* (Bartered Bride)	1974 (March 9)
9.	G. Verdi	*"Traviata"* (La Traviata)	1977 (April 9)

B. FOREIGN DANCE PERFORMANCES (MOSTLY BALLETS)

1.	B.V. Asaf'ev	*"Bakhchisarain orgilolt bulag"* (Bubbling Spring of Bakhchisarai)	1957
2.	G. Yarullin	*"Shurale (oin sawdag)"* (Lord of the Forest)	1958
3.	P. Tchaikovsky	*"Francheski da rimin"* (Francesca da Rimini)	1963 (March 12)
4.	N. Rimskii Korosakov	*"Shekherazada-Sindbad dalaichin"* (Scherazade)	1963 (March 12)
5.	J. Zorin	*"Chipolino-Songino khüü"* (Onion Boy)	1965 (May 7)
6.	L. Delibe	*"Kopelliya-Tsenkher nüden büsgüi"* (Copella-Blue-eyed Girl)	1966 (April 24)
7.	Ts. Puni	*"Esmeralida"* (Esmeralda)	1967 (May 3)
8.	L. Minkus	*"Don Kikhot"* (Don Quixote)	1971 (March 1)
9.	B.V. Asaf'ev	*"Parisyn döl"* (Flames of Paris)	1971 (July 12)
10.	S. Prokofiev	*"Zolushka"* (Cinderella)	1972 (November 7)
11.	I. Morozov	*"Aibolit doktor"* (Doctor Dolittle)	1975 (June 23)
12.	P. Tchaikovsky	*"Khunt nuur"* (Swan Lake)	1975 (June 28)

Figure 10. Dates of premieres of Russian and European operas and dance performances in the State Opera and Dance Theater (1957–1977) (Tsendorj 1983).

movements variously portray the "grief of the Mongolian people" prior to the Revolution, their "happiness after achieving victory and freedom," and their "dreams for the future" of the new society being built (*ibid.*). He says that the third movement, in particular, seeks to depict through music "the Mongolian people at a summer Naadam festival" (*ibid.*).

Mördorj's melding of the Mongolian and the European reflects his own cosmopolitan upbringing. He learned to play the two-stringed fiddle early in his life in his home city of Ulaanbaatar. By the 1930s, while still in his teens, he was one of the first musicians to study at the city's Theater Fine Arts School. Of the same generation as the fiddler Jamyan, Mördorj also studied with the same teachers at this school, and distinguished himself as a performer of the *khuuchir*. He entered an all-Mongolia national musician's competition in 1936 and won first prize, gaining the title of State Honored Musicians (*Ulsyn gawiyat khögjimchin*). In the 1940s he began to compose music, including popular songs (*niitiin duu*) and settings of revolutionary poetry. In 1950, he and fellow composer B. Damdinsüren composed the Mongolian national anthem, for which Marshal Choibalsang honored them both. That same year he entered the Moscow Conservatory where he continued his study of composition with Russian composers, under whose direction he began to work on the First Symphony.

His First Symphony was the first full-scale symphony written by a Mongolian composer and after the premiere of this work Soviet critics praised Mördorj for his mastery of the symphonic form. One described it as being rooted in the "Mongolian folk song and musical dialects," while showing "European thinking" interwoven with "reflections of the Motherland, Revolution, *Negdels* and their ways of life" (Natsagdorj 1989: 37).[9] As is typical of musical journalism of the Socialist period, however, nothing is written about how this music was received by Mongolian audiences. In fusing Mongolian folk musical elements with Russian and European classical musical structures as he did, Mördorj's symphonic style set an example to later the generations of Mongolian composers as to what a Mongolian national music could sound like.

The Party professionalized the field of composition with the establishment of the Mongolian Composers Union (*Mongol khögjim zokholchdyn kholboo*) in 1957. Like its counterpart in the field of literature, the Mongolian Writer's Union, the MCU quickly became a locus of musical power and authority in Mongolia. Membership was limited to those with the proper level of training, connections, or reputation. Once accepted, members were expected to meet annual compositional quotas. The Union decided when and for what type of ensemble or setting each composer should compose. At the same time, members were assured of performances of their works. Composers who were not members of the Union, in contrast, had few opportunities to get their works performed.

The leadership of the MCU was given a great deal of power to both define and control the music and musical performances that were undertaken in this period. Ensemble leaders, for instance, were responsible for determining the programs they were to present, but they were at the same time required to follow procedures established and supervised by the MCU in deciding the content of these programs. One of these procedures required that the ensembles perform a certain percentage of works written by members of the MCU. This made it difficult for ensembles to perform compositions written by non-MCU composers, such as those by local, regional, or amateur composers. These policies were ostensibly aimed at ensuring the quality of compositions performed at cultural centers throughout the nation. But, whether intended or not, they also further centralized the control of the MCU over musical performances in the country and contributed to the growing standardization and nationalization of musical style.

This filtering process continued to the point of performance. Ensembles were required to submit their program for approval by representatives of the MCU and the Party, who would then often come and sit in on dress rehearsals of ensembles. It was apparently not uncommon for individuals in these groups to call for changes to pieces, if not entire programs, the day before—or even of—the actual performances. S. Sündet, a senior conductor of the Folksong & Dance Ensemble for nearly four decades, recalls how much he hated these controls. "In that time," he said,

> everything that we did had to serve certain political views. Every piece we wanted to play had to go through an inspection by members of the State Political Committee [*Uls töriin towchoo*]. Before we could present a program, these guys would come in to hear our rehearsal. They could say to us, 'Change those words to that song,' or 'This piece can be presented, but this piece can't,' and so on. I was so happy when this ended! (Sündet 1997.08.01)

Some have described these controls as examples of the Party's tight artistic controls over musical expression, which might have been the case. But from another perspective, it could also have been the result of established composers within the MCU seeking to maintain controls over artistic standards and styles.

MODERNIZING NATIONAL INSTRUMENTS

The goals of professionalizing the performance of national music required that these instruments be redesigned, and in some instances newly created, to adapt to the changing performance contexts and aesthetics of the Mongolian music culture. These new contexts, including the large stages and ensemble settings, demanded instruments with capabilities that traditional instruments did not have, such as the ability to maintain their tuning, project their sound, and blending with the other instruments.

The "Great Ensemble" of the State Folksong & Dance Ensemble provides a good example of how the pantheon of national instruments was expanded during this period. When composers for the ensemble called for certain orchestral timbres that no existing national instrument could provide, the instruments were either drafted from other genres or created from scratch. Perhaps the most striking draftees included the monastic instruments, such as the Tibetan Buddhist long trumpet, the *ikh büree*, a long conical instrument made of brass, and a few percussion and wind instruments that were traditionally never used outside of the context of Tibetan Buddhist rituals. Other draftees included the European snare and timpani drums.

The new national folk instruments that the organizers created for this ensemble in the 1960s included the *ewer büree* and the *ikh khuur*. The *ewer büree* (literally "bull's horn") is shaped like a cow's horn and uses a clarinet mouthpiece, reeds, and keys. The modern *ewer büree* appears designed and crafted to imitate the timbre of a European clarinet. Badraa says that this instrument was adapted from the bull's horns (*uram*) that herders commonly used in ancient time (Badraa 1998e: 147). But there is no evidence to suggest that the *uram* was ever used as a *musical* instrument. Similarly the *ikh khuur*, or "great horse-head fiddle," introduced in the 1960s, is literally a very large horse-head fiddle that imitates the timbre of the European contrabass violin. Throughout the Soviet Union, instrument makers set to work creating entire "families" of folk instruments (cf. Slobin 1969; Bertkov 1963). The creation of the *ikh khuur* fits directly into this modern tradition.

The Great Ensemble bears striking similarities with the national "folk orchestras" common in Russia, Bulgaria, the PRC, and North Korea, among other places. As with other folk orchestras, the repertoire of the Great Ensemble includes arrangements of Mongolian folk song and European classical pieces and original compositions by professional composers. Two of the longtime "chestnuts" in the repertoire of the Great Ensemble is an arrangement of George Ionescu's "Romanian Rhapsody" for solo *khuuchir* and ensemble and an arrangement of Georges Bizet's overture to the opera *Carmen*.

The need for national instruments that meet the technical and aesthetic challenges of this kind of music forced instrument makers to reconsider how to modernize their design and construction. Instrumental parts traditionally fashioned from leather or animal skin were replaced with wood or metals; horsehair strings were replaced with nylon or cat-gut strings; traditional curved bows were replaced with European instrumental bows, and so on. The instruments were also constructed to be more durable so that their sound would project further into a hall and would better withstand the rigors of travel and changing climatic conditions from country to country. The strings of the fiddles were tightened to increase their projection and raise their pitch in order to meet orchestral standards.

The methods by which these modern folk musical instruments were constructed also underwent fundamental change. Instrument making and repair became a specialty in the new musical culture with the opening in the 1960s of a department devoted to it in the Music & Dance College. Youths here received training on how to construct, maintain, and repair national and European classical instruments, often from teachers sent from Russia and Eastern Europe. Talented graduates from this school often found work in the newly established State Musical Instrument Factory (*Ulsyn khögjim üildwer*) in Ulaanbaatar, where instruments were constructed to increasingly exacting—and standardized—measurements.

The mechanization of the instrument making process changed the traditional ways in which folk instruments were maintained and disseminated. The increasing complexity and quality of these modern national instruments made it more difficult for the performers themselves to maintain and repair them. Instead of fashioning one's own repair for a broken soundboard or bow, as a musician might have done with a traditionally constructed fiddle, he or she likely had to turn to an instrument repair specialist to have it repaired correctly. This development further exemplifies the growing specialization of professions within this new musical culture.

CULTURAL FESTIVALS AND MUSICAL COMPETITIONS

Despite early successes in its campaign of cultural uplift, Party officials were unhappy with the pace of modernization and professional development in the nation's cultural centers, and this in spite of the increasing number of trained performers being sent to them from music schools in Ulaanbaatar. Party literature of the mid- to late-1960s was filled with entreaties and complaints from local and national leaders about the poor state of controls over the quality of the activities taking place in the rural centers. In his speech to the Fifteenth Party Congress in 1966, Chairman Tsedenbal raised the specter that without the Party's constant attention to improving the content of these cultural activities, any gains made by raising the cultural levels of the workers and *arats* would quickly be lost. He called upon cultural workers to redouble their efforts in order not to lose any momentum towards cultural development they had already achieved. "It is necessary," he said, "to support and develop in every way various mass movements for knowledge and the new approach to labour and living, consolidating the positive results achieved in the years of the cultural offensive" (Tsedenbal 1966: 85–86).

One way of maintaining these "positive results" of their campaigns was for the Party to demand that the rural cultural organizations take greater responsibility in preparing and presenting its accomplishments to broader audiences. One of the more popular means of doing this was by organizing a "Ten Days of Culture and the Arts" (*Soyol urlagiin araw khonog*), a ten-day festival of the arts that was fashioned after the *Dekada* ten-day festival of the arts in the Soviet Union (Revin 1988). Each province was responsible for organizing a "Ten Days" festival in Ulaanbaatar at least once every five years as part of each province's five-year plan. Provincial cultural officials were expected to prepare performances that display their province's unique character, usually through concerts, theater productions, and gallery exhibitions. The elements of this "unique character" were expected to be both progressive and symbolic. Ethnic diversity within a province, for instance, was typically expressed through performers wearing costumes of each of the different "nationalities." The repertoire of these performances typically emphasized such themes as the homeland, happiness, labor, and progress.

The cultural center of Töw *aimag*, based in the town of Zuunmod, for example, held a "Ten Days" festival in Ulaanbaatar in early 1982 that included an exhibit entitled "The beautiful homeland Töw" (*Töw saikhan nutag*)," a concert entitled "Songs and Melodies of the People of the Töw Homeland" (*Töw nutgiinkhny aya duu*) and a theatrical performance entitled "The Hearth" (*Gal golomt*) ("Soyol urlag" 1982: 13). The festival was described in the press as drawing thousands of visitors "from morning to evening," and "providing a glance at this *aimag*'s workers' and herders' work and happy lives" (*ibid.*). While such festivals ostensibly provided the art workers of each province the opportunity to symbolically present their artistic creations to the Mongolian people, it also served as a means by which the Party could supervise and control the pace of cultural development in each province.

The Party also raised its expectations of participants in its nationwide "art examinations of the people" (*ard tümnii urlagiin üzleg*). The national competition of 1960, like those held in 1936, 1946, and 1956, tested the abilities of musicians to play national instruments and read musical notation (Chuluunbat 1972: 12). But later competitions were much more demanding. The competition in 1977, for instance, was open to both amateur and professional performers and required each to learn compositions by Russian and European classical music composers, as well as by national composers, and to play them on one of six different kinds of national instruments: the horse-head fiddle, *khuuchir*, *shudarga*, *yoochin*, *yatga* and *limbe* (Enebish 1982: 31). Enebish describes the expectation that Mongolian performers perform Western and Mongolian classical music as "a testament to the enormous growth of the musical abilities of our professional musicians and their high cultural mastery [of this art]" (*ibid.*). It was also a testament to the Party's ability to centralize, nationalize, and modernize the musical traditions in the country.

"PERFECTING" THE HORSE-HEAD FIDDLE

Despite the growth of the national musical arts in this period, the Party continued to invest most of its attention and resources on the development of European classical musical instruments and institutions. In this context, the modernization of the horse-head fiddle, for instance, was certainly low on its list of priorities. Although the fiddler Jamyan had initiated something of a mini-revolution in the teaching and performance of the horse-head fiddle in the 1950s, its substantial redesign would not come about until the late-1960s. It is also surprising that it came about through the initiative of a Russian violinmaker.

Denis Vladimirovich Yarovoi made violins in the Soviet Union that won high honors, including the top award in an international competition in Italy in 1959. Yarovoi was sent to Ulaanbaatar two or three times between 1966 and 1968 to conduct workshops for students in the department of musical instrument construction and repair at the Music & Dance College (Figure 11).

While there, Yaovoi became intrigued with the horse-head fiddle and about how it could be redesigned using European instrument making techniques to improve its sound and general acoustics. Yarovoi's most important contribution to these problems was to cover the face of the instrument with wood. While Mongolians had traditionally made horse-head fiddles with wooden faces,[10] Yarovoi taught his pupils how to design a wooden face similar to those used on European violins and violoncellos. Additional changes included the use of violoncello bridges, refinements in the treatment and lacquering of the wood, and the addition of two *f*-holes on the fiddle's face.[11] Like scholars and craftsmen in many fields in the Soviet era,

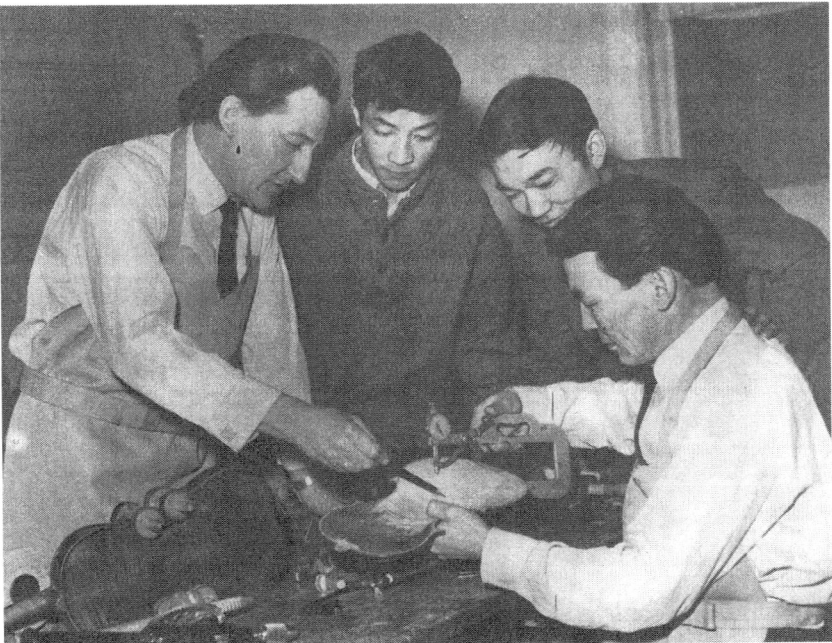

Figure 11. Soviet violinmaker Denis Yarovoi teaching his Mongolian pupils about the construction of a European violin. D. Buuran is seated (Enkhee 1968).

Yarovoi sought scientific methods to improve traditional arts and crafts, and devoted one of the two books he wrote to the construction of the horse-head fiddle (Enebish 1998.11.22).

Yarovoi presented his redesigned horse-head fiddle to Jamyan in 1967 or 1968, who promptly took it on a concert tour of European cities. After he returned, Jamyan was said to have praised the new fiddle "not only for protecting the rare quality that expresses the feelings of the Mongolian people, but also for having the sound of a large violin" (Enkhee 1968: 7). Jamyan and fiddle players after him were especially appreciative of how the wooden-faced fiddle better projected its sound into large concert halls and helped the instrument remain in tune as performance contexts shifted between dry and humid climates.

Yarovoi and his students applied their skills to improving other folk instruments, including the *khuuchir* and *yatga* (Enkhee 1968: 7; Enebish 1997.07.08). He also trained his students on how to construct a violin. One of the most talented, D. Buuran, became the first Mongolian to produce a European-style violin, which was played at a music festival in Ulaanbaatar in 1968. Yarovoi was impressed by the skills and professionalism of his students, particularly Buuran. "I am a man who has had many pupils," he said that year. "But only here have I encountered the most talented pupils. They have very good musical ears. Buuran was the very best at mastering the methods of making musical instruments" (Enkhee 1968: 7).

The Mongolians who worked with Yarovoi liked him as well, probably because he seemed to honestly appreciate them and their national music. A student of one of Yarovoi's pupils, a horse-head fiddle maker named D. Ulambayar, described Yarovoi as someone whose goals were "purely artistic," and not shaded by politics or ideology.

> He was very interested in and liked folk music. He was a specialist in music and believed that folk music was *real* music. He did his work in the call of his own heart. No one asked him to change or improve the horse-head fiddle. He did it by his own call. He was sent here to repair and teach the repair of string instruments and it was only after he arrived that he became interested in this instrument (Ulambayar 1998.04.01).

An important point in this assessment of Yarovoi was that he and his pupils undertook these refinements to the horse-head fiddle on their own initiative, rather than on order of the Party leadership. This fits with observations made by scholars of other Soviet era arts, such as Katerina Clark in her study of Soviet literature, who found that cultural authorities were generally much more interested in the political message of a work of art than in its aesthetic qualities (Clark 2000: xiii). The Party gave much more attention to the development of the European-oriented classical musical arts in Mongolia than to the national musical arts. This was likely because the classical arts provided a much clearer basis for comparing cultural achievement on an international stage than the national arts. For their part, Yarovoi's pupils appreciated his interest in the horse-head fiddle as a "serious professional musical instrument" (Ulambayar 1998.04.01).

In the 1970s and 1980s, Buuran and a handful of other students, including D. Baatar, Yargaa and Jügder[12] continued to make improvements to the sound quality and design of the horse-head fiddle (Enkhee 1968, Ulambayar 1998.04.01). Many of their pupils, in turn, went on to work in the State Music Instrument Factory where the improvements brought by Yarovoi and his pupils made their way into the instrument's design. As this factory remained the single source for modern horse-head fiddles in Mongolia until the early 1990s, the fiddle bearing them became the standard used to this day throughout the nation.

THE HORSE-HEAD FIDDLE AS A MUSICAL SYMBOL

Ulambayar's comment about folk music as being "real" points to a conflict that existed between artists and the Party officials about the role of the folk arts in a modern society. While the Party accepted that the horse-head fiddle and other national instruments had a place within the new musical culture, it also saw them as less important than those of European origin. Ulambayar even described a conversation he had with a Soviet-trained Mongolian cultural official who went so far as to say that he they did not consider the horse-head fiddle to have any vital part to play in the modern Mongolian musical culture (Ulambayar 1998.04.01).

The Party leadership instead appeared to envision such folk instruments as playing symbolic roles within a national musical context that was becoming increasingly global in scope. "Internationalism was the key," says D. Tserenpil, a member of the Mongolian Academy of Sciences. "The Party did not consider the horse-head fiddle to be 'bad,' only 'traditional.' [And thus] we needed only a little of it" (Tserenpil 2001.06.15). The fiddle maker Enkhjargal explained how the horse-head fiddle, like folk music in general, was considered to be like a "side dish" (*daivar*) in the new musical culture, "It was never the main meal" (Enkhjargal 1998.12.05).

In an article praising the importance of the horse-head fiddle in Mongolian history, the Enebish furthers this idea of symbolism: "Our people regard the horse-head fiddle as a superior symbol of our nation's music. The shape of the horse on the fiddle's head represents an emblem of contemporary Mongolian musical art" (Enebish 1991: 77). This fits closely with the idea that modern cosmopolitan nations need emblems to mark them as distinct from other modern cosmopolitan nations. The Mongolian traditional arts provided the material with which cosmopolitan nationalists could fashion emblems that marked national difference and the horse-head fiddle became one of these emblems. Though still a "side dish" in terms of its musical importance, the horse-head fiddle emerged as an important symbol of the new musical culture.

One of the earliest hints of this reimagination of the horse-head fiddle can be traced to the front-piece of a composition for wind instruments by S. Gonchigsümlaa, *Ulaan-baataryn Tukhai Duu (Val's)* (A Song About Ulaanbaatar [Waltz], 1961) (Figure 12). In this illustration, a horse's head rests atop a lyre-like figure that itself was often used as a symbol of European classical music. Despite the prominence of the horse-head in this illustration, however, the music is not written for the horse-head fiddle. Another composition, G. Jamyan's *Atryn öglöö* (Pristine Morning, 1978) for solo *shudarag*, includes a depiction on its front cover of an old-style horse-head fiddle and a grand piano, from the base of which shoots stylized rays of the morning sun (Figure 13). The horse-head fiddle depicted here is a traditional fiddle, its "ancientness" evident in the designs on its face, which are reminiscent of those painted onto skin faced fiddles; the curve of the fiddle's bow; and the especially detailed and high arcing horse's head. Like Gonchigsümlaa's waltz, Jamyan's composition was not written for the

Figure 12. The front cover to *Ulaan-baataryn Tukhai Duu (Val's)*, by S. Gonchigsümlaa (1961).

Figure 13. The front cover of G. Jamyan's *Atryn öglöö* (1978).

horse-head fiddle. What is important here is the symbolic use of this instrument. Each illustration represents both sides of the new national musical culture, the national and the international, as being united—rising together like the morning sun.[13]

The use of the horse-head fiddle as a symbol or emblem of the national musical culture was not meant to glorify the past, but rather to allude to those core cultural elements that characterize Mongolia's national identity within an increasingly international, specifically Soviet, cosmopolitan context. The fiddle and other such symbols were important signs that signified for Mongolians and the world at large how Mongolia was developing as an independent nation, albeit with the close friendship, support, and guidance from the Soviet Union. That the Mongolian Peoples' Republic was seeking entrance into the General Assembly of the United Nations in the early 1960s is perhaps not unrelated to the emergence of these national symbols at around the same time. Those UN member nations opposed to Mongolia's membership, including the United States, argued that the MPR was not an independent nation but rather a satellite of the Soviet Union. As a national symbol, the modernized horse-head fiddle argues against this point of view.

But what may have begun as a way of demonstrating Mongolia's uniqueness within the context of Soviet "internationalism" could just as easily have been picked up and used by Mongolian nationalists to promote much more narrow conceptions of national identity. There was a fine line between defining one's nation as a subordinate republic within the Great

Soviet community of nations and defining it as an independent entity within the international community at large. The distinction is largely rhetorical, and from its earliest days of the Revolution, the Party struggled within itself between tendencies to lean towards the Soviet Communist Party and at other times towards national independence, or at least towards greater autonomy from Soviet rule.

These struggles would continue through the 1960s and 1970s, culminating in the late 1980s with the rise in influence of a new generation of leaders who sought to cultivate a more distinctly national cultural identity. Though these leaders, including members of the musical elite, were adamant in their belief that a well-developed national identity was compatible with the goals of Marxism-Leninism, their notions of an independent national identity resonated with more overtly political and pro-independence-minded sentiments that were 'in the air' in this period. Their ideas helped to set the stage for the nationalist-fired political protests of the late 1980s and early 1990s that would bring about the downfall of the MPRP and the opening of a new era of true national independence.

3   Soviet Modernism and Cosmopolitan Nationalism

At the MPRP's Fourteenth Party Congress, held in Ulaanbaatar in early July 1961, Chairman Tsedenbal stood before a hall filled with the Party faithful and, with great fanfare, announced that, forty years after the Peoples Revolution, the Mongolian Peoples Republic had finally reached the historic stage of socialism. According to Marxist-Leninist ideology, this stage could only be reached when private ownership of capital, essentially all income-producing property, was eliminated in favor of either state or collective ownership. The Party had achieved this by successfully resettling nomadic herders onto state-owned or state-run agricultural collectives and by confiscating and redistributing their herds. In finishing this work, the Party could claim that it had successfully "eliminated the backwardness" of the Mongolian people and completed the nationalization and collectivization of the means of production.

According to Marxist theory, societies that practice the private ownership of capital are, ostensibly, capitalist. But Mongolia never reached this historic stage of evolution, in the Marxist sense. In fact, what made the MPR's passage to socialism especially historic for socialists around the Soviet bloc was that it had done so by "by-passing" the capitalist stage and moving directly from the feudalist to the socialist stage. At the Party Congress, praise was heaped upon the Communist Party of the USSR for its role in shepherding the MPR through this process. Tsedenbal himself declared the Soviet Union to be his nation's "'invariable and most loyal friend'" (Sterner 1961: 3). Looking forward, the next historical stage would be the attainment of Communism, and far beyond that, the ultimate attainment of a Communist Utopia, where the Mongolian people would essentially dissolve into a greater Soviet People.

In the mean time, however, as spelled out in the newly written 1960 Constitution, the Party was charged with "completing the construction of socialism" in the country and laying the foundation for the building of a communist society. Marxist-Leninist theorists, such as Viktor Kozlov, were more specific, describing the attainment of socialism as marking the historical point from which processes of "supra-ethnic" cultural assimilation could begin to accelerate. This was the final in a three-part process of assimilation in which nations or ethnic groups would naturally begin to loosen their allegiance to their own identities and to slowly adopt the language and culture of the dominant group, which in the case of Mongolia was the language and culture of the Soviet Union (Kozlov 1988: 154). For Kozlov, socialism was an historical period in which national groups were supposed to begin to look beyond their own nation and toward their eventual assimilation with international culture and lifestyles. He cites Lenin as describing this process of "ethnic integration" and "equalization" as one of "the objective laws of development" (*ibid.* 215). Indeed, had he visited Mongolia in the 1960s and 1970s, he would have found much to bolster his theory of natural assimilation. Many Mongolians in this period spoke Russian fluently and seemed at ease in an urban Mongolian lifestyle that bore the strong influence of Russian culture, especially in terms of food, clothing, customs, and even music.

As we saw in the previous chapter, however, this was also a period in which Mongolians began asserting a truly modern national culture, one that expressed a new cosmopolitan identity that was at once national and international. The State Folksong and Dance Ensemble, which played arrangements of music by European classical composers with a distinctively national style and sound, was an important symbol of this development. The modernized horse-head fiddle, which could play both national and international musical styles, was becoming another important symbol. As Mongolia entered into the international community of nations in the 1960s,[1] it was eager to prove to the world that it was unique from its brother socialist nations.

But this division between the national and the international had proved to be a fault line within the MPRP from its earliest days. Different factions within the organization struggled, often violently, to define just what kind of national identity the modern Mongolian state should have. Should it follow in line with the Soviet Union and accelerate its assimilation of international cultures? Or should it pursue a more conservative path towards modernity that embraced elements of the nation's heritage? Clifford Geertz suggests that newly formed nations typically go through periods where they struggle to find a point of balance between these two tensions, which he described as the desire for the "indigenous ways of life" or "essentialism" on the one hand and for the "the spirit of the age" or "epochalism" on the other (Geertz 1973: 240–241).

Despite its public displays of unity with the Soviet Union, the Mongolian political and intellectual elite, including those highly placed within the Party leadership, were at heart less Party ideologues than cosmopolitan nationalists. This is an argument made by Tom Ginsburg (1999), who adds that even those early Mongolian revolutionaries who helped to usher in the Socialist period in 1921 were generally concerned less with the nation's adoption of communist ideals than with its very survival and development. While all were opposed to maintaining the aristocratic and tradition-oriented society of the past, the question they faced was what to replace it with. Could Mongolia adopt modern ideas while still holding onto older ones that still had meaning, or must all older traditions be eliminated or kept as mere symbols of the past? At the core of these essentialist and epochalist debates lay varying definitions of the concepts of culture, tradition, and modernity.

Examining how these debates played out both in public and behind-the-scenes within the political and intellectual elite broadens our understanding of what the Revolution meant to Mongolians of the Socialist period. We will focus only on the debates within the elite, as they believed that they were speaking on behalf of the people of Mongolia. What becomes clear is that this leadership, particularly before and after the rule of the Stalinist Marshall Choibalsang, was no mere puppet of Soviet power. The Party was filled with a diversity of voices and points of view about how to relate to Soviet power that were either encouraged or suppressed at different times during the Socialist period depending upon external foreign relations. The ruling elite found what I call a shifting middle way between the essentialist and epochalist tensions through which it could assert a degree of independence or autonomy that separated the new nation from the extremes of outright assimilation with the Soviet Union and slipping "backward" towards the "feudalist" society of the past. It is from the debates discussed below that a new cultural identity would emerge to help fire the nationalist movement of the late 1980s.

MARXIST IDEOLOGY AND COSMOPOLITAN NATIONALISM

The politically oriented visual arts of Mongolia during the Socialist period can give us important clues as to how the Soviet Union viewed its relationship with the Mongolian Peoples Republic. As a political satellite of the USSR, Mongolia was not subject to the same political forces to which the national republics within the Soviet Union were subject. Soviet theorists did not consider the Mongolian people as being on an evolutionary trajectory towards unification with a Soviet people, except in some theoretical future society. And despite the efforts at "Sovietization" in Mongolia and the close relationships that developed between the Mongolian and Soviet peoples, neither the Mongolians nor Mongolian society ever became "Soviet."

Instead, the Soviets promoted the ideology of brotherhood between the Mongolian and Soviet peoples. The Mongolians were defined as a "younger brother" (*duu*) and the Soviet Union and the other Soviet political satellites were its "elder brothers" (*akh* or *akh nar*), which was often defined as an "Elder brother-Younger brother" relationship (*akh-duugiin khariltsaa*). Party propaganda in Mongolia was filled with the rhetoric of fraternalism, "brotherhood" and "friendship" (cf. Szynkiewicz 1990), which was

Figure 14. "Brothers Born from the Breast of Lenin." A
print by D. Amgalan (Tüdew 1986).

manifest in the national arts. The composer Choidog, for instance, premiered a ballet in 1964 entitled, *"Mönkhiin nökhörlöl"* (Eternal friendship). "Friendship" was often expressed symbolically through images and
imagery that made use of Soviet, Russian, and Mongolian symbols. A good
example of this is the print by D. Amgalan, *"Brothers Born from the Breast
of Lenin"* (Tüdew 1986) (Figure 14), portraying Lenin with two partisans,
a young Russian boy and a young Mongolian boy. They are "brothers" or
"friends," one being slightly taller than the other, symbolizing one's more
advanced development than or even dominance over the other. As the title
of the illustration implies, Lenin gave birth to the Russian and Mongolian
partisans, thus portraying them, and by extension the Soviet leadership, as
embodying an international phenomenon—one perhaps even greater than
the Soviet Union itself.

Figure 15. The meeting of the Mongolian and Soviet peoples on Red Square, Moscow. One part of a larger work (*zeegt naamal*) (Tüdew 1986).

Another example of "friendship" is found on one half of a dramatic piece of art that depicts Mongolian and Russian peoples meeting on Red Square in Moscow (Figure 15). This is a *zeegt naamal*, which is a traditional form of Mongolian art using sewn pieces of cloth. Each "people" is represented by symbolic representations of those "objective properties" that Soviet theorists used to define each nation's *ethnos*, or ethnic-national identity (Bromely and Kozlov 1989: 429). While the two couples in the center of the image are in the process of greeting each other or expressing their friendship, the figures standing behind them function to identify the *ethno-nation* from which each comes. It is striking how the Mongolian couple in the back appears to represent more traditional forms of Mongolian traditions than the couple in front of them. This is evident in the "hair horn" that the woman is wearing, which was common in pre-Revolutionary Mongolian culture, and in the up-turned traditional style of boots both are wearing. The woman in front, in contrast, wears her hair in a long braid, along with what appear to be Western styled shoes. Most curious of all, the man in the back is holding a horse-head fiddle. It is an old-fashioned fiddle, evident in the designs on the face of the instrument typical of skin-faced fiddles. The colors of the instrument (visible in the original) also designate it as an old-fashioned fiddle, including a green fiddle face, a red sound-box (body), and a green horse's head. Both the "hair horns" and the fiddle together symbolize "old Mongolia," a time past, with the horse-head fiddle also alluding to Mongolia's horse-centered, nomadic ways of life. This couple stands in the background, static; they are present but silent, motionless. While not actively taking part in greeting the Russians, they are, perhaps, watching approvingly from a distance.

It is also interesting to note in this image how the horse-head fiddle is used as a marker of the Mongolian *ethnos*, which seems to reflect the instrument's emergence in the Mongolian political rhetoric of the 1960s and 1970s as a resonant symbol of a national socialist identity, albeit one constructed within the context of Soviet internationalism. Such representations of the fiddle would be picked up by Party members in the 1980s, as we will see later, to argue for a more autonomous and explicitly nationalistic expression of this socialist identity.

Unlike the previous illustration, there are no hierarchies of power between peoples being suggested in the *zegt naamal* art work. Instead, it is the location itself, Red Square in Moscow, with modern skyscrapers and the walls of the Kremlin set against the background, that becomes central to its meaning. It seems to provide a symbolic common ground upon which all peoples of the Soviet world, each with their own distinct identity, can meet and interact, thereby reaffirming their equality and unity as socialist nations. It is in this sense that the socialist national identity was cosmopolitan. It defined the nation as a distinct entity within the family of nations defined by Soviet internationalism. Its new national culture was at once connected to its own ancient national heritage and to a modern and progressive international Soviet culture. This larger identity was framed by the broader evolutionary and progressivist aims of Marxist-Leninist thought, which assumed that all workers of the Soviet world were moving arm-in-arm towards a communist future.

But while the Mongolian political and cultural elite expressed its allegiance to these Soviet ideals by sponsoring politically oriented visual arts like these, it appeared to be driven by its own, more practical goals. Tom Ginsburg (1999) suggests that the close ties that the Mongolians established and maintained with the Soviet leadership throughout the twentieth century were motivated not by strong desires to become loyal communist citizens but instead, ironically, to maintain national independence. He points out that the Mongols, being historically surrounded by—and at various times and in various ways subject to—two of the most populace and powerful nations in the world, have long feared the loss of their national identity to one of them. While the fear of Russian assimilation was less intense than Chinese assimilation, the fear of both nations has long shaped the strategies by which the Mongols have related to the rest of the world.

Ginsburg argues that they learned long ago how ensuring national independence meant giving their neighbors a stake in maintaining it. The Mongols sought a pragmatic relationship with the Soviet Union in which they would agree to give up something valuable to them in exchange for independence or at least relative autonomy. Soon after the Peoples' Revolution, the Mongolians understood that they had to trade in their dreams of regional, pan-Mongolic unity and national independence in exchange for Russian protection from Chinese claims of sovereignty. In this way, cosmopolitan nationalism represented a new kind of political idea in Mongolia

Most of those involved with the Revolution and the subsequent Mongolian Peoples' Party were at heart, says Ginsburg, really "cosmopolitan nationalists." He describes the early revolutionaries as being motivated by "the quest for national survival in a changing international environment" (Ginsburg 1999: 248). When we look back at them and their successors in the Party, we see individuals who had a strong sense of Mongolia's position within the international context. While they longed to see their homeland develop in relation to other modern nations of the world, they also did not want to see the demise of their own nation or its eventual assimilation into a Greater Soviet or Greater Chinese people. An examination of these political elite shows them struggling amongst themselves over the best ways to achieve national development: while some, at times, identified closely with the Soviet Union, others, at other times, sought a more independent or autonomous approach.

ZHAMTSARANO AND EARLY SOCIALIST CULTURE

Tsyben Zhamtsaranovich Zhamtsarano was one of the most interesting and influential figures in the early cultural development of the People's Republic during the Revolutionary period. Famous for his revolutionary zeal, Zhamtsarano was a well-educated man from the Buriatia, Russia, who was deeply concerned with the cultural uplift (*soyolyn deeshlüülelt*) of the Mongolian people. He was responsible for establishing, often single-handedly, many of the cosmopolitan cultural institutions of the modern Mongolian state. He was one of a loose-knit group of Buriat intellectuals from Russia who came to Mongolia in the first decades of the twentieth century whose goals were to help the Mongolian people attain lasting independence and cultural modernization. The most influential of his Buriat compatriots included Elbekdorzhi Rinchino, Erdeni Batukhan, and Dashi Sampilon.

All these men were intellectual exiles from their homeland in the late nineteenth and early twentieth centuries. They came to Mongolia after it became clear to them that the pressures from the Tsarist land reforms, which favored the rights of Russian and Ukrainian migrants over those of the native peoples, as well as its policies of ethnic assimilation and Russification, were not going to end before the significant decline of Buriat cultural identity. Fearing the weakening of Buriat political rights and loss of a distinct cultural identity within their ancestral homeland, these intellectuals encouraged the Buriat people to support political parties that opposed the Tsarist policies and favored the Buriat language and ways of life, particularly their unique folklore, language, religion and history (Rupen 1956: 398).

With Tsarist oppression intensifying in the first two decades of the twentieth century, however, these intellectuals and other Buriats began to look to Mongolia, which after 1911–1912 had declared its independence from the collapsing Qing dynasty, as a place to protect a strong Mongolian identity. Most of these Buriats were sympathetic to the creation of a pan-Mongol or pan-Buddhist state, which would be centered in the capital Urga (later Ulaanbaatar) and would include all the Mongol peoples of Mongolia, Russia, and China. And while they supported an alliance with Russia as a protectorate, many of them also wanted to create a separate state that "could defend Mongolian integrity against Russian incursion from the north and Chinese invasion from the south" (*ibid.*, 384).

What separated these intellectuals from many common Buriats was that they were intellectuals and cosmopolitans. Though raised in traditional Mongol contexts, most were fluent in Russian, graduated from prestigious Russian universities, collaborated with Russian Orientalists, translated Russian works into Mongolian, and were widely traveled in Asia and European Russia—some even worked in Germany and France (*ibid.*). They were as comfortable in the Russian and European cultural worlds as they were in those of their Mongols brethren. Like the Mongolian youth of later generations, these intellectuals recognized that the Mongols needed to adopt elements of the progress and civilization of the West in order to survive as a distinct people in the world.

It is also apparent that these Buriats were deeply influenced by Russian and European attitudes and prejudices toward nomadic peoples (cf. Karpat 1986). Since at least the nineteenth century, Russian popular and scholarly literature has portrayed the nomadic societies of Asia in negative terms (Becker 1986a, 1986b, 1991; also Forsyth 1996). These works tended to portray Asia in monolithic terms as stagnant and caught in the earliest stages of evolutionary development. Asians were typically portrayed as a people without history, whose lives were marked by savagery and ignorance (Becker 1991: 54–55). At the same time, many Russians continued to view Asia, and particularly Mongolia, as a threat, given their strong collective memory of having suffered for centuries under the "Tatar yoke," referring to the period when the descendents of Chinggis Khan ruled over the Russian people. Russian colonization of the nineteenth century was often justified as a process of bringing the "fruits of civilization" to the peoples of the "East" (Becker 1986b: 40). This was one of the reasons why the Tsarist government in this period intensified its efforts at Russifying the Buriats, including increased the opportunities for Buriats to attend Russian schools and universities.

The writings of the Russian-trained Buriat nationalists employ much of the same terminology that their Soviet counterparts used to describe the Mongol people. The need for the Mongolian people to be "enlightened" through the introduction of science and a common language was a common theme. As such, they approached the answers to these problems in ways similar to the Russians (and later Bolsheviks), even though the Buriats saw a very different end. The Russians saw these Buriat intellectuals, with their cosmopolitan background and outlook, as ideal mediators between the Tsarist leadership and the Mongolian people, and they drafted many of them to do their political work in Mongolia. That these Buriats should ally themselves with the Russian mission in Mongolia is ironic considering that most sought to escape from Russian cultural and linguistic imperialism in their own homeland.

While staunchly against the effects of Russification among the Mongols, the Buriats' work of "uplifting" the Mongolian people nonetheless promoted it. Rupen even describes these Buriats as "Russian agents" in Mongolia. When Zhamtsarano came to Urga in 1912, for example, the newly placed Russian envoy to Mongolia, I.Ya. Korostovets, selected him to head a Russian-sponsored secular school and a Mongolian language publication called *Sine toli kemekü bičig* (New Mirror) (Rupen 1956: 131). In the same period, Zhamtsarano also began his work of collecting and publishing Mongolian folklore, making transcriptions of Mongolian epics, and publishing in Mongolian his translations of a number of Russian and European literary works (*ibid.*, 132). These projects helped to bring the ideas of European and Russian internationalism to his adopted homeland.

These Buriat's affinity for Russian learning and culture came from their own background as deeply Russified individuals. As an increasingly large number of Russians and Ukrainians migrated to Buriatia, everyday life in the province became progressively more dominated by Russian ways of life. As in other colonial contexts of the same period, Buriats who could speak Russian and assimilate Russian culture often found upward mobility in the new society. They maintained their Mongol identity, while also developing a Russian one, and in this way they came to represent Russia and to extend Russian influence in Mongolia. As Rupen says, "wherever they went in the Mongolian world, they bore the stamp of Russia, as well as the stamp of Mongolia. They were both related and foreign, and [for this] the Khalkhas of Outer Mongolia hated them" (Rupen 1958: 392). While hatred of the Buriats may be an exaggeration, there were very likely feelings of ambivalence about them among the Khalkha Mongolians.

Despite these feelings, however, the Khalkha revolutionaries recognized the importance of these Russian-educated Buriats in mediating between themselves and the Russian government and in securing Russian military aid. The Buriats, particularly Rinchino and Zhamtsarano, helped to translate the language and culture of each to the other. In addition, however, the Buriats were also important proponents of the early revolutionary ideology. Zhamtsarano participated in the first congress meeting in Kiakhta in 1921 of what would later become the Mongolian People's Revolutionary Party. He even wrote the Party's platform, which, interestingly, called for the restoration of an autonomous Mongolian nation—albeit one under Russian or Chinese protectorate—and for Mongolian "power and culture" to "be raised to a level comparable to that of other people" (Rupen 1964: 142). In the platform, Zhamtsarano and other revolutionaries cite the need to bring change to the status quo in Mongolia once autonomy was again achieved:

> Questions of external and internal policy, and also of religious life, questions of change of long-observed customs, traditions, and economy ways-of-life, our Party will resolve according to the spirit of our times, the experience of the peoples of the world, and in conformity with the character of future changes in world events, in the interests of the welfare and progress of the Mongolian people. Thus, branches which are useless or inimical, not conforming to the spirit of the times, or which are dying out, will be removed through sheer necessity, as obsolete and unhealthy, as far as possible by mild, and in border-cases by firm, measures (*ibid.*).

Zhamtsarano's call to cut off the branches of tradition-oriented society that do not conform to "the spirit of the times" closely resembles Geertz's description of epochalism, that is, the felt need of people in young nations to put aside their "indigenous ways of life" and pick up those more in line with the "spirit of the age" (Geertz 1973: 240).

Zhamtsarano was not advocating the wholesale replacement of traditional society with modern international society. He instead wanted to preserve the essential aspects of Mongolia culture. The list of cultural institutions he helped to establish in Mongolia includes the State Library, a museum, and the Mongolian Scientific Committee (*Mongyol sudur bičigün küriyeleng*), the forerunner to the Mongolian Academy of Sciences. He also continued to publish translations of Russian and European works into Mongolian,[2] conducted archaeological and ethnographical investigations, and discovered and published a large number of historical documents. Zhamtsarano was a dominant figure in the Mongolian cultural and intellectual life in the 1920s (Rupen 1956: 389).

As Soviet policy became increasingly hard-line towards the end of the 1920s, the Buriats' strongly nationalistic and pan-Mongolist points of view became increasingly passé. By the early 1930s the Party had forced most of these Buriats to the sideline or exiled them from the country altogether. None lived to see the end of World War II (*ibid.*, 397). After being exiled from Mongolia in 1932, Zhamtsarano was sent to work in Leningrad, where he was later arrested. He died in prison in Russia in 1942 (Sanders 1996: 108–109).

Zhamtsarano provides a good example of a new generation of revolutionaries who passionately believed that the survival of the Mongolian people as an independent entity required them to adopt modern practices, beliefs, and institutions from more advanced nations. They used their privileged status as mediators between Tsarist Russia and the Mongolian people to promote their aims. In the end, however, this liminality made them suspect to the very people they were seeking to help. The Buriat intellectuals were often frustrated, in particular, by those in the Party who took more hard-line approaches to modernization of Mongolian society, who saw the traditional ways of life as a threat to the nation and who advocated the need for a much closer alliance with the Soviet Communist Party. We can see this conflict in action through transcripts of early Party meetings.

THE THIRD PARTY CONGRESS

The Third Congress of the Mongolian Peoples Party (MPP) took place only three years after the People's Revolution, but already two different ideologies within the Party elite were coming into conflict. On the one side were those who sought to accelerate the Party's affiliation with the Soviet Union and on the other were those who sought a slower, more deliberative approach. From a broader perspective, the arguments were between those who saw the need to define modernity as the absence of traditionalism and those who sought a more negotiated approach between the two.

Detailed notes taken during the twenty-three "sittings" of the Congress in August 1924 allow us to see many of the different personalities that made up the Party leadership coalition in this early stage of the Revolution and to see the growing splits between them. It is especially instructive to watch the two principal characters at these meetings, the Commander-in-Chief of the Mongolian Army and Vice-President of the Council of Ministers Danzan and an outspoken member of the Party's Central Committee E. R. Rinchino. Ts. Zhamtsarano was also present at these meetings.

Rinchino made his voice heard on nearly every issue under discussion, despite his relatively low status as a member of the Central Committee. More often than not, he advocated a position of closer alliance between Mongolia and the Soviet Union and the international community in order to expand national defense and social development. He even urged the Congress to move quickly, lest the nation miss out on the coming world revolution of the proletariat.

> [We] must carefully watch the general state of things in the world. The whole word [*sic*] is on the brink of great and radical reforms, and such backward countries as Mongolia will inevitably be drowned in

the general socialistic upbuilding. We are an atom on the wave of a
great upheaval (*Mongolia* n.d.: 33).

He urged the Congress to expand the size and depth of the nation's military, warning that "Chinese generals" and "Imperialists" were "ready to
swallow us up" (*ibid*. n.d.: 22), an act, he said, that the Soviet Union would
not allow to succeed (*ibid*. n.d.: 21). He also declared that the People's Revolution should both foment revolution among the "toilers" of China and
actively support the Inner Mongolians in their quest for freedom (*ibid*.).
Danzan, in contrast, spoke about the need to better equip and train the
army, but made no mention of either foreign campaigns or the need to prepare for an attack by foreign armies (*ibid*. n.d.: 19).

In regards to the problem of feudalism in Mongolia, both agreed it needed
to be ended, but Rinchino was adamant that it be ended right away and with
great force. "You know that the complete abolition of the feudal system is
one of the chief problems of the Party. This problem must be revolved forthwith and I move the question of the abolition, once and for all, of the last
bits of feudalism in Mongolia" (*ibid*. n.d.: 35). Danzan, for his part, was
more skeptical of Rinchino's rhetoric about social classes in the country. He
urged the Congress to take a more even-handed approach to the problem of
ending feudalism, suggesting that even members of the old aristocracy could
still play a positive role in building the new nation. "It must be kept in mind
that not all princes and nobles are reactionaries nor are all common people
honest. Yet it must be found out whether this or that member of the Party is
reliable. People have been entering our Party for different purposes; all this
must now be investigated" (*ibid*. n.d.: 28). Furthermore, Danzan did not
share Rinchino's concern over the pace by which the old system was being
ended. "Why should measure be taken to abolish what is by itself falling to
pieces. We have more important tasks on hand" (*ibid*. n.d.: 35).

When the discussion turned to the question of whether the Party should
support the practice of Tibetan (Buddhist) traditional medicine or turn
entirely to the practice of the so-called Western medicine, the Party leadership split along the same lines. Zhamtsarano was positive about the practice of Western medicine, but worried that bringing it to Mongolia would
be a long and difficult practice. Instead he suggested that Mongolians be
sent to study in medical schools and Buddhist lamas be trained in Western
medicine. He also suggested that Tibetan medicine be improved with Western science, "making use of everything that is good in it" (*ibid*. n.d.: 47).
But Rinchino saw little to trust in Tibetan medicine, in large part because
it was practiced by Buddhist lamas, whom he saw as untrustworthy. "That
is why I am very skeptical as to the revival with us of Tibetan medicine"
(*ibid*.). The Japanese, he said as a counter example, had given up on "old
medicine" and adopted Western medicine entirely.

Though not entirely evident in the notes, the dispute between the two
sides was growing in intensity throughout the Congress. In the eighteenth

sitting of the Congress, Danzan and Rinchino began to argue with each other. Their dispute must have been intense since the next day, before the beginning of the next sitting, Rinchino arranged for Danzan and an associate to be arrested, sentenced, and shot. Soon after, the representative of the Soviet Union, Comrade Vassiliev, who was attending the Congress, declared that the "'carried out sentence would contribute to the strengthening of the alliance between Mongolia and the Union of Socialist Soviet Republics'" (*ibid*. n.d.: 62), suggesting which side of these debates the Soviet leadership hoped would win.

When the Congress resumed a few days later, the divisions between the two sides were clear for all to see. Rinchino and his supporters maintained the opinion that unless Mongolia dropped its reliance on traditional and "old" ways of doing things, it will be left behind by the world and disappear in significance. The more deliberative pace of development and change advocated by Danzan, Zhamtsarano, and their supporters, on the other hand, suggested that they saw the need for a more balanced approach to change and development. While those on both sides supported the Revolution and the goal of national development and modernization—perhaps, ironically, none with as much force as Zhamtsarano[3] himself—they were at odds over how much of a break from the old social order was needed. Zhamtsarano, for his part, called for combining the "best" of either system so long as it contributed to national development.

It is important to note that the arguments on both sides of the ideological divide during this Congress were framed in terms of what was best for the progress and independence of Mongolia, and not for the sake of the Soviet Union or Lenin's world revolution. Even Rinchino's close association with the Soviet representative during this meeting and his role in assassinating the more moderate Danzan were in line with his aim of ensuring the survival and development of the Mongolian nation and people. When looked at from a broader perspective, the ideological differences that divided Party officials in this congress were still not as great as those that distanced the Party collectively from what it termed the "traditionalists"—the so-called "lamaists," "feudalists," and all others who were sympathetic to them. The Party associated all of them with an old, corrupt, and dying social order.

In fact, Party ideology generally defined the question of national development in stark terms, i.e., as a conflict between the "modern" and "traditional" and the "progressive" and "backward." Party ideology held that the modern and progressive societies will always succeed the traditional and backward ones. We see this in the deliberations between Party members above. Even those sympathetic to the traditional figures of authority, for instance, did not question the need for Mongolia to abandon its traditional ways of life. Haslund-Christensen held similar views when writing about the dissolution of the traditional musical culture in Inner Mongolia in the 1930s. Though he was, of course, no advocate of Party ideology, he too adopted the same modernist frames of reference, seeing the increasing pace of industrial modernization as inevitably destroying the traditional cultures and ways of life.

Another characteristic of these debates over modernity in Mongolia was the absence of the voices of the traditionalists. Both Danzan and Zhamtsarano supported the idea of incorporating the most loyal or skilled of the traditionalists into the Revolutionary movement, but the voices of these individuals themselves were not heard. These figures were mute, not unlike the Mongolian couple in traditional costumes representing "old" Mongolia in Figure 15 above. As such, they were much easier to objectify, define, and, ultimately, to destroy. In fact, those periods when the MPRP was most closely aligned with the Soviet Communist Party tended to correspond with those periods when more moderate voices within the MPRP were silenced by more conservative leaders, as happened to Danzan in 1924.

NATSAGDORJ AND THE 'NEW LITERATURE'

Zhamtsarano, Danzan, and Rinchino are only three examples of early Mongolian cosmopolitans—those who had traveled or studied in Russia and Europe, and who sought to bring about the regeneration of Mongolian culture and society through contact with the best of the West. In writing about the development of Mongolian society, B. Shirendew, another important cosmopolitan about whom we will learn more below, makes the point that

> from the beginning of the twentieth century there were some intellectuals in Mongolia who sought progress and European culture. Leading figures in our government, such as N. Khayankhyarvaa, D. Chagdarjav, A. Danzan, and others traveled abroad and on returning home promoted many important ideas concerning the direction of national development, a fact which I repeatedly mentioned in articles I published (Shirendew 1997: 112).

The author and poet Dashdorjiin Natsagdorj (1906–1937) was a cosmopolitan intellectual of the Revolutionary Period who brought modernist and nationalist approaches to Mongolian literature, and his works exemplify some of the most successful attempts by artists of this period to combine epochalist and essentialist points of view. His poem *Minii nutag* (My Homeland, 1933), for instance, has become one of the most famous and beloved poems in Mongolian literature. It is a paean to the Mongolian nation, praising the steppe lands, rivers, mountains, forests, blue sky and other dramatic features of the Mongolian landscape (Natsagdorj 1989: 13–14). Much of the poem's power comes from the poet's use of specific geographic places in the country (e.g. Lake Khöwsgöl, Orkhon and Selenge rivers, Gowi desert) that Mongolians relate to as unique and important to defining their nation. He also uses specific clichés (e.g., the "crystal rivers," "eternally snow-capped mountains," "Blue Sky") that have long been a part of traditional Mongolian oral and written literature. The poet constantly reiterates the point that what he is describing is "my native land . . . my Mongolia," thus connecting his concept of the Mongolian nation to not only an ancient homeland but also to the land that the Mongolians now occupy. This emphasizes, even essentializes, the continuity of the connection of the land and the Mongolian people, which is a technique common to other forms of nationalist literature and rhetoric (cf. Smith 1997, 1984; Abrahams 1993). The poem works to portray his "native land," which his Mongolian readers understand as "*our* native land," as an essential—unchanging and eternal—symbol of Mongolian national identity.

At the same time, the poem also acknowledges the changing character of the Mongolian people and their growing interaction with the world at large. The poet tells us in the seventh stanza that his homeland is a country "where all may ride and drive at will" and "where people live freely in all seasons," referring to the new freedoms of movement that accompanied the end of Qing dynastic rule. In the same stanza, he tells us that this is a land on which "five grains" grow, referring to the Party's early attempts to expand agricultural production. In the eleventh stanza, we hear that land has "fit" the Mongols from the time of the ancestors to the time when "the land [is] overspread by the Red Banner of New Mongolia." Significantly, this reference to Communism is indirect; it is the land and nation that are the direct objects of this line.

The poem is also interesting for what it leaves unstated. Just as the land is rich in symbolism for the Mongolians, so too has it become something of a common denominator upon which all Mongolians could agree. Absent is mention of more contentious or problematic associations, such as about those places famously associated with Chinggis Khan, the Mongol empire, Buddhist deities, or shamanic spirits (although other poems by him do make these associations). The poem makes only a veiled reference to places that Mongolians identify as sacred, e.g., those places marked with an *owoo*, usually a pile of rocks and other items, which he simply describes as "ancient."

Also absent is any mention of a Greater Mongolia—the idea that the Mongolian nation encompasses lands that, at least by the 1930s, were no longer a part of the physical geography of modern Mongolia. The long-held but ultimately doomed dream of pan-Mongolism, of uniting all Mongols into a greater nation, was on the minds of early Party members in the 1920s. In defining what makes Mongolia a nation in this poem of the 1930s, Natsagdorj was contributing to the new and "politically correct" idea that the Mongolian homeland is exactly contiguous with the political boundaries of the modern state—one that includes neither other lands, such as parts of contemporary Russia and China, nor the Mongols who lived in them.

Likewise, the emphasis throughout the poem appears to be focused on contemporary Khalkha Mongolia and the Khalkha Mongols, once again excluding all other Mongol ethnic groups. While he makes reference to Uws

Lake and the Altai Mountains in the west, most of his imagery is focused upon the steppelands of central and northern Mongolia and the *gowi* (or desert) of the south, typically understood as part of Khalkha Mongolia. This is a point Natsagdorj emphasizes with his reference in the fifth stanza to the "vast land of Khalkha among the deserts and highlands." In these ways, Natsagdorj is referring to a politically defined nation-state populated by a single, ethnically homogeneous people. Such an appeal to a unified and homogenous "people" is a common trope of nationalist literature.

While his poetry can draw upon nationalistic or essentialistic imagery and themes, Natsagdorj was no traditionalist. He wrote poetry that praised the Peoples Revolution as it occurred in Mongolia, Russia, and Eastern Europe (e.g., his poem "The October Revolution"). More commonly, however, Natsagdorj would work epochalist themes and ideas into stories set in traditional contexts. Such is the case in his allegory, "Son of the Old World," which examines the life of an unnamed "son" living with his family in a herding encampment deep in the country. Throughout the story the narrator presents images of how closed in and trapped these people were in their traditional world, both in their physical remoteness from their neighbors and by the limiting nature of their traditional understandings the world around them. The narrator's voice is often judgmental, portraying the views of one who knows better than these simple people:

> The Mongols thought that there were no villages beyond the mountains and that the horizon was the end of the earth. They knew nothing of what was going on in the world. Living in their remote corner day after day, the Mongols prayed to God in the mornings and in the evenings bowed to the sky. They lived this way until they died (Natsagdorj 1974: 1).

This repetitive and seemingly pointless life of the people continues from generation to generation. The "son of the old world," he continues, "could not imagine any other life than the roaming from one pasture to another spring, summer, fall and winter. He knew of no other truth except the words of his ancestors and his elders. What a blighted and ignorant life! How his young years had been wasted!" (*ibid.*, 2). This ignorance is not a product of stupidity, the narrator seeks to make clear, but rather of lack of opportunities: "By nature the son of the old world was not a dull-witted person; his life, however, passed within the confines of but three or four *örtöö*" (*ibid.*). This confinement was both intellectual and physical: "Living according to their ancient customs, mistaking suffering for happiness, gloom and ignorance for prosperity, a whole people most of whom, like the son of the old world, closing their eyes and ears, were unaware of the world and had nearly forever remained cut off in their desolated steppe" (*ibid.*, 3).

The narrator's story ends, however, with these people being "awakened from their slumber" by the "rays of light [that have] penetrated beneath the overturned cauldron"; this light was brought about by "the marvelous man

[who] had made a revolution in the north" (*ibid*.), referring to Lenin. Only by opening these rural, countryside people up to the "new world" are they able to transform their lives and find happiness and fulfillment.

> Everybody now learned that there was more land beyond the horizon, that there were five oceans and five continents. The road to a new world was opened to the people, the road to development. The son of the old world became the son of the new world. Happiness and rejoicing were now the lot of the people! (*ibid*.)

The narrator's "son of the new world" has become cosmopolitan in every sense—he understands that he and his people are an integral part of a much larger and interconnected world. This awareness is for him a source of happiness and freedom. It is also the first step to achieving true progress and development.

It is easy to pass off such a poem as a piece of Party propaganda. The shallowness of the characters and the simplicity of the solutions open to them are characteristic of such forms of political writing. But it is interesting that even in such a political work, Natsagdorj focuses upon the revival or reawakening of the Mongolian spirit and not on promoting more overt symbols of communist ideology. While the "rays of light" of the new day were indeed common symbols of Soviet Communism, they appear in this poem as the means of bringing about the social transformation of his people rather than their absorption into a greater Soviet People.

In these poems, Natsagdorj addresses the question of modernity in typically cosmopolitan nationalist ways. The Mongolian people should be proud of their homeland and ancient ways of life since they connect them to a homeland and to each other. These ancient ways help Mongolians identify themselves as a "people" who are indelibly identified with a land. To Natsagdorj, these images were meant to be symbolic rather than actual. They help the Mongolian people to tell the story of who they are and where they came from, but their true destiny is as part of a modern world. Like those counterparts we examined above, Natsagdorj sees the need to make a clear break with the traditional world. He draws a clear line between cosmopolitans like himself and those still living "traditional" ("blighted" and "ignorant") ways of life. Using quasi-religious imagery, Natsagdorj seems to be saying that only by crossing over from that old world to the new will the Mongolians find happiness and freedom.

SHIRENDEW AND THE INSTITUTIONALIZING
OF COSMOPOLITANISM

The efforts of the Party and government to expand and improve the state of education during the late 1940s and 1950s contributed to the rise of a largely literate and better-educated populace and a new generation of intellectuals. At the end of World War II, the Ministry of Education was charged with the duty of raising the level of literacy among young and middle-aged adults in the country. A teacher-training institute was opened in Ulaanbaatar in 1952 that gave special emphasis to the training of teachers, or "cadres," for rural schools (Shirendew 1997: 131). At the same period, the Party increased the number of school buildings sought was to reduce the rates of student drop-out. The Party passed resolution 281/75 in 1952 that declared the need to greatly increase the quality of the education in the nation's schools, including setting minimum standards for teacher training, increasing educational resources, and expanding the number and improving the maintenance of school buildings. The resolution also called for schools to begin teaching Marxist-Leninist doctrine to "young children" (*ibid.*, 132).

Under these plans Russian and Soviet influence also greatly increased. Plans were made to send teachers to the Soviet Union for advanced training and for the Soviets to send educational materials to Mongolia. Teachers and educational advisors from the Soviet Union came to the country in answer to an appeal by the Mongolian Ministry of Education. They, along with Soviet specialists and advisors working in the Ministry, helped expand the country's educational system (*ibid.*, 132–133). The establishment of training courses for Russian language teachers in 1954 helped lay the groundwork for the eventual mandate that all students learn the language.

At the level of higher education, however, this close working relationship with Russian and Soviet educational institutions had already been established by the 1940s. The first major institution of higher education in the country, Mongolian State University, was opened in 1942, and two years later the Party appointed B. Shirendew as its first rector. Shirendew was a part of the first generation of Mongolians sent to the Soviet Union for advanced training in the 1930s. He went to the same school in Ulan-Ude, Russia, as Yu. Tsedenbal, who was a few years ahead of him and who would later become Prime Minister. Returning to Ulaanbaatar in 1941,[4] Shirendew quickly found work in the government as an assistant to Prime Minister Choibalsang. The government and Party sought the skills of Shirendew and others who had studied in the Soviet Union for their fluency with the Russian language and Russian culture. Shirendew worked closely with Soviet specialists and Russian deputy rectors as rector of the State University (*ibid.*, 124–125). He was charged with overseeing a distinguished faculty of Mongolian professors and scholars who were also trained in the Soviet Union as well as a core of Soviet professors and scholars (*ibid.*, 124–125). Shirendew says that his duties included improving the student's knowledge of the Russian language and their understanding of Marxist-Leninism (*ibid.*, 124). But mastering teaching methods from the Soviet teachers was also an important task. "We used these skills when teaching in the universities and middle schools and paid attention to turning out highly-trained cadres. The progress and conclusion of the Soviet

Patriotic War and the international situation occupied an important place in the teaching" (*ibid.*).

Such training by Soviet and Soviet-trained teachers, conducted in close association with Soviet institutions, gave the Mongolians a much greater awareness and understanding of the outside world than was typical of those earlier generations who studied only in Mongolia. When Shirendew first worked for Prime Minister Choibalsang, for instance, he was given the task of translating Russian for him during official occasions, since Choibalsang had only a conversational grasp of the Russian language. He also gave him weekly lessons in Mongolian, Soviet, and world history, as well as literature and art (*ibid.*, 92–94). The Prime Minister also relied on Shirendew in his meetings with Russian officials. Younger, Soviet-trained Mongolian officials, on the other hand, such as the Party Chariman Yu. Tsedenbal, were typically fluent in Russian and had no trouble communicating with Soviet officials and specialists. Shriendew hints at the level of insecurity that Choibalsang felt about his abilities to understand Russian well. He mentions, for instance, that Choibalsang felt obligated to seek the opinions of Tsedenbal in regards to Russian-language books. "Choibalsan had to show every book to Tsedenbal and accept his opinions about them" (*ibid.*, 94).

In his autobiography, Shirendew comments about how the high Party and government leadership of the early 1940s generally had relatively little formal education, which in his opinion hindered their abilities to deal with complex issues (*ibid.*, 95). Part of the reason for the lack of highly trained cadres in the 1940s and 1950s was the result, Shirendew admits, "of the cruel death of thousands of select cadres in the Party, government, army and other branches of the economy, education, and science between 1937 and 1949" (*ibid.*, 91). He is referring in part to the period of purges the Party carried out against Buddhist monks, lamas, and other "anti-revolutionaries," which were at their most intense between 1937 and 1939 and which were largely directed by Choibalsang. This is one of the few times when Shirendew passes a negative opinion about Party policies of this period. The historian Shagdaryn Sandag (2000) presents a good overview of the young Mongolians the Party sent abroad for advanced training in the beginning of the Revolutionary period. Most of these early students, around 180 of them, studied in the Soviet Union, but a large group, around 43, also went to Western Europe, including Germany and France (Sandag and Kendall 2000: 134–136). A significant number of these early intellectuals disappeared during the period of political purges in the late 1930s. The lack of highly trained cadres was one of the reasons motivating the enormous growth and attention to the expansion of the educational system after World War II (Shriendew 1997: 91).

Shirendew's account provides clues to the depth of Soviet involvement in the leadership of the Mongolian Peoples Republic. In nearly every position that he held, he had to work closely with Soviet advisors, consultants, and specialists, and he often described them as his friends and as individuals whose ideas and advice he respected. Like other Mongolian intellectuals and officials of the period, Shriendew traveled between Russia and Mongolia often, married a Russian woman, and wrote about life in Russia as if it were as comfortable and familiar to him as life in his own country. Ginsburg makes the point that these Soviet-trained Mongolian officials and intellectuals who were put in positions of authority in the MPR were generally closer to life in the Soviet world than with the traditional life in their own country.

> Mongolians quickly became integrated into Russian patterns of life, and one person interviewed explained that Mongolia and Russia were so similar that there was no experience of culture shock going form one to the other. Mongolians ate Russian food, spoke Russian, and some-times lived with Russians (Ginsburg 1999: 260).

In adopting modern Russian cultural ways, Shirendew appears to have turned away from his upbringing in the traditional world in which he was raised. He recalls this world with great relish in the first chapters of his autobiography, giving detailed narratives about his life as a youth in the countryside. He tells the reader many stories about how he learned tradi-tional songs and dances, rode horses, herded sheep, and memorized Bud-dhist prayers as a child. But these narratives disappear almost completely in the subsequent chapters when he arrives in the big city of Ulaanbaatar and begins his personal transformation.

He comments on the alienation that he came to feel from those he describes as the "ordinary people." He recounts, for instance, an encounter he had one winter with a group of herders in the countryside, during which he gave a speech about Party goals. He said that after his talk the leader of the group dismissed him and his ideas outright. Upon reflection, he realized and lamented the distance that had come to exist between the Party ideolo-gies that he represented and the actual realities facing these herding fami-lies. He comments on how he himself had become "separated from ordinary life" (Shirendew 1997: 109). This feeling of alienation was also evident in his description of the difficulties he experienced years earlier in relating to his parents after returning home from school in the distant village (*ibid.*, 55). The process of adopting modern ways had changed him profoundly, making him a very different person than he was before he left.

Alienation also marks the ways in which Shirendew speaks about music and literature in the new society. After coming into the world of books, schools, and trips to Russia, he makes no more mention of the traditional Mongolian music he loved as a youth. He does write about occasionally going to ballroom dances or singing Russian songs (*ibid.*, 74, 112). The only mention he makes of the Mongolian national musical arts is when, later in his text, he praises their professional development and progress since the Revolution (*ibid.*, 149). It is as if in his transformation from being a son of the old world to a son of the new, what had been once an integral part of his everyday life—singing, playing music, and dancing—had became merely another object that could be improved with the help of Soviet ideas and experience.

TS. DAMDINSÜREN AND THE CULTURAL HERITAGE

Ts. Damdinsüren (1908–1987) was one of the most respected Mongolian intellectuals in the twentieth century and he was not afraid to speak out against those who sought to deny the achievements of Mongolia's past. While advocating the modernization of Mongolian literature, Damdinsüren emphasized the need to hold onto what he termed progressive elements of the ancient literary tradition:

> 'In building up of our new popular literature we ought to examine our old cultural heritage, and exploit whatever is useful and good. There are many useful and good items in our seven hundred year old literature. It is a holy duty of us to study these and exploit them in building out new culture' (Bawden 1989: 414).

Damdinsüren clearly respected the traditional cultural achievements of the past, but he did not advocate their wholesale return. He saw a place for the "best" of the traditional arts and wisdom in modern society and believed, in particular, that it would be foolish for the Party to disregard the achievements of earlier generations of Mongolian writers when building a new popular Mongolian literature. He believed, for instance, that oral literary forms of the past could serve as a basis for new literary compositions, so long as their content reflected life in the new society. He praised the pre-Revolutionary singer Luwsan *khuurch*, for instance, for composing the words and melody to the new song, "Aeroplane" (Damdinsüren 2001: 51). "Despite the development of literature and the increases in literacy in the new Mongolian nation," he writes,

> the folk oral literary basis of our storytellers and fiddle players has not been lost. [These artists] are [instead] composing the songs that praise the new Mongolian renaissance, development, and victories of the Red Army . . . (*ibid.*). We should not be seeking to change the form of folk oral literary compositions. We should, instead, be creating compositions that feature new content presented in a folk oral literary style (*ibid.*, 52).

Damdinsüren took to task iconoclastic and strongly epochalist sentiments that a colleague named Mishig made about older works of literature.

> 'Since the 1921 revolution the Mongol people have flourished and have produced many specialists, and have brought their culture to a level

never reached before. But in praising these fine achievements we must not deny the earlier ones. If Mishig thinks to make today's achievements stand out the more by decrying earlier achievements, he is in error. It is desirable that the previous state of culture and present developments should be described on a basis of truth' (Bawden 1989: 415).

In 1959, he published *Mongyol uran jokiyal-un degeji jayun bilig orusibai* (One Hundred Masterpieces of Mongolian Literature), a literary anthology that contained his selections of the "best" works of Mongolian literature, including poems, stories, legends, and religious writings. It was published in the Mongol, or vertical, script and in a small print run. The Party allowed it to be published perhaps in part because the early 1950s was a period of relatively liberal cultural policies and perhaps also because the leadership viewed it as a harmless collection of dusty old stories. But several years later, when the Party's cultural policies became more conservative, Party officials criticized the work as being "'completely without interest even from an artistic point of view'" (Bawden 1989: 415–416). Damdinsüren believed that there was something essentially good in the best examples of the old cultural traditions that should be retained and developed for use in the new culture.

THE 'CHINGGIS KHAN' INCIDENT

Perhaps no event better exemplifies the shifting between epochalism and essentialism among the political and intellectual elite than the so-called Chinggis Khan Incident of 1962. In 1961 scholars and intellectuals of the Academy of Sciences began to discuss how the MPR should commemorate the eight hundredth anniversary of the birth of the founder of the Mongol Empire, Chinggis Khan. They devised proposals for a series of events to take place around the anniversary date in the last week in May 1962. These included organizing a scientific conference to discuss Chinggis' role in Mongolian history, issuing "Chinggis Khan" stamps, building a memorial to him in his "homeland" of Khentii *aimag*, and publishing a series of papers and books about his life. Enebish says that Mongolian writers and composers were also involved and composed songs and poems about Chinggis Khan for the event (Enebish 1998.11.22).

The Central Committee's Department of Ideology surprised many of these scholars by giving its initial approval to their proposals, which were then discussed at a general meeting in 1962 of the Central Committee led by the Prime Minister Yu. Tsedenbal. The supporters of the proposal made their cases as to the benefit of undertaking such a commemoration, suggesting that it "would promote proper appreciation of the Mongols' contribution to world history" (Boldbaatar 1999: 238). Party Secretary D. Tömör-Ochir had earlier suggested to members of the Academy that such a commemoration would "'show equally both the good and bad sides of Chinggis'" (*ibid*.). At this meeting with Tsedenbal, Tömör-Ochir added that Chinggis had "'overcome the disjointed feudal situation'" to establish a unified state (*ibid*., 239). This is a form of praise of Chinggis Khan by a high Party official that would have been unthinkable in earlier decades, and it exemplifies the shifting and contextual nature of the essentialist-epochalist debates.

It was agreed that the events should proceed, but very carefully. Members of the Academy, working closely with Prime Minister Tsedenbal's office, prepared a speech entitled "'Chinggis Khan: Founder of the Mongolian Unified State'" (*ibid*., 241). Eager not to offend or cause political tensions with either Russia or China, Tsedenbal wanted reassurances that Chinggis Khan's "'reactionary activities'" be given special attention in the speech and other literature prepared for the event (*ibid*.). The article that was finally published in the Party newspaper *Ünen* on May 31, 1962, described Chinggis as the founder of an independent Mongolian state, adding that modern Mongolia "'owes its principles of peace, friendship, and justice to the people's revolution,'" and that its people "'are fully determined to build socialism and communism in their Motherland'" (*ibid*.).

In the scientific conference that took place during the event, the first scholar to speak was the head of the Institute of History at the Mongolian Academy of Sciences. He described Chinggis as a wise leader and military commander who successfully unified disparate tribes into a nation, codified a set of laws, and established a national script. He added, however, that Chinggis' association with the noble classes and his penchant for expensive military campaigns meant that he could never be hailed as a national hero (*ibid*., 242). This tone of balance, however, was soon lost in subsequent speakers. As the historian Boldbaatar writes, the distinction between Chinggis Khan as a distant historical figure and a contemporary symbol of Mongolian nationalism became noticeably less clear as the conference continued (*ibid*.).

The MPRP's response to the conference in succeeding days was quick and sharp. Likely pushed by Soviet Communist Party officials, the Party leadership began to criticize the event's organizers and participants soon after the event ended. It blocked the publication of the proceedings of the conference and in the following months stopped the Mongolian distribution of stamps commemorating Chinggis Khan (although they were still sold internationally). The Party also attempted (but failed) to halt efforts to build a Chinggis Khan monument in Khentii *aimag*. Many of those who participated in the conference and publication of the newspaper article were questioned about their nationalist leanings. Tömör-Ochir was formally condemned by the Party for having "'supported 'nationalist' ideologies in opposition to the 'internationalist' philosophy of the party'" (*ibid*., 244). He was both dismissed from both his post and kicked out of the Party, a severe punishment in this era (*ibid*.).

The long simmering disputes between those holding epochalist and essentialist points of view within the Party leadership became very public during this event. Fearing that the Soviet Communist Party would begin to suspect the nationalist leanings of the Mongolian leadership, the MPRP leadership went out of its way in the succeeding months to reaffirm its commitment to the path of Leninism and friendship of the Soviet peoples. Party criticism of Damdinsüren and other intellectuals, whether or not they directly participated in the affair was stepped up (cf. Bawden 1989: 415). Tsedenbal even alluded to the struggle between these two different points of view in a speech he gave at a meeting of the Congress a few years later, insinuating that the essentialist points of view were downright reactionary and anti-revolutionary.

> The Congress notes that socialist construction in our country and the acute struggle of the two opposing ideologies in the world arena require insistently that the internationalist education of working people be made more effective and the reactionary ideology of anti-communism, nationalism, and of alien views be lucidly exposed (MPRP 1966: 207).

Even though he had signed off on these commemorations, Tsedenbal demanded a new focus on ideological single-mindedness in an era of international threats.

The early to mid-1960s was a sensitive time for the MPRP. The Soviet leadership was eager to increase the accelerated development of the Mongolian nation. But at the same time, the increasingly difficult relations between the Soviet Union and China on the one hand and the United States on the other obligated the MPRP to close ranks with the Soviet leadership. The Party responded by clamping down on what it viewed as overly nationalistic expressions of national identity. It reasserted in speeches and in other ways that there was "no middle way" towards national development. Those who expressed nationalist sentiments came to be viewed as an enemy of the state and all Party members were charged with the task of looking out for such "anti-Party" behavior.

In his speech to the Party leadership in 1966, for example, Tsedenbal praised the growing economy and flowering culture and the "advancing and strengthening ... unbreakable friendship and all-round co-operation of the Mongolian People's Republic and the Soviet Union" (Tsedenbal 1966: 40). But he also warned that the Party must be constantly alert to the dangerous expression of "bourgeois nationalism" and "reactionary nationalist ideology," adding that "socialist patriotism," while acceptable, must be tempered by "proletarian internationalism." Here, once again, is that "middle way" that cosmopolitan nationalists used to define the MPR's national identity within an international context. Tsedenbal was giving voice to the two sides of the disputes taking place among the Party's cosmopolitan leaders. While "nationalism," or *ündesnii üzel* in Mongolian, was considered a dirty word, "patriotism," or *ekh oromch üzel*, was acceptable, so long as it supported the socialist—and cosmopolitan—goals of internationalization. The difference, however, in the meanings of these two words in Mongolian—as in English—is small and largely based on the context in which they are used.

The Chinggis Khan Incident marked the beginning of a period in which epochalist points of view became ascendant within the MPRP leadership. It paralleled a similar development in the same period within the CPSU, which was concerned with the rise of expressions of "nationalism" throughout the Soviet Union. Shanin describes how by the late-1960s and early 1970s, under Brezhnev's leadership of the CPSU, Soviet social scientists were being warned against publishing any conclusions about ethnicity that would be politically sensitive, or otherwise "unpleasant," for the Party leadership. He tells a "good Muscovite joke" that highlighted the CPSU's "ignorance is bliss" attitudes towards the Soviet ethnic policies of this period:

> Riding on a train when the track suddenly ends, Brezhnev simply has curtains drawn (while Stalin has the conductor shot, and Khrushchev orders the passengers to drag the train forward). As to Soviet scholars [of ethnicity], their tools were left to rust. Ethnic evidence was collected (the 'plan' of the Academy of Sciences had to be fulfilled), but the resulting conclusions carefully avoided political implications. Most of the social scientists, paid and pampered to praise and reassure, dozed in one of the compartments on Brezhnev's train (Shanin 1989: 421).

Despite the CPSU's demands during the 1960s to 1980s for increased allegiance to the rule of the Soviet ideology, the system that put ethnic leadership in charge of the Soviet republics and that allowed the existence and development of cosmopolitan nationalism, remained strong and even strengthened. It was only a matter of time before the native political and intellectual elite in each of these republics would begin to assertively question the legitimacy of total Soviet rule—a process that would lead, by the late 1980s and early 1990s, to the rapid dissolution of the Soviet system on the whole.

BADRAA AND CULTURAL NATIONALISM

There were some Mongolian scholars, however, who refused to follow the MPRP's epochalist lead and censor themselves on issues of cultural policy, even during this period of increased ideological diligence. A well-known example of such rebelliousness, and the Party's reaction to it, is found in the story of the famous Mongolian cultural intellectual, B. Rinchen, whose penchant to praise Mongolian traditions was criticized by the Party practically until the day he died in late 1977. But there is also the example of Jamtsyn Badraa, an editor, translator, and scholar who had his own ideas about the direction of contemporary national folk music.

While not a trained music researcher or critic, Badraa published articles about traditional music and culture in the 1960s and 1970s that were welcomed by music scholars and criticized by the Party leadership. In them, he praised the historic development of the Mongolian folk arts while also criticizing recent trends in their national development. In his 1968 article, "The Mongolian Folk Long Song" (1998b), Badraa wrote about the long song and its important place in traditional Mongolian culture. He describes practitioners of this song genre in pre-Revolutionary society and faulted the Party for not paying greater attention to its history and development. In his 1966 article, "Musical Abilities" (1998c), he laments the decline in the abilities of contemporary professionally trained musical performers. While acknowledging their new technical prowess, for example, he bemoans their inability to improvise melodies just as the folk musicians of the past could do and the lack of feeling they bring to their music. He complained that contemporary musicians often were merely "playing for their salary" (Badraa 1998c: 118).

Badraa's advocacy of the maintenance and study of traditional forms of music and art and his criticism of professional musical practice irritated Party officials. Lacking the international fame and institutional stature of such figures as Rinchen and Damdinsüren, Badraa suffered professionally for his outspokenness. He was dismissed from his work at Mongol Radio in 1959 after Tömör-Ochir, then head of the Central Committee's Department of Ideology, accused him of "non-Marxist minded activities" in the Party newspaper *Ünen*. He was then essentially exiled to teach high school in the far western *aimag* of Khowd. While he returned to Ulaanbaatar less than a year later, Badraa was not allowed to work for the Party nor any academic organizations, and in fact the Central Committee took it upon itself to decide which positions he was to hold (Badarch, J. Badraa's wife, personal communication). Badraa's trouble with the Party, caused by his outspoken "nationalism," as his actions are characterized today, as well as his willingness to criticize Party policies towards culture and the arts, likely served as a powerful example to other like-minded Mongolian scholars of the period, prompting them to choose "dozing" in their compartments on Tsedenbal's train instead of pushing the boundaries of official interpretations.

Throughout the Socialist period in Mongolia, but perhaps no more so than during the 1960s and 1970s, the top leadership of the Mongolian Peoples Revolutionary Party made great efforts to cultivate close relationships with the leadership of the Soviet Communist Party. They sought to control the presentation of cultural expressions so as to portray the eternal friendship of the Mongolia and Soviet peoples, the Mongolians' loyalty to the Soviet mission in Mongolia, and their adherence to the principles of Marxism-Leninism. The closeness of the Mongolian political leadership with their Soviet counterparts, as well as their willingness to criticize and even suppress prominent Party members for their nationalist ideas, has led a number of contemporary scholars to dismiss this period as a time when the Party leadership was little more than a "puppet regime," merely followed the biddings of the Soviet Union.

Seen from another perspective, however, the political and intellectual elites who shaped the development of modern Mongolian society in the twentieth century were from the very beginning cosmopolitan nationalists. We can see in their writings and activities that many were generally more inclined towards enabling national development than towards promoting the assimilationist goals of Soviet ideology. Following the ideas of Ginsburg, we can see how these elites cultivated close relationships with their Soviet counterparts as a calculated political strategy, like those common among other colonized peoples in history, i.e., learning to use the tools of power colonialists hold in order to claim a degree of control over themselves (Chatterjee 1986). In the case of the Mongolian elites, the goal was both the survival of Mongolia as an independent entity and its development into a modern nation.

As we see in the debates highlighted in this chapter, the questions were generally not over whether or not Mongolians should adopt modern ways of life, but instead on the degree to which these modern ways should reflect national or international characteristics. What is telling about them is how they were built upon the very assumptions of modernity that underlay Marxism-Leninism and the Soviet colonialist mission in Mongolia. We may compare these elites with the subjects of nineteenth century European colonization described by Partha Chatterjee that is, as subjects challenging "the political claim to political domination" of the colonial power by using the "very intellectual premises of 'modernity' on which colonial domination were based" (Chatterjee 1986: 30).

The contrasting tensions they struggled to define were essentially two sides of the same coin. The dominance of one faction of the Party leadership would usually set the stage for the reappearance of the other. The unsettled nature of international relations in the 1970s, particularly between the Soviet Union and the PRC, forced the MPRP to reassert its close alliance with the CPSU and its commitment to "proletariat internationalism." In this type of political climate, the Party suppressed the ideas of those, such as Badraa, who advocated positions of "socialist patriotism." But even figures like Badraa knew that the tables could turn and those advocating more essentialist points of view, like himself, could—and would—regain positions of power and authority.

In the following chapter we will focus on the life and career of the Mongolian composer who helped to reassert the essentialist argument in national politics. N. Jantsannorow, one of the most influential of the late twentieth century cultural elites, was part of a new generation of Soviet-trained cosmopolitan nationalists that rose to positions of power in the Party establishment in the early 1980s. He stressed the need for the Party to support the development of a distinctly national cultural identity and saw music as the medium through which it would be most succinctly expressed. As we will see, his efforts helped spur another reimagination of the horse-head fiddle, this time as a popular nationalist icon.

4 N. Jantsannorow and the Reshaping of Mongolian Musical Nationalism

Growing Cold War tensions in the early to mid-1960s between the Soviet Union and other nations, particularly the United States and the Peoples Republic of China, ended the trend towards cultural liberalization that Khrushchev had initiated in the previous decade with the goal of de-Stalinizing Soviet culture. Khrushchev himself was forced from power in 1964 and replaced with the aging Leonid Brezhnev, who sought to reassert the power of the political center. The MPRP leadership felt the need to close ranks with the Soviet leadership in this period, especially after the posting of Red Army troops on Mongolia's border with the PRC. At the same time, the MPRP tightened its control over expressions of what it saw as overly nationalist sentiments, which led to the censure of figures such as J. Badraa, and outwardly favored the policies of cultural assimilation with Russia. Few dared criticize such priorities of the Party leadership in this period.

Music was as subject to overt Russian influence as were other elements of Mongolian culture, which was evident in the new productions of Russian operas and symphonies in Mongolia, the growing quantity of Russian classical and popular musical genres entering the musical culture, and the increasing number of Russian and Soviet performers, teachers, and advisors working in Ulaanbaatar and elsewhere in the country. By the late 1970s, however, there were increasing signs of discontent, particularly among urban Mongolians, with what many saw as a one-sided, Western approach to musical development in particular, and cultural development in general. Many began to realize how few people were still alive who could remember actually experiencing life in Mongolia before the Revolution. With this realization came a sense of sadness, even fear, over the continuous loss of the past ways of life. While many welcomed the benefits of industrialization, urbanization, and modernization, many also disliked the ills these processes had brought to their country, and increasingly looked to the distant past as a time of glory and wholeness.

While such romanticization of and nostalgia for the distant past was likely a part of Mongolian society from the earliest years of the Revolution, it intensified with the acceleration of urbanization and industrialization from the 1960s on. A new generation of cosmopolitan nationalists was coming onto the national scene that was less afraid to speak out in promotion of national interests, even if these conflicted with stated Soviet interests in their nation. This contrasted them with members of previous generations, individuals like the fiddler Jamyan and the fiddle maker Buuran, who were relatively content to work quietly behind the scenes, helping to modernize the Mongolian national culture without drawing any political attention to themselves and their work.

In this chapter we will examine the career of one of this new generation, the composer, musicologist, and politician Natsagiin Jantsannorow. Though a Party member and committed to the ideology of modernity in Mongolia, he chafed at what he saw as the overt influence of Russian ideas on modern Mongolian music. He instead set his mind to reshaping cultural policies in ways that celebrated distinctly Mongolian national characteristics, and he was not afraid to take a political stand within the Party leadership to bring this about. For Jantsannorow, music was the medium through which he could best contribute to the cultural resurgence of the Mongolian people, and by the late 1980s the horse-head fiddle became the focus of his aspirations.

His abilities as a musician and politician helped him rise to a position of great visibility and influence in Mongolian society beginning in the mid 1980s, and his subsequent efforts contributed to the MPRP's move away from its overtly Russian and epochalist stance and towards one more sympathetic to the development of a distinctly national culture. Jantsannorow's essentialist ideas about Mongolian culture also helped to lay the groundwork for more overtly exclusive and nationalist expressions of national identity that would, by the end of that decade, begin to seriously challenge the legitimacy of Party rule.

THE EARLY DECADES—FINDING HIS VOICE

Jantsannorow was raised in the countryside, but he quickly learned how to navigate within the new national musical culture. He was born in Ölziit sum, Öwörkhangai aimag, in 1949, and went to school in the town of Khujirt, located close to the town of Kharakhorin (medieval Khara-Khorum), the thirteenth century location of the empirical capital and home of Erdene Zuu monastery, which was constructed from its ruins. In Khujirt, Jantsannorow learned to read musical notation and to play a variety of instruments, including the accordion. By his early to mid-20s he began to develop a reputation as a composer of popular songs, particularly *niitiin duu* or "common songs" and *zokhiolson duu* or "composed songs." His friend and colleague of later years, Jigjid Boldbaatar, says that his songs were popular in part because of their "unique new melodies" (Boldbaatar 1996: 150). After graduating from the Music and Dance College in Ulaanbaatar in 1971, Jantsannorow studied at the Tchaikovsky Conservatory of Music, in Kiev, Ukraine. After graduating in the early 1980s,

Jantsannorow returned to Ulaanbaatar and began to work with the State Folksong and Dance Ensemble (Sanders 1996: 109) and the Central Committee's Department of Ideology (Boldbaatar 1996: 153)—a high political position for a young man just out of school.

He also continued to compose. One of his assignments soon after returning to Ulaanbaatar was to compose music for a new radio series that the Party was developing to teach basic economics to rural herders. The head of the Ministry of Culture at that time ordered him to compose a melody "that herders would accept as their own" (*ibid.*, 154). Jantsannorow responded by composing his piece "Mongol ayalguu" (Mongolian melody), which he scored for strings, guitar, and horse-head fiddle (*ibid.*). The composition became popular with radio listeners and has since, especially in his arrangement for the State Horse-head Fiddle Ensemble, become one of his most popular works.

As he worked in Ulaanbaatar he continued to develop his own opinions about the state of cultural development in Mongolia and considered what he would do should he ever be placed in a position powerful enough to do something about it. He believed that the national culture and the arts were becoming increasingly Russified—one of the signs of which was the influence of the Mongolian President's Russian wife, Anastasya Ivanovna Tsedenbal-Filatova. Comrade Tsedenbal-Filatova, as she was called, had long been involved with the cultural and youth activities of the Party, including her leadership of a commission overseeing the building of child-care facilities. In 1980, on her sixtieth birthday, she was awarded the Order of Sükhbaatar, the highest civilian honor in Mongolia, for her humanitarian work. How someone of such relatively low political position as she was could achieve such great honors was a question pondered by many in Mongolia (Sanders 1989: 428). To Jantsannorow and others it was clear that Tsedenbal-Filatova wielded more power over government policies than her official position would suggest.

Her influence in the realm of culture and the arts were particularly evident to Jantsannorow. He describes Tsedenbal-Filatova as having had her own opinions about how Mongolian culture should develop, and since she was the President's wife, "all the important people in our country listened to her words." One result of this, he says, was "that our culture became very Russian in nature" (Jantsannorow 1999.10.09).

While the trends toward Russification had been developing for quite some time, Tsedenbal-Filatova personified for Jantsannorow the overbearing nature of the Soviet relationship with the MPRP. Like others in the Mongolian intellectual and political elite, he felt that the relationship between the CPSU and the MPRP was too close. He believed that the Party leadership was too eager to follow Soviet models of cultural development and he looked for ways of putting himself in a position where he could have some say over the development of culture and the arts.

Jantsannorow particularly respected the man who held the position of Deputy Minister of Culture, whom he called "clever and adaptable." Jantsannorow recognized the power that someone in this position would have over the development of musical composition in Mongolia, given that this Ministry "always gave instruction about how to compose songs and music." Jantsannorow felt that the person in this position "should be someone very experienced and talented"—someone like himself. To his surprise, he was offered the job in 1981 when he was just 32 years old. It is curious that someone as young as he was should be offered a job with as much responsibility as the Deputy Minister of Culture. It perhaps shows the confidence that he and his ideas inspired in more powerful members of the Party and government.

Jantsannorow says that his new position in the Ministry of Culture made him "responsible for all of the art and culture" in Mongolia (*ibid.*). It also gave him "the opportunity to speak with Tsedenbal-Filatova as someone in the Ministry." And from that time one, he says, the Party leadership also began to listen to his ideas. He set to work bringing changes to the ways in which the Ministry carried out its cultural activities. An important first sign of what was to come was his selection of J. Badraa as one of his main advisors, a controversial move since the Party had long criticized him as a nationalist. As Jantsannorow describes Badraa, it is clear that the two shared similar ideas about the development of Mongolian culture, as well as a good friendship.

Badraa's ideas about the need for the preservation of Mongolian traditional musical cultures were evident in Jantsannorow's first large-scale project, a resolution for a "national inspection of traditional art" in Mongolia, which he undertook within the first year of arriving at the Ministry. Boldbaatar says that Jantsannorow took the idea to Yu. Tsedenbal himself, "presenting him with documentary evidence that Mongolian traditional art was disappearing" (Boldbaatar 1996: 156–157). He convinced the Party leader of the need for the project and soon after the Central Committee passed a resolution supporting it. "It was a very large project," Jantsannorow explains.

> First I myself went to the *aimag*s and chose the people myself. Then I brought them back to Ulaanbaatar where we organized a central concert. Over three hundred people participated. Most of them were herders and not professionals. When the people [both the performers and the people who came to see them] saw this, I explained to them, 'We have such rich culture and we should stop the Russian influence in the culture' (Jantsannorow 1999.10.09).

Such sentiments critical of Russian culture were likely greeted with surprise by all involved given Jantsannorow's position in the Ministry of Culture.

He expressed similar views in a newspaper interview published the same year. When asked what he believed was the reason for the People's Revolution of 1921, Jantsannorow said he answered that "it was the result of our people's struggle for their rights," adding that both Queen Mandukhai[1] and Chinggis Khan were also struggling for the rights of the Mongolian people (*ibid*.). He says that while the people who heard his statements welcomed them warmly, the Party responded by punishing him, though he would not say how. Some of his supporters at the time cautioned him to be careful. The day after his interview was published in the Party newspaper, *Ünen*, he says, "the chief of the Gandan Monastery called me and said that what I said was a very new idea, but that it might be too early for it" (*ibid*.).[2]

Jantsannorow stressed the degree to which the common people (*ard tümen*) of Mongolia welcomed his ideas. When asked how much resistance he felt from the Party leadership to his ideas, he responded,

> There were many people resisting me. But there were lots of people who were also happy about these ideas. Usually, our people loved me, and even on the street everybody knew me. And so I think that many people were waiting for the Revolution [of 1990] and for these things to come because of my work in helping folk arts to develop (*ibid*.).

It is, of course, unlikely that many Mongolians foresaw the events of 1990 in the early 1980s. But Jantsannorow's larger point is that by contributing to a general resurgence of interest and pride in traditional culture in the latter half of the 1980s, he helped to initiate a series of events that would lead to the collapse of Party rule in 1990.

Jantsannorow went to pains to make the point, however, that in this time he was not seeking to challenge socialist rule in Mongolia or its replacement with a multi-party democracy. He stressed that he was not a "nationalist," or anti-Party activist as it was understood in this period. His intent was instead to urge the Party to distance itself from the policies of the CPSU and to allow more room for Mongolians to identify with their own national culture. And for him, developing the national folk arts was a way of accomplishing such goals.

> This was not about nationalism, which the government was suppressing in this time. I just started to think that we should develop our traditional music and traditional instruments. You see, the policy of the Russians was such that we had to accept Russian or European art and culture, [while at the same time] we had to leave behind the traditional arts. Thus, our people moved away from playing the horse-head fiddle in the same way as they moved away from riding a horse to driving a car (*ibid*.).

Jantsannorow believed that developing a modern musical culture could not be achieved by merely accepting the ways of the international community at the expense of the national culture. He wanted to convince the Party leadership that cultural development required both learning from the outside world and applying this new-found knowledge to the development of the national arts.

> But we should instead pay attention to both sides. If we consider only our traditional folk art, only looking at that and not considering the arts and cultures of other nations, then we will surely not develop or improve. Instead we need to see how the Russians or Germans have developed their music and life, [in order] to see how we can develop our music and life (Jantsannorow 1999.10.13).

Jantsannorow saw the need to improve Mongolian culture through the selective borrowing of ideas and models from the "developed" nations of the West. Doing so, he argues, will help Mongolia prove to the international community that it could become as developed and modern as any other nation while simultaneously retaining its own unique cultural identity. Such cosmopolitan nationalist approaches to cultural development were not nationalist or anti-Party from his point of view, but rather approaches that reflected the more essentialist interpretations of Marxist-Leninist ideology.

REORIENTING MUSICAL COMPOSITION

From the time of his appointment in the Ministry of Culture, Jantsannorow had the goal of fundamentally reorienting the nature of Mongolian composition. He wanted Mongolian composers to not merely copy or imitate Russian compositional models, but to develop a uniquely national compositional style, one rooted in traditional musical forms that could, in turn, distinguish Mongolian composers from those of all other nations. Jantsannorow spoke about how he tried to convince the Party leadership of the national need for these new musical styles.

> The government always sponsored operatic performances [in the socialist era], but none of the leadership ever went to them. So, one day I organized a new opera performance and invited all the government leaders to attend. Before the opera began I made a little speech telling people that in Italy and Russia there was opera that was based on the traditional music and traditional customs of the Italian and Russian people (Jantsannorow 1999.10.09).

He said he was trying to stress to the Party leadership the importance of supporting the development of a truly national style of composition. He says that in this way he was trying to solve the debates going on within the

Party, i.e., between the epochalists and the essentialists, in a non-argumentative or, as he put it, a "soft way" (*ibid.*), in contrast to the more direct and assertive ways of Damdinsüren, Rinchen, and Badraa, which we saw in the previous chapter.

> The Russian government wanted to instruct the people of Mongolia on how they should live, and the Mongolian government went along with this without any changes. But the people want to live by themselves; they want to think and do what they want. The people of Mongolia want to live freely. [If this is so,] then there should be national or traditional things. The important thing is not about capitalism or socialism. It's more about the Mongolian government just copying from Russia and then conveying this to the people. But the people didn't want this principle. They wanted to live by their own opinions (*ibid.*).

In spite of his obvious devotion to establishing a modern national culture, Jantsannorow says he had to continually reassure the Party leadership that he was no "bourgeois nationalist." To this end, in 1982, the same year as the folk music festival and his comments about Russian cultural influence in Mongolia, Jantsannorow organized the first of what would become an annual festival of modern music, called *Altan namar* (Golden Autumn), modeled after an annual autumn music festival in the Soviet Union called *Moskovskaya Osen* (Moscow Autumn). The three-day festival features concerts of recently-composed songs and instrumental works in the classical and popular genres, particularly those influenced by Russian traditions and aesthetics. He believes that founding the *Altan namar* festival gave hard-liners in the Party less to criticize him about: "the government began to think that I'm not just biased toward Mongolian folk music, but that I also support modern songs, as well as Russian music and performers" (*ibid.*). But overall, the fact that Jantsannorow was merely criticized for his ideas and not dismissed from the Party or his position is an indication of the shifting dynamics of power in the Party leadership between the 1960s and 1980s, to say nothing to the change from the Revolutionary era. Jantsannorow must have received considerable support from powerful figures within the Party and government that allowed him to stay in his position in spite of the criticism he says that he had to endure.

Indeed, the Party continued to support his work throughout the 1980s. In 1983 it appointed him to the position of Secretary of the Mongolian Composer's Union (MCU), a position that allowed him almost complete control over the future direction and development of Mongolian composition. He held this position until 1990 and has sighted his accomplishments as Secretary as including a significant increase in the number of composers. He says that he also raised the Mongolian composers' general level of ability and productivity, and believes that he helped Mongolian composition develop "a strong foundation in the musical soil" of their country (Jantsannorow 1989: 6). He encouraged Mongolian composers to look to the "national traditional music" as "an immeasurably rich treasury and main source of their creations" (*ibid.*, 19). He encouraged composers to work more closely with Mongolian musical ethnographers, who were charged with collecting and analyzing the folk music of the many different Mongolian subcultures. He authorized the MCU to establish preservation archives for recordings of Mongolian folk song and music. "Folk music research," he said in 1989, "is becoming the foundation of the music sciences and has important significance to the study and analysis of contemporary musical compositions" (*ibid.*, 20).

At the same time, he encouraged Mongolian composers to continue to master modern European compositional techniques. He persuaded them to view the symphony orchestra as the musical genre most fitting for the development of Mongolian music within the realm of a broader, internationally-oriented Soviet musical world:

> Mongolian music composers in this period [the 1980s] have been able to master all of the large types and forms of musical composition. . . . Symphonic musical compositions are an essential part of establishing the principles of socialist realism in our musical art in the past, present, and future. The most important quality of Mongolian symphonic and chamber orchestral compositions are their civil and internationalist orientations (*ibid.*, 6).

What set Jantsannorow apart from those of his predecessors, however, was his call to young and middle-aged composers to create a new national style, one that combined "modern music skills, folk music tunes, and national thinking" (*üdesnii setgelgee*). Examples that he gives of works in this new style include a symphony by S. Baatarsükh (*ibid.*, 7), as well as compositions for orchestra by the young composers Bilegjargal, Chinzorig, Sharav, and Natsagdorj, all of whom were his students. One of his more important achievements was his introduction of the orchestral concerto for folk instruments:

> I composed the first concerto for the horse-head fiddle, *yatga*, *yochin* and *shanz*. The young composers listened to these works and then started composing good quality music [in this genre]. These include Sharav's horse-head fiddle concerto, and one by Khangal, which is actually a very good concerto. Chinzorig's *yatga* concerto was very well written. You see, I was in a high political position in the arts and so I was able to start all of these things. There was no one else around to who would undertake this protection [of our heritage]. The democracy of culture in the arts came before the democracy of the economic and political! (Jantsannorow 1999.10.09)

Jantsannorow once again suggests that the efforts of Mongolian composers like himself to strengthen the national musical culture preceded—and even contributed to—the rise of democratic sentiments in other realms of Mongolian society.

It needs to be added, however, that the 1980s was a period of rapid change in other sectors of Mongolian society. In 1984 members of the high Party leadership engineered the removal of President Yu. Tsedenbal from power with the approval of the Soviet Communist Party. Tsedenbal had been increasingly seen by others in the Party leadership as being too pro-Russian and possibly senile. Many were also frustrated by the influence of his wife in running the national affairs. His removal followed the death of Leonid Brezhnev and the appointment of Yuri Andropov as Party Secretary of the CPSU. Andropov began to introduce modest reforms to the ways in which the USSR related to its satellite republics, and the removal of Tsedenbal might have been a part of this plan. Andropov's death two years later was followed by the ascendancy of Mikhail Gorbachev to the post of Party Secretary and the launch of his programs of *glastnost* (openness) and *perestroika* (restructuring). The new Prime Minister of Mongolia, J. Batmönkh, quickly adopted similar policies of *il tod* (openness) and *öörchlön shinechlel* (renewal). By 1986–1987 these policies were beginning to be felt by Mongolian cultural institutions in the form of less ideological pressure from the Party. Thus, by the time Jantsannorow became head of the MCU, the ideological space for new ideas in composition was already beginning to clear. He does deserve credit, however, for initiating his reforms several years earlier, in the early 1980s, when ideological pressure from the Party was still strong.

DEVELOPING A MODERN 'ASIAN' STYLE OF COMPOSITION

Jantsannorow was particular about the quality of the "Western" or "modern" musical ideas and styles that the composers were drawing upon in modeling their compositions. He felt that the older generations of composers had stuck too closely to the styles of late-romantic Russian composers, and described their music as being in the "traditional European style" (*traditsionnii evropeiskii stili*). He described three of the most famous and established composers of the 1950s and '60s, S. Gonchigsümlaa, E. Choidog, and L. Mördorj, as belonging to "the nineteenth century European school of composers" (Jantsannorow 1999.10.09.). They developed well as composers, he says, but "they were influenced by Tchaikovsky, Rachmaninov, Mahler, and Shostakovich" (*ibid.*). He also cites the influence of Gliere and Khatchaturian, describing Choidog's 1964 ballet, *Mönkhiin nökhörlöl* (Eternal friendship), as "just like a copy of Katchaturian's ballet *Gayne*" (*ibid.*). After Choidog's graduation from Moscow University in 1962, Jantsannorow says, the Party sent no other

Mongolian composers to Russia for advanced training until the composer Khangal, nearly a decade later. Composers instead studied in Mongolian schools and institutions where he says they continued to learn late-Romantic compositional styles and techniques, adding that "seventy percent of the teachers at the Music & Dance College were Russian" (*ibid.*).

It was not until Khangal rose to prominence in the 1970s that composers began to compose in what Jantsannorow calls the "new European style" (*shine Evropyn stili*). "In 1972, while still a student, Khangal composed a string quartet that brought to Mongolia the European musical arts of the 1960s. Khangal brought the influences of Stravinsky, Schoenberg and others—all of the new music of Europe" (*ibid.*). He later added Bartok, Debussy, and Ravel to this list, adding that the 1960s was much too late for the arrival of these early twentieth century influences (*ibid.*).

Mongolian composers were not looking only towards Russia for ideas about modern musical development. While studying at institutions in Moscow and Leningrad, Mongolian students of composition were introduced to the music of other Asian Soviet republics, including Armenia and Azerbaijan. Azerbaijan, in particular, had a very highly developed modern musical culture, one whose roots had developed before the Soviet era. Jantsannorow says that Azerbaijani composers had developed a uniquely national sound to which, for their part, young Mongolian composers were paying attention, listening to recordings and reading the scores of contemporary composers from this region.

> The Mongolians already had a European musical understanding, but many Armenian and Azerbaijani composers were composing with a mixture of European and Asian styles. These composers composed their music based on traditional Asian music with European style. These new ideas were very influential for us Mongolians (*ibid.*).

With their "Asian style," Azerbaijani composers provided an example to the Mongolians of how to further develop their own national musical style and to distinguish it from the Russians classical traditions. As we will see in the next section, Jantsannorow found in the horse-head fiddle both a symbol and a sound that would further help focus the efforts of Mongolian composers in developing a distinctly national style of music.

The example of the Azerbaijani's explicitly "Asian" style of modern music must have had great symbolic importance to the Mongolians. Russian policies toward the Asians, particularly the Central Asians, typically assumed their backwardness in relation to Russian and European nationalities. The success of the Azerbaijanis in establishing a national style that drew the respect of Russian composers likely symbolized to many Asian nations within the Soviet Union the growing maturity of the Asian peoples in relation to the developed West.

THE ROLE OF THE "CHINESE" IN THE
EMERGENCE OF THE HORSE-HEAD FIDDLE

In Mongolia, the West is commonly referred to as the "North" (primarily Russia and Europe), whereas Peoples Republic of China is referred to as the "South." So far, we have examined how artists like Jantsannarov conceived of a national musical style in terms of their nation's relationship with the "North." But Mongolia's relationship with the "South" in this period was just as important in defining the modern Mongolian nation.

The general anti-Chinese sentiments of the MPRP lessened after it officially recognized the PRC in 1949. But by the late 1960s whatever warmth there was in the relationship between the two neighbors had again dissipated. While the PRC made no overt moves against the MPR, the threat that it posed to the sovereignty of the nation, and with it to the Soviet Union, as well, was woven into the Party's rhetoric about national security and national identity. In 1969 the Party "invited" the Soviet Red Army to station its troops along the MPR's southern border. Verbal sparring marked the relationship between the two nations in this period, including, as Bawden writes, "Mongolian charges of Chinese 'annexationism' towards Mongolia, and Chinese charges of Soviet 'colonialism' towards Mongolia" (Bawden 1989: 426). In 1979, the Party expelled many Chinese residents from Mongolia for what Sanders calls "crimes against the state" (Sanders 1996: xxxix).

This tense political atmosphere further distanced Mongolians from their kinsmen in China, the Inner Mongolians. Travel between the two countries was tightly controlled and largely prohibited, leading to the nearly total break in communication between the Mongolians and the Inner Mongols. Little was taught about Chinese history and civilization in Mongolian schools and universities and few Mongolians learned read or speak Chinese. Even historians who could read Chinese or who used Chinese sources were commonly viewed with suspicion. The Mongolian historian G. Sükhbaatar, a member of the Mongolian Academy of Sciences, for example, published works in the late 1960s and early 1970s on the ancient history of the Mongols and Mongol ancestors, including those on the Khünnü (Xiongnu/Hsiung-nu), Hsien-pi, and Kitan peoples who occupied different parts of the Inner Asian region long before the rise of the Mongols. Though his works were strictly historical, his use of Chinese sources drew the attention of some Party officials. In the 1970s, despite his own strongly nationalist sentiments, Sükhbaatar was dismissed from the Party and slipped into a life of relative obscurity (cf. Dashpürew and Soni 1992).

This near complete lack of information about or communication with China led many in this period to speculate about what life was like in Inner Mongolia, especially during the period of the Maoist Cultural Revolution. One of the first signs of the thaw in the chilled relations between the two neighbors occurred in the mid-1980s when a scholar from the Mongolian

Academy of Sciences was allowed to visit an academic conference in the capital of the Inner Mongolian province, Höhhot. Professor D. Tserenpil of the National University remembers what it was like when this scholar returned to the Academy to talk to his colleagues about what he saw and experienced.

> To us it was as if he had visited another planet. We learned that the Inner Mongolians had created a film about Chinggis Khan around this time. This raised great interest among us. So people got the film and brought it to the Academy. We paid a lot of money to show the film on video. It was so hot and uncomfortable in that room in the Academy of Sciences, but everyone was so interested to see the film. Life in China seemed so interesting to us. We heard about the Mongolians in China, but the border was completely closed. Even in books, there was no mention of the Mongolians in China. We were completely closed off—people rarely went there. It was so interesting just to see an Inner Mongolian film (Tserenpil 2001.06.15).

Despite such curiosity in the lives of the Mongols living in China, however, the Mongolians continued to view the Chinese with suspicion. The historian Uradyn Bulag has written about the relationships between the Mongolians and Inner Mongolians and one of his consistent arguments is that the Mongolians of Mongolia have long viewed themselves as those best able to maintain Mongolian cultural heritage (cf. Bulag 1998). To many Mongolians, the Chinese Mongols have lost their true Mongol identity: they have become like Chinese citizens, having adopted their culture, customs and language. Many Mongolians believe that Inner Mongolian blood has been polluted by Chinese blood. This attitude is no doubt tied to the Mongolian tendency to speak of Inner Mongolians as "Chinese."

So it was with special interest that the Inner Mongolian horse-head fiddle player Chi. Bulag arrived in Ulaanbaatar to perform a series of concerts organized in the late 1980s as part of a cultural exchange initiative. Mongolian musicians were especially eager to see him perform. His reputation as a great horse-head fiddle player in Inner Mongolia was known among those of the professional music world in Mongolia. But this was also a rare opportunity to see a musician from China. Horse-head fiddle players were particularly interested in learning more about the horse-head fiddle traditions among the Inner Mongolians. The musicologist L. Erdenechimeg, at that time a teacher of music theory and an amateur horse-head fiddle player in Ulaanbaatar, says that she and her colleagues were excited to meet Chi. Bulag and hear him and his troupe perform. "His horse-head fiddle was not like our Mongolian fiddles, but different. The strings were made from [nylon] fishing line and the fiddle's face was made of wood with beautiful designs carved into it. The sound of the fiddle was very strong, stronger than we were accustomed to in Mongolia, and this excited everyone" (Erdenechimeg 1999.10.03).

Chi. Bulag says that his first visit to Mongolia in December 1988 came after years of being refused a visa by the Chinese government.

> Jamyan *bagsh* [teacher] sent me an invitation to visit him in Mongolia in 1982, saying that since my teacher was a student of his, he would like to meet with me and to build a relationship between our two cultures. So I petitioned the Chinese government, asking for permission to visit the MPR, but the high officials consistently refused to let me go. They wondered why I wanted to go, asking if I liked Outer Mongolia more than the Chinese people, and then word came down from the [Chinese] Community Party that if I go to the MPR I will not to be allowed back in. So when they did not give me this permission to travel, I went to Japan for four years. But I kept petitioning the Ministry of Foreign Relations and finally in 1988, after six years, they let me visit Ulaanbaatar (Chi. Bulag 2004.01.07).

Chi. Bulag recalls the excitement he felt in coming into Mongolia by train. He recounts how he saw cattle on the steppe wearing woolen blankets to protect them from the cold winter weather. He says his wife commented on how Mongolia must be a rich nation "if even its animals wear woolen blankets." He was struck by the beauty of Ulaanbaatar with its tall white buildings and by the politeness of the Mongolian people towards him.

But even in Mongolia, Chi. Bulag was not free from the political pressures imposed on cultural performances. During his first meeting with the fiddle players Jamyan and Batchuluun in a small apartment in the city, he says that Jantsannorow came in and told him that he must not speak about Chinggis Khan nor play any music about him, as this would be considered an "anti-Party" activity (*ibid.*). They organized a concert performance for him at the Music and Dance College that was well-attended by many musicians and scholars. Erdenechimeg recalls how, after the concert, he told his Mongolian audiences about how difficult it was to maintain the traditional Mongol arts in Inner Mongolia during the Cultural Revolution, and even wept as he told them how the Chinese authorities imprisoned him during this period (Erdenechimeg 1999.10.03).

While Chi. Bulag's visit excited most in the musical community, not everyone was pleased with what they saw and heard. To the horse-head fiddle maker Ulambayar and his colleagues, his visit provided an indication of how far behind the Mongolians had become in developing the art of the horse-head fiddle. His accomplishments in Inner Mongolia challenged their conception of what they had achieved to that point in history.

> When Chi. Bulag came to perform in Ulaanbaatar, several times with a troupe, people realized how advanced the horse-head fiddle in Inner Mongolia had become from the fiddle in Mongolia. We found their fiddles and the music they played as essentially different in composition,

style, sound and the way we played our fiddles. These guys played on horse-head fiddles that were very distinctive—smaller, with very different styles of playing from our own. The music was different too. The improvement of the horse-head fiddle is all related; the style, sound, and other factors [need to come together] to improve the horse-head fiddle. We began to realize that the Inner Mongolians had made more progress than us. Those Chinese [i.e. Inner Mongolians] improved the horse-head fiddle a lot; they rose to another level of development. Being introduced to these players, they made us ask ourselves what is going on? Why did their horse-head fiddle become so much more advanced? Maybe they improved it and we are falling behind (Ulambayar 1998.07.17).

Chi. Bulag's visit startled the Mongolians working with the horse-head fiddle. They began to fear that the Inner Mongolians were paying more attention to the state of their folk arts than were the Mongolians themselves. This attention, in turn, was translating into the quicker advancement of the horse-head fiddle traditions than even the Mongolians themselves had been able to achieve, and this was worrisome. While he admired the advancements that the Inner Mongolians made with their fiddles, Ulambayar's account suggests that he did not see them as legitimately Mongolian but rather as being shaped by "Chinese" culture.

The Khalkha horse-head fiddle was different, but I can't say the Inner Mongolian horse-head fiddle is worse than it. But I do feel that the Inner Mongolian fiddle has declined more from the influence from Chinese culture, and especially from the influence of Chinese music. Of course, the fiddle had to be adapted to Chinese culture given that there are so many [Han] Chinese people in Inner Mongolia. So, this Chinese influence is to be expected (*ibid.*).

For Ulambayar and the others involved with the horse-head fiddle in Mongolia, the visit by the Inner Mongolians spurred them to reassess their goals and methods in regards to these traditions. The question of how the "Chinese" could have advanced so far beyond the Mongolians in the development of the fiddle was perplexing and prompted great discussions about the state of the folk culture and what could be done to accelerate its development. National pride seems clearly to have been at stake in these discussions.

With these clarifying distinctions [in the fiddles of Chi. Bulag and his ensemble], many in the folk music community felt moved to act. Seeing them in concert gave us many things to think about. We began to talk about how we could improve the folk arts. The Chinese have developed the horse-head fiddle to a high level, and so what should we do? All the people specializing in the horse-head fiddle got together to talk, and after a while we decided to organize the Horse-head Fiddle Center [*Morin khuuryn töw*]. Jantsannorow was one of the main organizers of this center and Jamyan was its first president. In the center there was a nine-member committee and I [Ulambayar] was one of them. One of our first projects was to develop the shape, sound and music of the horse-head fiddle (*ibid.*).

This Center does not appear to have been an actual place, but rather consisted of a virtual community of fiddlers, fiddle makers, and composers who sought to determine how they could accelerate the development of the horse-head fiddle and its spread to other nations. Chi. Bulag's visit did more than raise interest in the development of a folk fiddle. It touched a nerve of national sentiment and helped to raise the fiddle's political visibility. Given these new stakes, it is not surprising that Jantsannorow took a leadership role in this effort.

A few months after Chi. Bulag's first visit in 1988, Jantsannorow and Jamyan accepted his invitation to make a reciprocal visit to Höhhot, Inner Mongolia, to see his ensemble of horse-head fiddle players. Jantsannorow remembers being impressed with the organizations he saw there but not with the quality of the developments.

> I and other two men were invited by Chi. Bulag to go to Inner Mongolia. I was trying to set up the Horse-head Fiddle Center around that same time. While I was there, I saw [Chi. Bulag's] Horse-head Fiddle Ensemble and remember thinking that it did not have the real Mongolian horse-head fiddle sound. The Inner Mongolian fiddle has a relatively higher tuning than in Mongolia. They use a tuning called *raliya*. As a result their fiddles do not have the pure horse-head fiddle sound [*tsewer morin khuuryn duulal bish*] like our fiddles. So I started to think that if we want to disseminate the horse-head fiddle all over the world then we Mongolians should set up a center for Mongolians to study. Also I was with Jamyan, and he said to me that Mongolians should be doing this work [with the horse-head fiddle] and not the Inner Mongolians. After my return to Mongolia, I composed the first Mongolian horse-head fiddle *Symphonia* [i.e., his horse-head fiddle concerto] (Jantsannorow 1999.10.09).

Jantsannorow's use of the word "pure" is important. Note how he is trying the make the case that only a "pure" Mongolian horse-head fiddle sound can be acceptable to the Mongolian people. One of the major distinctions that the Mongolians make between themselves and the Inner Mongolians is that they have been able to maintain ethnic "purity," whereas the Inner Mongolians have intermixed with the Chinese. For the historian U. Bulag, the issue of purity in blood and food lies at the core of Khalkha chauvinism towards the Inner Mongolians (Bulag 1998). The use of the term *tsewer*, or pure, as in *tsewer Khalkha*, "pure Khalkha," is common in Mongolia when designating ethnic identity. Like Ulambayar, Jantsannorow appears to be alluding to the same nationalist trope of purity when he describes its absence in the sound of the Inner Mongolian fiddles that he heard.

Instead of building closer relationships between the two communities, as Jamyan had intended, Chi. Bulag's visits in the late 1980s appear to have had the effect of making the Mongolians more aware of their fundamental differences with their neighbors to the south. While Chi. Bulag wanted to celebrate an important shared element of a historically common culture, his efforts instead seem to have moved Mongolians to reclaim the horse-head fiddle as their own unique symbol of national identity. As we will see in the following section, efforts to do so led to the emergence of the horse-head fiddle as a popular symbol of national identity, as well as contributing to the formation of a more exclusive and aggressive form of nationalism.

THE FIRST HORSE-HEAD FIDDLE NAADAM

Upon his return from Inner Mongolia, Jantsannorow began to develop his ideas of holding a grand *naadam* or festival in celebration of the horse-head fiddle, which he decided needed to take place in the following autumn of 1989, in lieu of the *Altan namar* festival for that year. Given his influence in the government, this was easily accomplished, and the *Morin Khuuryn Naadam*, "Horse-head Fiddle Festival," began on October 10, 1989, in Ulaanbaatar. Unlike the usual *Altan namar* festival, the Horse-head Fiddle Festival lasted five days and featured many different kinds of activities, including a series of concerts and workshops, ceremonies honoring past achievements and celebrating new ones, a horse-head fiddle making competition, and an exhibition of horse-head fiddles from around the nation. The organization of the Festival was mostly accomplished by the newly organized Horse-head Fiddle Center, which Jantsannorow had set up in the months prior to the Naadam. At the time of the Festival, the Center was run by a nine-person committee consisting of famous and respected fiddle makers, players, and composers. G. Jamyan was appointed its first President. With the support of the MPRP, the Center invited several hundred people from around the country to participate in this event. Chi. Bulag was also invited to attend.

Jantsannorow said that he had set four goals to be achieved by the Festival. The first of these was to encourage the development of the compositions for the horse-head fiddle; the second was to encourage horse-head fiddle players to experiment with new ideas and playing techniques; the third, to improve the making of the horse-head fiddle; and the fourth, to encourage popular interest in the horse-head fiddle among the Mongolian people.

Even though the Festival was devoted to the horse-head fiddle, the Party still expected new musical compositions to be premiered and performed and to this end Jantsannorow scheduled one concert of modern music. But the additional three major concerts during the Festival were restricted to music for the horse-head fiddle, which ranged from traditional to contemporary works. Jantsannarov, for instance, premiered *Simphonia*, his concerto for horse-head fiddle and string orchestra during the Festival.

These concerts featured many of the most talented and respected fiddlers in the country and abroad, including G. Jamyan, Ts. Tserendorj, Ts. Batchuluun, Ch. Batsaikhan, Ch. Tsogbadrakh and D. Tsogsaikhan, as well as Chi. Bulag. Ensembles of horse-head fiddles also played an important role in this Naadam. A well respected horse-head fiddle quartet performed. Formed in 1981, this quartet consisted of some of these great fiddle players of the day, including Batchuluun, Batsaikhan and Tsogtsaikhan, and it was known for performing challenging works of music, including chamber music by Tchaikovsky and Chopin.

Jantsannorow intended the third goal of the Naadam to be to promote the improvement in the design and construction of the horse-head fiddle. To this end, the Mongolian Art Worker's Union and the Mongolian Composer's Union jointly sponsored a fiddle competition that looked for the fiddles that most successfully combined appearance, design, and sound. The winners were chosen by a committee chaired by the fiddle maker B. Ulambayar, then director of the State Music Instrument Factory in Ulaanbaatar. The winner of the competition that year was P. Baigaljaw, a young worker at the Factory who made a modern wooden-faced

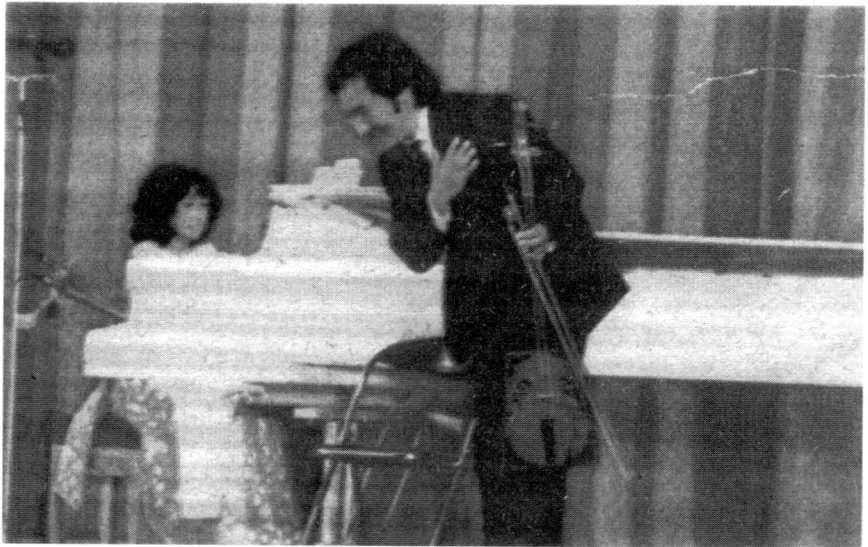

Figure 16.   Inner Mongolian fiddle player Chi. Bulag with an unnamed accompanist during a performance at the Horse-head Fiddle Naadam, Ulaanbaatar 1989 (Dulmaa 1989).

horse-head fiddle. Ulambayar admits that fiddle makers from Ulaanbaatar had an advantage over those from the countryside, given the resources and training they received in the Factory (Ulambayar 1998.07.17). Those who organized and ran the competition likely shared the sentiments of Sh. Dulmaa, writing about the festival in the Party's *Youth* magazine, that "the horse-head fiddle must be well made in order to develop the horse-head fiddle art" (Dulmaa 1989: 14). Ulambayar feels that devoting a major national festival to this one instrument did indeed contribute to its development. "Many composers participated [in this festival]," he says, "which meant that there also had to be many good horse-head fiddle performers and makers there, as well. In this way, the festival gave a push to the development of the horse-head fiddle" (Ulambayar 1998.07.17).

The accompanying exhibition, however, also showed many of the more traditional fiddle making practices. Sixty-four horse-head fiddles were entered by fifty craftsmen from around the nation and put on display. Dulmaa's account of the festival gave special attention to the work of traditional fiddle makers, such as G. Darisüren, a fiddle maker from Dund-gowi aimag, who incorporates symbolic designs in the construction of his fiddle.

> On the wood between the two ears of the fiddle, a pair of swans is gliding on water, symbolizing the happiness of couples in this world. On the bow was carved a male camel being chased by a wolf, reminding us of a legend. On the hilt of the bow, the shape of a tiger is carved, while on the cross beam, the image of a lion is carved. These images symbolize the strength of the fiddle's melody and its invincible braveness. On the wooden side below the strings two fish of peace are carved,[3] symbolizing eternal friendship. What this shows fundamentally is that we should support those who so skillfully craft musical instruments (Dulmaa 1989: 14).

It is not clear how widely recognized were Dulmaa's interpretations of these symbols, but Darisüren's fiddle did represent more traditional ways of crafting fiddles. These were traditions generally falling out of practice with the increase in use and popularity of modern fiddles, many of which were being constructed in the State Instrument Factory. Dulmaa also recognized the old tradition of using goatskin to cover the face of the two-stringed fiddle and of carving the sound holes in the shape of symbolic designs. She even wondered about the role they could play in the development of the modern fiddle-making traditions:

> The art of making fiddles with goatskin has come down to the Mongolian people from our ancestors. It is necessary to support this way of making the national instruments, like making the face of wood. Probably most horse-head fiddles have a sound hole. But instead of making them in the shape of those used on European instruments, it

would be better to make the holes in the form of national decorations or styles (*ibid.*).

Dulmaa goes on to advocate the building of centers to train people in such traditional techniques of constructing fiddles.

> We should establish a school that prepares both talented musicians and skilled instruments makers. How can the sole State Music Instrument Factory be sufficient for everything? Therefore, it would be good to create an education-training center to make horse-head fiddles in each aimag, sum and large city. It will require a real Mongolian spirit to organize this. We must learn how to make the horse-head fiddle from such people as D. Bandi of Dund-gowi aimag, who are skilled at making fiddles in a variety of ways. D. Bandi has been making horse-head fiddles since 1972 and has given them to artists, schools and private people (*khuwi khün*). He has made more than 80 different kinds of fiddles, including children's, intermediate (*dund garyn*), and great fiddles (*Ikh khuur*). He has continued until now to make suitable fiddles for every occasion. It is necessary for future generations to learn to make the fiddle well (*ibid.*).

With the fiddles constructed in the State Music Instrument Factory winning the awards and representing the new standard for modernization and

Figure 17. An "orchestra" of horse-head fiddles during the Horse-head Fiddle Naadam (Dulmaa 1989).

progress in the horse-head fiddle tradition in Mongolia, it is interesting that Dulmaa should voice support for the continuation, even nationalization, of such traditional methods.

Jantsannarov and the Center hoped that in organizing a final concert with a massed ensemble of fiddle players they would achieve their fourth goal of the Festival, i.e., raising the popularity of the instrument among the Mongolian people. The Festival organizers arranged for Mongol Television to record this concert for subsequent broadcast across the nation and Jantsannorow hoped that it would wake people up: "We wanted people once again to pay attention to the horse-head fiddle, because for a while people didn't care about the instrument. But I expected that when 180 horse-head fiddle players would perform together on one stage, people would be impressed and take notice" (Jantsannorow 1999.10.13). About the concert, Dulmaa wrote: "When the beautiful sound of a hundred horse-head fiddle players on stage thundered, [the expression was heard] among the audience members, 'What a beautiful thing. So many horse-head fiddles, it's not worse than a symphony orchestra! How many years we were careless about such beautiful national music'" (Dulmaa 1989: 14). The narratives about the fiddle to which Dulmaa was beginning to give voice in her article were those that described the instrument in almost primordialist and essentialist terms.

> No foreigner could understand Mongolia without a fiddle. This beautiful instrument can play any type of melody, long songs, short songs or classical. If we are to preserve it from generation to generation (*üyeiin üyed öwlüülen üldeewel*) then how much better it is for us to perform on our own fiddle, rather than the instruments of the world's stages! How wonderful it was in the recent Horse-head Fiddle Naadam to listen to one hundred fiddles playing simultaneously. All of this shows us that our horse-head fiddle is a musical instrument that cannot be rejected in any century (*ibid.*, 15).

Dulmaa sees the fiddle is an essential element of contemporary Mongolian national identity, one that must therefore be promoted through schools and popular culture. In addition, the instrument's uniqueness will grab people's attention around the world.

> From what Chi. Bulag says there is no doubt that setting up horse-head fiddle groups in secondary schools, in youth organizations, and even pop groups, would be an important indicator of our national culture (*ündesnii soyolyn chukhal negen üzüülelt*[4] *bolokh ni damjiggüi*). The horse-head fiddle creates a sense of national pride among our people with an ancient culture. We will surely draw great attention if we bring our horse-head fiddle to the stages of the world, and if we enter a horse-head fiddle ensemble in Olympic performances, youth festivals, regional, and world art festivals. All that is needed to organize and

initiate this is a pure Mongolian heart (*jinkhene mongol zürkh setgel l kheregtei baina*). The melody of the horse-head fiddle, which was [an object of] respect for us from the time of the ancestors, will continue to sound for hundreds of years (*ibid.*).

In Dulmaa and Jantsannorow's descriptions of the Horse-head Fiddle Naadam, we see the beginnings of a new narrative about the horse-head fiddle that would shape people's perception of the instrument in the approaching period of political and cultural upheaval. They both speak about the fiddle as being uniquely Mongolian—an object that was indigenous to Mongolia and that had been progressively developed by the Mongolian people over the course of centuries from ancient times to the present. In the hands of true masters, the quality of this instrument was being perfected and raised to international standards of excellence. Through such rhetoric, the instrument was emerging as a "great tradition" that connected contemporary national culture directly with the ancient past. At the same time, the instrument was also becoming a symbol of a new national consciousness, one that reflected the worldly aspirations of a people increasingly aware of their essential national identity.

In promoting the Horse-head Fiddle Naadam and the narratives that surrounded it, Jantsannorow and his colleagues sought to advance a redefinition, or *reimagination*, of the horse-head fiddle in the popular consciousness, from being a dusty and largely overlooked folk fiddle at the start of the Revolution to being a vital symbol of a newly emerging national musical identity in its end. Jamyan in the 1940s and 1950s and Yarovoi and his Mongolian students in the 1960s brought about important advancements in the development of this instrument. But Jantsannorow, with his charisma, enthusiasm, and political influence, succeeded where others did not in reimagining the horse-head fiddle as an important new symbol of national identity. More than any other cosmopolitan nationalist up to that point in history, he helped to articulate the importance of the horse-head fiddle in a modern Mongolian socialist state. He also helped to set the stage for the emergence of this instrument as an iconic symbol of national identity in the post-Socialist period.

5 The Folk "Revival" and the Reimagination of the Horse-head Fiddle

The decision by the Mongolian Peoples Revolutionary Party to relinquish its hold on political power in the face of persistent popular street demonstrations in early spring 1990 led to a series of events that would transform Mongolian society in the coming years. In this new environment, the horse-head fiddle began to become much more visible than ever before, as well as much more explicitly displayed as a national symbol. In 1992, the Mongolian President, Punsalmaagiin Ochirbat, issued a decree ordering the creation of the *Töriin khan khuur* or "State Sovereign Fiddle," a horse-head fiddle modeled after pre-Revolutionary horse-head fiddles, which was then formally installed in the State Parliament Building along with other newly sanctioned national symbols. In the same year, this time by Parliamentary resolution, the State Horse-head Fiddle Ensemble was created and became one of leading State-run musical institutions along side of the State Folksong & Dance Ensemble and the State Philharmonic. The decision was made to reinstate the use of the horse-head fiddle in the opening ceremonies of the State Naadam, a national festival of traditional arts and sports held each year in downtown Ulaanbaatar. And the decision was also made to pair a performance of a horse-head fiddle with the Mongolian President's annual, nationally televised address to the nation on the first day of the Lunar New Year or *Tsagaan sar*, which many consider to be the most important festival on the Mongolian calendar.

This rise in status of the horse-head fiddle from a minor symbol of the national musical culture in the Socialist period to an explicit symbol, if not icon, of national identity in the post-Socialist period paralleled the general rise in interest Mongolians had for their nation's cultural past. In the newly liberated national media, for instance, newspapers began to be published that were devoted solely to the use and promotion of the Mongol (also called vertical) script, which predated the Cyrillic script that was introduced during the Socialist period. New television game shows featured Mongolian contestants testing their knowledge of old Mongolian proverbs and customs. The practice of Buddhism and shamanism reemerged and began again to flourish in many rural and urban areas around the country. And it became acceptable again to wear the traditional Mongolian *deel* in formal settings. In fact, doing so was seen as an expression of national pride.

Perhaps the most important national symbol to reemerge in the years following the 1990 revolution was that of Chinggis Khan, whom many Mongolians revere as the founder of the nation. It was to the spirit and ideals of the Great Khan that the Mongolian political elite pledged their allegiance. Even members of the struggling Mongolian Peoples Revolutionary Party began to sing the praises of the man their party had condemned decades earlier. Anthropologist Caroline Humphrey describes what occurred in Mongolia in this period as a shift of "moral authority" backward in time to the *deer üyed* or "deep past," a vague concept that has come to refer generally to any period before socialism in Mongolia (Humphrey 1992: 375).

The events of 1990 marked a point at which Mongolians dramatically turned away from the as yet unfulfilled epochalist promises of the Soviet Union. Even with the consequences of doing so, including the loss of Soviet subsidies and a resulting period of severe economic crisis, there was a strong feeling among the population that the nation was better off on its own. Many believed that by following the example—if not the practice—of Chinggis Khan, as well as by tapping into a collective cultural heritage that had formed over centuries, they could glean indigenous or home-grown solutions for how their nation could survive in the modern world.

Looking for inspiration and authority in the *deer üyed*, however, did not mean the rejection of all Mongolia had gained from its nearly seven-decade long alliance with the Soviet Union. The nation's cultural institutions remained by and large intact and little changed between the Socialist and post-Socialist periods. What did change, however, were their goals. The socialist national myth was quickly replaced by a nationalist one, in which the nation's modern identity was rooted in narratives of a Golden Age under the leadership of Chinggis Khan and the accumulation of an ancient nomadic cultural heritage. Similarly, the idea of incorporating elements of this deep past into a modern national culture was by no means new in Mongolia. Ts. Zhamtsarano gave voice to this idea in the years following the 1921 Revolution, and it continued to find expression in the essentialist arguments of the political and intellectual elite throughout the Socialist period, all the way to N. Jantsannorow's Horse-head Fiddle Naadam on the eve of the 1990 Revolution. This point reaffirms the argument that socialism and nationalism grew up together in Mongolia in the twentieth century. When the former was rejected in the 1990s, the latter emerged as dominant.

Residing at the heart of a complex of symbolic meanings surrounding the key symbol of Chinggis Khan (Ortner 1973), the horse-head fiddle came to play an important role in the narratives surrounding and supporting the new national myths. This is seen in particular in the narratives that connect the instrument to Chinggis Khan, the Mongol Empire, and the national cultural heritage. As in many other parts of the world, the historical accuracy of these narratives often falls apart under close scrutiny. But while it is important for historians to analyze such narratives and point out inconsistencies where they are found, it is just as important for them to understand the broader role these narratives play in contemporary culture. In analyzing some of the most widely promoted historical narratives told about the horse-head fiddle, we find that they play an important role in defining modern Mongolian self-identity.

THE HORSE-HEAD FIDDLE IN HISTORICAL NARRATIVES

We begin by examining several core "facts" or widely accepted ideas about the horse-head fiddle that are found in the historical narratives promoted and maintained by Mongolian scholars, particularly from the early 1980s to the late 1990s. These narratives are drawn from academic articles and books, the mainstream mass media (principally newspapers and news magazines), liner notes to professional recordings, and poetry. In 1980 the Mongolian scholar Battsengel contributed this statement about the horse-head fiddle to a collection of articles about Asian music published in Japan. It was likely written for her visit to Tokyo in 1978 to participate in a conference of Asian music.

> The *morin xuur* is one of several bowed string instruments in Mongolia. At first, its surface was made in the shape of a scoop like the churn for horse's milk liquor. Its face was covered with hide and it was used to play melodies of prayer and praise using a horse hair bow. *Morin xuur* was called *sanagai xuur* [*sic*] (scoop violin). The *xuur* music came to be used at home and at feast more and more. The shape and structure of the instrument were changed and its melodies were also developed. Since the 1940s, the surface of the *morin xuur* was changed to wood and its timbre and volume became much wider and greater. Thus *morin xuur* came to be worthy of playing contemporary music and works of excellent composers of the world. . . . As *morin xuur* music is the traditional music which our people have mastered, there have appeared many famous performers. These include such great *xuurč* (performer of *xuur*) as Argasun in the thirteenth century, Sandag in the nineteenth century, Darigagiin [*sic*] Sar Damdin Očir early in the twentieth century, and later Tudew, Tuwden, and Luwsan (Batzengel 1980: 53).

According to Battsengel (Batzengel), the fiddle originated among a people—whether Mongol or not, she does not clarify—who created it out of a ladle used for the beverage *airag*, or fermented mare's milk, a summer drink common among the nomads of different Mongol and Turkic peoples of Inner Asian. The early fiddle, she says, was named after the implement from which it originated, the *shanaga* (misspelled in the article as *sanagai*), meaning a ladle or large spoon. She also says that one of its earliest masters was a Mongolian named "Argasun the fiddler" who, legend says, was a beloved servant to Chinggis Khan at the height of the Mongol Empire in the thirteenth century. She lists other great fiddle masters (Sandag, Očir, Tudew, Tuwden, and Luwsan) who carried on these fiddle traditions from the thirteenth to the early twentieth centuries. Throughout this period, she tells us, the "shape and structure" of the fiddle developed, emerging after the Revolution as a professional instrument capable of performing the music "of excellent composers of the world."

In 1987, the musicologist D. Nansalmaa wrote about the horse-head fiddle in her entry on Khalkha Mongolian folk music for a multi-volume ethnography edited by the ethnographer S. Badamkhatan. Her entry bears interesting similarities with Battsengel's:

> [The bowed instruments among the Khalkha Mongolian people] include the *morin khuur, khuuchir*, and *shanagan khuur*. These three are two-stringed, bowed instruments that have been handed down from the very early period of the Mongolian people to the present. The horse-head fiddle is a very ancient stringed and bowed instrument. In the shape of a ladle, it was first used among the Khünnü people, though it was called 'pi-pa.' In their own development, it was made with the carved shape of a *gardi* [a form of mythical deity], goose, crocodile and dragon's head. Later it was given the head of a horse and the name 'horse-head fiddle.' The horse-head fiddle is a national musical instrument that was produced by the Mongolian people, who gave rise to many famous fiddle players, not just Argasun, but also Sandag (nineteenth century), the favorite fiddle player Jigjid, and in the beginning of the twentieth century, Tüdew and Tüwden (Nansalmaa 1987: 349–350).

Like Battsengel, Nansalmaa points to a continuous line of development of the two-stringed bowed fiddle from "the very early period of the Mongolian people" to the present and cites nearly the same list of fiddle players through history, i.e. Argasun, Sandag, Jigjid, Tüdew, and Tüwden.

What is new in her account is that the horse-head fiddle "was first used among the Khünnü people." The Khünnü is the name created by Soviet historians to refer to a confederacy of nomadic tribes that rose to prominence in the region of modern Mongolia in the third to second centuries BCE, establishing an empire that extended into neighboring Central Asia, Manchuria, and parts of Siberia. It was an empire that made repeated invasions into northern China, prompting the Chinese to begin construction on what would become the Great Wall. Chinese dynastic records name this confederacy as the Xiongnu (Hsiung-nu), but some Russian scholars have generally adhered to the identification of them as the European Hun tribes of the fourth and fifth centuries. Thus, the composite word "Khünnü" was formulated and has become the common designation of this confederacy by Mongolian scholars. For accuracy, however, this study will refer to them using the Chinese designation, Xiongnu.

Mongolian scholars for decades have tried to find connections between the Xiongnu and the modern Mongols, who first appeared in the historical record only in the tenth century CE. The lack of evidence of an ancestral or historical connection between the two has not stopped some scholars from claiming connections through cultural affinity. In her entry above, Nansalmaa is referring to a theory that the Mongolian two-stringed fiddle is a direct descendent from a similar instrument used by the Xiongnu, which she says they called the "pi-pa."

The musicologist J. Enebish also emphasized the indigenous development of the two-stringed fiddle among the Mongolian people in an article published in the same year as that by Nansalmaa.

> Our historians have established that the forefather of the horse-head fiddle is the 'ladle fiddle.' This name refers to the stretching of the strings over the wooden *kumiss* [Mongolian *airag*] ladles and using it as a musical instrument. The tradition was established from an early time to carve on the heads of the ladle fiddles the figures of various animals. The ladle fiddle with its carvings in the forms of lions' or dragons' heads, even up to our present time, is being handed down through the generations of our people and is widely known by its melodies. But now in our country, the fiddle with the head of a horse and a square body is being widely used (Enebish 1991: 78).

In an interview, Enebish described how the combination of bows to hunt and horses for transportation and food are clearly connected with the origin and development of the Mongol fiddles.

> The nomadic peoples trace their origins back thousands and thousands of years ago, and the horse came out in an early period in the lives of the Mongol people. The horse-head fiddle is connected with animal husbandry because the fiddle is made up of the hairs of the horse's tail. So we can say that the fiddle originated before the Khünnü period. One way to establish the age of the fiddle is to examine the bows. We can do this through comparisons. So far we have studied and observed that people hunting with bows and arrows are portrayed in rock paintings. The arrows are undeniably connected with bowed instruments. Ancient peoples called their bows *khawchaakhai*, and not *nom sums*, as they do today. We have to compare the origins of the horse-head fiddle with the origins of bowed instruments (Enebish 1998.10.25).

In comparing these three entries, we begin to see the repetition of a core set of ideas, including that the fiddle originated in an ancient time as a ladle used to scoop or churn *airag*; that it was used by the Xiongnu tribes; and that one of the first in a long line of "masters" of the fiddle was a man named Aragsun in the thirteenth century. Before we go further, we should stop to examine these three ideas in more detail in order to understand what they say, how they rose to importance, and whether or not they can withstand historical scrutiny.

THE "LADLE" FIDDLE

The music scholar G. Badrakh was probably the first to write about this idea in his *Mongol khögjmiin tüükhees* (From the History of Mongolian Music), written in 1937, though not published until 1960. He says that in its beginnings the instrument that would become the horse-head fiddle was carved into the shape of an *airag* ladle, strung with strings, and called the *shanagan khuyur* or "ladle fiddle" (Badrakh 1960: 57–58). Writing in the 1960s and 1970s, J. Badraa cites Badrakh as his source for this theory (1998a; see also [1963] 1998d). Badraa theorizes that over time this simple ladle fiddle diversified into several different kinds of instruments, including the *biiwaa* (or *pipa* in Chinese [Badraa 1998a: 136]); the plucked *tow-shuur*, most commonly used in the western regions and which has retained its "ladle" shape; and the bowed two-string fiddle, which changed into the form of a box shape in the recent period (*ibid.*, 91).

Unfortunately, neither Badrakh nor Badraa provide historical sources for their theory about this "*airag* ladle" origin of the fiddle. That these fiddles were shaped like ladles and called "ladle" fiddles in the past, does not, of course, prove that they originated from ladles. Their claim that it originated from an *airag* ladle is even more difficult to prove. Ladle-shaped stringed instruments have been common to both nomadic and settled societies throughout Central Asia for centuries, if not millennia, and they often go by other metaphoric titles, including "bowl"-shaped and "pear"-shaped (cf. Slobin 1969, Vyzgo 1980).

THE "XIONGNU" FIDDLE

Badrakh was again perhaps the first to introduce the idea that the fiddle originated among an early nomadic people of the Mongolian steppe, which he called the Xi tribe. He says that the instrument they had, called the *dün-xui*, was later adopted by the Xiongnu people (Badrakh 1960: 58). Badraa pursued this idea as well, stating that this instrument, present among the Xiongnu of the third to second centuries BCE, could indeed be historically linked to the Mongol peoples (Badraa [1982] 1997). He drew upon Chinese and some Western language historical sources to make his point that the Xiongnu actually had an early form of the Mongolian fiddle:

Our earliest knowledge of the words 'fiddle' and 'to play the fiddle' comes from the many core documents of Chinese history that relate to the period of the Mongolian Xiongnu nation. For example, Fan Ye writes in *Hou Han-shu* (or *History of the Eastern Han Dynasty*): 'Emperor Lingdi liked Xiongnu clothes, Xiongnu houses, Xiongnu beds, Xiongnu *konghou*, Xiongnu *bishgüür* (a woodwind instrument), and Xiongnu dances' (Badraa 1998d: 86).

Badraa focuses upon this "Xiongnu *konghou*," citing other historians and scholars, including the French scholar Paul Pelliot and Japanese music researcher Shigeo Kishibe, who, he says, have determined that this instrument indeed could be a fiddle-like musical instrument. In the end, however, Badraa gives us his own opinion:

> Based on linguistic, historical and musical analyses, [we can say that] the root of the word *kun-xeü* is Mongolian. Therefore we have reached the result that the word *kong* is the word for the 'swan,' and the word *hou* is the word for 'fiddle,' or in other words, the 'swan-headed fiddle' (*ibid.*, 87).

In fact, there was little musical or historical evidence available for Badraa to make this point. His argument rests almost entirely upon his own linguistic interpretation of the name of the instrument in this Chinese historical document. Badraa was determined to show that the word *kong* is really an early form of the modern Mongolian word *khun* (swan), and that *hou* is an early variant of the word *khuur* (fiddle). Badraa cites Paul Pelliot as making the connection between the *konghou* and the Turkic *kobuz*, which he believes is linguistically related to the modern Mongolian word *khuur*:

> In my opinion, the origin of the name '*khuur*' is related to the words '*kög-khög*' of the root '*kö-khö*' which have the meaning 'to move, to sing.' From this '*kö-khö*' root come a considerable number of other words, including *khög khögjim* (a dance song), *khögjim khögjim-dökh* (to play a musical instrument), *khögjil* (development), *khöör* (joy), *khöörög* (snuff bottle), *khödölgöön* (movement). Although these root words are distinguished by a number of alternate consonant and vowel sounds, they line up with many words with the roots '*kho, khu, khü, go, gu, gö*,' which have related meanings. Therefore, if we translate the word *khuur* in contemporary Mongolian language, we find that it has the meaning 'the sound stirring of an instrument,' and it is related to a family of musical instrument names, such as the instruments that spread among the Turkish Mongols called '*kubos, kubiiz, kobuz, kobiiz, kumiiz, komuz, komus, komiik*, and *komiiz*' (*ibid.*, 86).

Paul Pelliot did say that the Mongol word *khuur* (*quɣur*) is related to the Turkic word *kobuz* (*qobuz/qopuz*), with a possible etymology being the Chinese word *k'ong-hou* (Doerfer 1963: 445). But Gerhard Doerfer counters that "the *kuŋhou* was a type of harp, and thus essentially incomparable" with a bowed fiddle like the *khuur* or *kobuz* (*ibid.*). Badraa's idea that the word *konghou* is Mongolian is pure speculation. His idea that the Xiongnu word *kong* is related with the Mongolian word *khuɣur* through the phoneme *kö-khö* is a misunderstanding of Mongolian etymology and linguistic theory. Nor did Badraa make any attempt to show anything other than a similarity between two words in the language of two peoples separated by many centuries. Furthermore, we may presume that the words used in the Chinese historical sources were Chinese interpretations of Xiongnu speech, which raises further doubts about Badraa's interpretation. In the end, his evidence and analysis are much too weak to prove any direct connection to, much less the existence of, a "Xiongnu fiddle."

As happened with his theory about the "ladle" fiddle, however, a number of influential Mongolian scholars uncritically accepted Badraa's theory about the Xiongnu origins of the two-stringed fiddle. In his history about the Xiongnu, for instance, the historian G. Sükhbaatar, reported that Badraa's research has "made it clear that the Xiongnu had a fiddle" (Sükhbaatar 1980: 132). He goes even further, however, misquoting Paul Pelliot, and saying, "it is possible that a very early pronunciation of the word *kunkhou* was the Mongolian word *khuur*" (*ibid.*).

ARGASUN KHUURCH

The legend of "Argasun the fiddle player" is one of the most well-known modern legends about the horse-head fiddle. The scholar Ts. Damdinsüren brought the legend to popular attention with the publication of his *Mongɣol uran jokiyal-un degeji jaɣun bilig orusibai* (1959), a collection of "masterworks" of Mongolian literature. "*Arɣasun quɣurči-yin domog*" (The Legend of Argasun the Fiddler) was one of the selected passages that was copied from Lobsangdajin's seventeenth century historical chronicle, the *Altan tobči* (Golden Summary).

In short, the story begins with Chinggis Khan far away on campaign in Korea. After three years of not hearing from him, his Queen Qulan decides to send the palace fiddle player, Argasun (*Arɣasun quɣurči*), to find and encourage him to return home soon. After a long journey, Argasun arrives at Chinggis' camp and delivers the Queen's message, but he does so in such poetic way (i.e. through a series of riddles), that no one save for the Great Khan himself could understand what was being said. Having understood the hidden meaning of the message, Chinggis Khan returned home to his Queen. That night in the palace, Argasun becomes drunk and takes the Great Khan's Golden Fiddle (*altan quɣur*) from the palace and spends the night playing and drinking with friends. In that time there was a law (*jasaɣ*) stating that anyone who takes the Golden Fiddle from the palace will be sentenced to death. Upon hearing what Argasun had done, Chinggis Khan orders that he be killed immediately and "without commotion." When the guards sent to do this find Argasun, they instead warn him of what they were ordered to do and encourage him to go and seek the Khan's forgiveness. Argasun agrees and when he is brought before Chinggis Khan, he gives an apology so poetic that the Great Khan is moved to stay his execution.

Damdinsüren transliterated this story from an older form of the Mongolian language, the Uighur (or vertical) script, into a modern form. And since then debate has flared among scholars about his interpretations. One of the first to question his version of the story was Sh. Gaadamba who in 1971 published an article stating that Argasun was not someone charged with caring for the Khan's golden fiddle (*quɣurči*), but rather someone charged with caring for the Khan's golden arrow quiver (*qorči*) (Tsend 2000: 17). The difference, he points out, essentially rests upon the transliteration of a single letter—whether or not a word has one "u" or two—which could change the meaning of the word "fiddle" to that of a "quiver." When spelled correctly in vertical script, the difference between these two words is clear. But these old documents were hand-written and medieval scribes were prone to making mistakes in their spelling or to misread the meanings of words. Thus, if misspelled, the difference between the words "fiddle" and "arrow" can become ambiguous.

To complicate matter, Damdinsüren made his transliteration not from an original copy of the seventeenth century manuscript, but a nineteenth century copy of it made by the German scholar Isaac Jacob Schmidt (1829). In this version of the text, the words "fiddle" and "fiddler" vary between *quɣur* (fiddle), *qor* (quiver), and *quur*, which is an ambiguous word, a spelling that lies somewhere between the other two.

When faced with such irregularities, scholars usually turn to other forms of justifications for one interpretation or another. Some scholars say that because Argasun was such a multi-talented and poetic speaker, he must certainly have been a fiddle player; others say that because fiddles have long been used to bring happiness to homes and royal palaces, it makes sense that it was a fiddle, instead of a quiver (*ibid.*). But Gaadamba, for his part, turned to the Yüan dynasty histories, saying that they contain information about there being an official *khorchi* (quiver bearer) in the royal Mongolian palace (*ibid.*). Linguist and historian Györgi Kara says that the word *qorči* (quiver bearer) was common in the era of the Mongol Empire (twelfth to thirteenth centuries). There was even an administrative or military unit with the same name during this period, presumably named after their assigned duties. These units were later transformed into a clan-like social group that came to be known as the Khorchin people of eastern Inner Mongolia. By as early as the fourteenth century, Kara says, the word was beginning to fall out of use. After a time the word and its meaning became forgotten, and even the Khorchin people themselves forgot the source and meaning of their own ethnonym.

The word, however, was preserved in Chinese transliterations of the original Mongol sources, including the 1389 transliteration of the *Secret History of the Mongols*. This version speaks about a hero named Argasun who had a quiver. While there is often ambiguity in dealing with such ancient texts, about the reading of this source, Kara says, "there is no doubt" (personal communication). Furthermore, when we examine the sources that Damdinsüren was using to create his version of the story, we see that they included Russian translations (Kozin) and transcriptions (Palladius) of these Chinese transliterations, suggesting that Damdinsüren was using sources far removed from the originals. Despite being criticized for his interpretation of these words, Damdinsüren continued to hold that his interpretation of this word as a "fiddle" was entirely possible. Among scholars in the Mongolian Academy of Sciences, this debate is at something of a draw between those supporting either side (D. Tserenpil, personal communication).

As often happens, however, such arcane debates among top intellectuals have had little effect upon the popularity of this legend among the general population. Nansalmaa and Enebish quickly picked up on the idea of Argasun, calling him one of the great fiddlers of Mongolian history. Their scholarly stature has helped to further popularize and legitimate the legend. Once set in motion, this story of "Argasun the fiddler" has become a powerful part of the national myth of the Mongolian people.

ARGA-BILEG

Another powerful idea about the horse-head fiddle that has been promoted by Mongolian scholars and intellectuals is the Mongolian philosophical concept of *arga-bileg*. This concept is similar to the Chinese concept of *yin-yang* and is related to the Buddhist ideas of *prajna* (wisdom) and *upaya* (skill in means). In the early 1990s there were numerous articles written in the popular press that openly considered the usefulness of this philosophy in addressing some of the existential problems the Mongolian people were facing in that period.

The well-known journalist and translator, G. Akim, for instance, wrote an article in a newspaper he founded (*Il Towchoo*) about this concept, adding his own twist to the theory. He began by describing what he saw as the depth to which *arga-bileg* was centered in traditional Mongolian culture. "Being as they are a part of the Oriental cultural frame," he writes, "Mongolians consider all phenomena in the world by the principle of *arga-bileg*, which expresses the struggle and unification of opposites" (Akim 1991: 6). To bolster this point he quotes a verse from a poem by the famous nineteenth century Mongolian poet Noyon Khutagt Danzinrabjai:

Birth and death,
Creation and destruction,
Father and mother,
[All this is] *arga-bileg* (*ibid.*).

Akim goes on to say that herders of the past embodied their understanding of this essential duality in the construction of the two-stringed fiddle: "As the Mongolians worshipped the principle of *arga-bileg*, so they made the horse-head fiddle with two strings" (*ibid.*). He extends this idea by quoting an excerpt of a famous poem about the horse-head fiddle written in the mid-1960s by the well-known poet Mishigiin Tsedendorj:

The world consists of only two colors,
While and black are pairs,
The people are a pair of lovers
Suffering and happiness are pairs;
The whole world has only two strings.
There is a day and there is a night,
The mass of people has only two occurrences,
There is meeting and there is separation.
Everything in this world is explained by the principles of *arga-bileg*.
Even though the world is wide,
Even though the people are many,
This is why they say that all can be put within only two strings
    (*ibid.*).

Akim paints a picture of traditional Mongolian herders as almost natural philosophers, men whose thoughts took into consideration such a broad ranges of ideas "as to include the sun moon, sky [*tengger*] and all the world" (*ibid.*). These Mongolians, he seems to be saying, were in touch with an indigenous cosmology that gave a sense of order to the world, and that was expressed in the construction and sound of the horse-head fiddle. In the process of becoming a modern nation, however, Mongolians have lost touch with these traditional philosophies, and as a result have lost the sense of order and power that they once generated. "We kill each other during the Lunar New Year," he says, "a time which should symbolize *buyan zayaa* [virtuous fate]. We kill the horse that wins at Naadam, which should instead be respected. We do all of these things because our mind has become poor" (*ibid.*).

Akim's portrayal of the traditional herder is almost completely opposite the portrayal that the writer Natsagdorj presented in his story "Son of the Old World" (cf. Chapter Three). In Natsagdorj's story, the herder of the "Old World" lives in ignorance of the larger world outside of his own provincial homeland. The herder knew "no other truth except the words of his ancestors and his elders," which, as the author made clear, was "a blighted and ignorant life" (Natsagdorj 1974: 2). Only after following the road to development, at the end of his story, did the herder realize his ignorance and find true happiness. In Akim's portrayal of the traditional herder, however, he seems to suggest that Mongolians will find a sense of balance and happiness again by remembering the ways of the deep past—ways inscribed into the very shape and sound of the horse-head fiddle. Such contrasting views reflect the contrasting aims of socialism and nationalism in contemporary Mongolia: where the first seeks to draw the local and traditional nature of the Mongolian population towards the international and modern, the second seeks the opposite, thus confirming the essentialist-epochalist tensions that underlie contemporary approaches to culture in Mongolia.

Akim was no pure traditionalist, however. He was not advocating a return to the past. Rather, he saw how contemporary Mongolian society could be regenerated through contact with the traditional past. That he acknowledges the essentially cosmopolitan nature of Mongolia's national culture is evident in his plea to the Mongolian people at the end of his article to pay more attention to the horse-head fiddle. Many modern nations, he says, use traditional instruments as a cultural symbol that defines their unique identity.

> Africans are proud of their tam tam drums. The Finnish are proud of their harps. The Scottish praise their bagpipes. The Kazakhs praise their *dombra*. The Ukrainians talk about their *bandore*. Every nation is proud of their national music instruments. We are Mongolians, and we are respectful toward our horse-head fiddle, which embodies within itself all the people and songs of the world (Akim 1991: 6).

Akim's ideas suggest something of the excitement and bewilderment that Mongolians felt in that period of newly won independence, a time when many believed that they, finally, were in charge of their own destiny. For many intellectuals like him, this was a time to turn to the "wisdom of the people" (*ardyn bileg*) for guidance on how to proceed in the future.

The musicologist L. Erdenechimeg was in the same period writing her dissertation in Ulaanbaatar on the subject of the relationship between the horse-head fiddle and *arga-bileg*. Her dissertation for the Department of Culture and Art in the Mongolian National University of the Arts was entitled, *Morin khuuryn awiag arga bilgiin onolyn üügnees sudlakh ni* (A study of the sound of the horse-head fiddle from the perspective of the theory of *arga-bileg*), which she defended in 1993. She approached the relationship between *arga-bileg* and the fiddle from highly theoretical points of view, relating elements of sound analysis with the concepts of *arga-bileg* among other ancient Mongolian and Buddhist theories of reality. Her work is deeply theoretical and makes little mention of contemporary contexts of fiddle performance aside from brief historical remarks in her introduction.

While her ideas about *arga-bileg* do not appear to have penetrated into the broader discourse about the horse-head fiddle, the fact that a Mongolian scholar has written a dissertation on this subject is a point of pride for some Mongolians. Writing in his encyclopedia about the Mongolian horse, S. Jambaldorj, for instance, praised her dissertation as being "the first large-scale scientific work on the topic of the horse-head fiddle" (Jambaldorj 1996: 105).[1]

Whether or not they were influenced by Akim or Erdenechimeg's works, some professional musicians refer to the theory of *arga-bileg* to describe the instrument's power to communicate with the world of the spirits:

> The Mongolian people have faith in *arga-bileg*. This is a pair of things, like good-evil, mother-father, heaven-land, and male-female. This is why the fiddle has two strings. The Mongolian people talk with Tengger ["Heaven"] through their fiddle. For example, if there is a drought in the homeland, they can ask for rain from heaven by playing the fiddle (Enkhjargal 1998.12.05)

Since the 1980s, the research that scholars have conducted into the history of the horse-head fiddle has profoundly shaped what is known about the instrument in Mongolia. While the theories that connect the instrument to the "ladle fiddle," the Khünnü, and a fiddle player named Aragsun, do not stand up well to historical analysis, they have, along with the idea of *arga-bileg*, succeeded in working their way into the stories that Mongolians tell each other about this instrument.[2] It is common to meet Mongolians who fervently believe that the horse-head fiddle is "thousands of years old," that it "originated in Mongolia," and that "Chinggis Khan had his own horse-head fiddle player."[3] Whether or not these beliefs are historically accurate, they have become a part of the popular Mongolian self-identity. This point was most clearly exemplified in the words of a 77 year-old fiddle player name D. Luwsan, who had started to play the horse-head fiddle just seven years earlier. Reflecting on the importance of the horse-head fiddle in Mongolia, he insisted that playing the fiddle is a patriotic activity: "To me, anyone who does not play the horse-head fiddle is not a real Mongolian!" (Luwsan 1997.09.19)

THE HORSE-HEAD FIDDLE IN POLITICAL RITUAL

Our examination of the horse-head fiddle as national icon has so far been limited to representations found in literary resources. But another important medium through which the fiddle is represented in post-Socialist society is through political ritual. In each of the rituals described below, we find the horse-head fiddle used to symbolize a connection to different periods in the *deer üyed* or "deep past." Whether directed by government institutions or individual inspiration, the representation of the horse-head fiddle in these rituals reflects the new cosmopolitan nature of the national musical culture. The instrument is clearly meant to symbolize some aspect of the deep past within a modern and internationalist context. In spite of the discourse of "ancientness" in these representations, we are seeing a decidedly modern tradition.

STATE NAADAM FESTIVAL

One of the most signs that the post-Socialist period had begun was the reappearance of the horse-head fiddle and long song at the opening ceremonies of the State Naadam in Ulaanbaatar. The *naadam* is an ancient Mongolian summer festival that features contests of the traditional sports of wrestling, archery, and horse racing. Communities throughout the nation organize local *naadam* festivals in the summer months, but the State Naadam in Ulaanbaatar is the largest and most important in the nation. It is attended by all of the political elite, including the President and Prime Minister, and many foreign dignitaries. And, as befitting such an important event, the State Naadam is televised live to every corner of the nation.

History books report that the Khalkha Mongols traditionally opened their *naadam* festivals with the singing and playing of the song *Tümen ekh* (First of Ten Thousand), which was written in 1696 by the Darkhan Mongol Chin Wang (Nansalmaa 1987: 336). At some point during the Communist era, however, this tradition was stopped and replaced by the singing of more contemporary song genres. After 1990, the tradition of singing *Tümen ekh* was reinstated. Every year the festival organizers vary the make-up of the ensemble performing this song. In 1997, for instance, the song was performed by two singers and two horse-head fiddle players located on a raised platform situated at one end of the oval-shaped Naadam Stadium in Ulaanbaatar. In 1999, however, it was performed by a large vocal choir accompanied by ten horse-head fiddle players, all located directly in front of the box seats where the President and other dignitaries sat. To commemorate the eight hundredth anniversary of the founding of the Mongol state in 2006, the opening ceremonies featured a mass performance by one thousand horse-head fiddle players and long song singers. Despite the changing make-up of the performers, the performance of the song always involves a horse-head fiddle player and long song singer.

In this new era, however, the song's specific historical context has changed, with the new emphasis being placed on the symbol of Chinggis Khan as national unifier. While it was long considered a marker of Khalkha Mongol identity in pre-Revolutionary days, *Tümen ekh* accompanied by the horse-head fiddle has been drafted into a set of historic elements that make up what is essentially a grand theatrical performance that annually commemorates the nation's founding. The opening and closing ceremonies of the festival are part entertainment and part sacred ritual, with the emphasis on invoking a thirteenth century ethos in the modern-day stadium.

Costuming is important to this effect. The horse-head fiddle players always wear a stylized thirteenth century Mongol army uniform, as do the members of the police and army honor guards who participate in and oversee the running of the opening and closing ceremonies. In the opening ceremony, a group of police in thirteenth century army regalia enter the Naadam Stadium on horseback conveying the "Nine White Standards"[4] from their home in the Government Palace to the Stadium. Placing the standards in the center of the Naadam Stadium during the course of the festival, which are guarded by honor guards in the same regalia, is meant convey the presence and blessing of the founding father's spirit. In some years, the procession is even led by a man dressed like Chinggis Khan and flanked by soldiers so dressed.

In many of the opening ceremonies, after the planting of the Nine White Standards, dancers and musicians from the State Folksong & Dance Ensemble run onto the field and perform dances. They too wear brightly colored uniforms styled after thirteenth century army regalia. Musicians with tympanis and bass drums are also stationed in various parts of the stadium and, when the Standard-bearing retinue enters and leaves the stadium in the opening and closing ceremonies, they play in dramatic ways—arms with mallets raised high—referring to the Mongol drummers that Marco Polo claimed he saw in his *Travels*.

Through exhibiting these symbols of imperial glory, the State appears to be invoking a direct spiritual link between these modern rituals and those it is imagined Chinggis Khan oversaw during the period of the Mongol Empire. While Mongolian viewers intrinsically understand that the political symbols, uniforms, and even fiddles used in these ceremonies are modern creations, there is a widespread belief that they represent what really occurred in the thirteenth century. In summoning these symbols on an annual basis, regardless of the modern variations brought to their performance or representation, the State seeks to imply an unbroken continuity in their practice from the present to the deep past. Caroline Humphrey (1992) calls this "historical mimicry," a symbolic enactment that gives rise to "past-oriented" meanings. The past, however, can be re-imagined to include any number of desired elements. There is no evidence, for instance, that the horse-head fiddle, or any two-string bowed lute, was ever used in the opening ceremonies of the *naadam* festivals during the time of the Mongol Empire. But the inclusion of this instrument in such a symbolically important event as the opening of the State Naadam gives weight to the popular idea that the horse-head fiddle is indeed ancient and essential to the very idea of the Mongolian nation itself.

THE LUNAR NEW YEAR (TSAGAAN SAR)

The return of the horse-head fiddle to the rituals surrounding the *Tsagaan sar* or Lunar New Year was welcomed by many Mongolians in the post-Socialist period. *Tsagaan sar* is a celebration associated with very old rituals of rebirth and renewal in Mongolia. It marks not only the beginning of the new lunar year but also the first day of spring. As we saw in Chapter One, many Mongolian ethnic groups have long had traditions of performing the two-stringed fiddle on the first day of the *Tsagaan sar* festivities as a means of welcoming in the New Year, purifying the home, and bringing luck and happiness to the family or *ail*. For a variety of reasons, the Party banned the celebration of *Tsagaan sar* and replaced it with a Worker's holiday known as "Collective Herder's Day." The performance of the horse-head fiddle and many other rituals associated with this holiday were also generally suppressed, though they likely continued in the countryside and in the privacy of people's homes.

Since 1990, however, there has been something of a resurgence of the tradition of playing the horse-head fiddle during *Tsagaan sar*. Professional fiddle players in Ulaanbaatar report that they are especially busy performing for families and friends during this holiday, at times for payment and at times as a gesture of good will. The senior fiddler with the State Folksong & Dance Ensemble, Kh. Altantog, says that he gets more requests to play during this holiday than he can handle. But this is a festival where even amateur performers are often nudged into playing simple tunes on a fiddle to mark the occasion. It is as if the mere sound of the fiddle on this day becomes more important than the tune played or the quality of the performance, and thus in this way older, pre-Revolutionary forms of the fiddle traditions are re-invoked. Curiously, the interest in sounding the fiddle on this day does not appear to extend to the sounding of other folk instruments, either traditional or modern. In addition, the fiddle's reappearance during *Tsagaan sar* is one of the few instances we can find in the post-Socialist period where an older, pre-Revolutionary musical tradition was reinstated on the basis of popular memory. The re-emergence of this tradition does not appear to be something instituted from "above," such as from the political or intellectual elite. Rather it is something that emerged from people's own memory of *Tsagaan sar* rituals from the past.

The Mongolian government did introduce one important new fiddle tradition that is associated with this holiday. On the first day of *Tsagaan sar*, the Mongolian President presents a televised address to the nation where he outlines his hopes for the nation in the New Year. Beginning in 1992, this address has been immediately followed by a short performance of a piece by a horse-head fiddle player. In earlier years, the televised image of the president switches to the inside of a special *ger* set up within the Government Palace. There a fiddle player, dressed in a *deel* and sitting on a small stool, immediately began to perform a short piece of music called the *Morin khuuryn süld ayalguu* (Anthem of the Horse-head Fiddle) or sometimes just the *töriin süld* (State Anthem).[5] This is a modern piece of music with no words, lasting just under two minutes, whose structure and rhythm are reminiscent of fiddle tunes that accompany epic songs. This particular piece sounds very close in style to the famous *Khökhöö namjiliin domog* or "Legend of Khökhöö Namjil," the origin legend of the horse-head fiddle itself. Perhaps fittingly, the "Anthem" was commissioned by the government to commemorate the creation and official installation of another important state symbol, the *Töriin khan khuur* or "State Sovereign Fiddle."

THE STATE SOVEREIGN FIDDLE

The *Töriin khan khuur* is, in essence, a large horse-head fiddle constructed in 1992 by Presidential decree. The instrument has since resided in a special *ger* known as the *Töriin yoslolyn örgöö* (State Ritual Palace), which has been set up within the Government Palace. Sitting in a cabinet beside a larger-then-life sized statue of Chinggis Khan, the *Töriin khan khuur* has become one of the official state symbols of the post-Communist era.

The idea for the creation of the *Töriin khan khuur* is credited to Honored Culture and Arts Worker Ts. Tserendorj, a widely known and respected fiddle performer and singer of folksongs. In the early 1990s he was head of the Horse-head Fiddle Center, an organization set up following the Horse-head Fiddle Naadam of 1989 with the aim of promoting the development of the instrument. Tserendorj worked closely with Jantsannorow, Jamyan, and other respected fiddle players and artists in Ulaanbaatar. In 1995, he told an interviewer that the idea of the *Töriin khan khuur* came to him when he was pondering the legend of Argasun the fiddler.

> I read about this legend and the idea came to me that a *Töriin khan khuur* could be created and placed in the State Ceremonial Ger. One day [in 1992] I visited the Presidential Counselor, Tümen, and handed my suggestion to him on a *khadag*[6] (Bazarragchaa 1995: 8).

President Ochirbat liked the idea and issued a presidential declaration that called for the musical instrument to be made and placed within the Government Palace. The job of constructing the *Töriin khan khuur* went to D. Ulambayar, one of the first fiddle makers to establish a private workshop in the country after 1990, which he named, ironically, the 'Argasun' Factory (*'Argasun' üildwer*). This factory, actually a workshop, is located in a non-descript converted warehouse on the east side of Ulaanbaatar, between two large apartment complexes. Wood shavings and sawdust cover nearly everything in this space where Ulambayar and his two associates work, shaving, sawing, sanding and lacquering the wood for their fiddles.

In the early 1990s, Ulambayar represented one of the new generation of fiddle makers in Mongolia who, given their advanced training, approached the construction of the fiddle from the perspective of "science," as he puts it, rather than art or tradition. A graduate of the State Technical University in Ulaanbaatar, Ulambayar says that instrument making these days "is all about the technical side of music, and not the playing side. What we do is related to physical science and acoustics—you can say it is really a field of physics" (Ulambayar 1998.07.17). Even while a university student during the Socialist period, he often visited the State Music Instrument Factory to train and do research. He wrote his diploma paper on the technology of making the horse-head fiddles and upon his graduation in 1986 began to work in the Factory as a musical instrument repairman.

Ulambayar has brought important advances in technology and training to bear on the task of making musical instruments. But he is also aware of the fiddle-making lineage he represents. His teacher at the Technical University was the famous fiddle maker named Jügchid, a student of Jügder, who was one of the students taught by the Russian violin maker Yerovoi. Ulambayar acknowledges the debt that he and contemporary fiddle makers owe to their teachers, saying that they had taught his generation to bring a scientific frame of mind to the construction of the horse-head fiddle. "Starting in the 1960s with Yarovoi," he says,

> we worked to improve the horse-head fiddle. Yerovoi was critical to this mission. He was the first person who applied a general scientific method to the construction of the instrument. He used modern technology to improve its construction, such as the use of the wooden face and an entirely different tuning than was common before. But any musical instrument is a whole system; all the different parts are related to one another. Thus, to improve the instrument, we needed to address the entire system. We had many tries and many failures. It took us about twenty years. But by the 1990s the improvement of the horse-head fiddle was nearing the final stage of this process. In our mind, all the different parts of the fiddle needed to have their own optimal quality. They needed to be perfect. And by the 1990s, as a musical instrument, the horse-head fiddle came very close to being perfect (*ibid.*).

President Ochirbat's decree of 1992, ordering the creation of the *Töriin khan khuur*, however, forced Ulambayar to lay aside his commitment to modernizing the fiddle and instead to imagine the design and construction of a self-consciously "old" fiddle. "This project came about," he says, "when Mongolians were trying to bring back all kinds of traditions, like the *Yösön tsagaan tug* (Nine White Banners), the *Töriin khar num* (State Black Bow) and other traditions related to the State and State symbols. The government wanted to reestablish everything the Mongolian state had before, in the time of Chinggis Khan. The *Töriin khan khuur* was one of these." (*ibid.*)

Figure 18. "*Öwgön khuurch*" (The Old Fiddle Player, 1963) by Ü. Yadamsüren (Anonymous 1986).

When he received the order to construct the instrument, he had to decide what a state fiddle should look like. "I needed to research this question. I talked to many historians and ethnographers. It's impossible to go by our own idea. In the end, I came to the conclusion that we had to keep a traditional design." He decided to model the fiddle after a fiddle shown in a famous painting by the Mongolian artist Ü. Yadamsüren, called "*Övgön khuurch*" (The Old Fiddle Player, Figure 18), from 1963, depicting an old man with a long white beard sitting cross-legged on a carpet, playing a horse-head fiddle. The painting is remarkable in its detail, as much as in its subject and treatment. "Yadamsüren was a State prizewinner and also a highly educated man. He was a kind of ethnographic painter. I know he painted it based on his research and ethnographic materials. That's why I decided to model the *Töriin khan khuur* after this painting" (*ibid.*).

In keeping with traditional design, Ulambayar constructed the fiddle with a skin face. The neck was long, like many traditional fiddles, extending beyond the length of typical modern fiddles. He also strung his *khuur* with the tail hairs of a black haired horse. The decorations that Ulambayar

painted on carved into the fiddle were both traditional and deeply symbolic, the most prominent of which was the *Yösön erdene* (Nine Jewels).
He felt it especially important for his fiddle to symbolize the unity of the
Mongolian people. "Mongolia is like a unit, one family," he told me, "and
so the fiddle that I made is for this country as a whole. I tried to create a
fiddle for the whole of Mongolia. That's why I put the symbol of the *Yösön
erdene* on it" (*ibid.*).

At the same time that Ulambayar was completing the *Töriin khan khuur*,
other artists and officials were at work creating a place for it to stay, devising rituals for its use, and composing music for it to play. It was decided
that the *Töriin khan khuur* would be placed in the *Töriin yoslolyn örgöö*
(State Ritual Palace), in a large wooden cabinet crafted by the sculptor B.
Bayasgalan. Interestingly, he created a base for the *khuur* that is carved to
resemble a blossoming lotus flower (Santaro 1999: 144).[7] In the upper part
of the case is carved symbols of the sun, moon, and fire; interweaving them
from above and below them are auspicious designs called *khee* (*ibid.*).

The "installation" of the *Töriin khan khuur*, its placement into this
cabinet, occurred at the "hour of the horse" (Pegg 2001: 287), on April
20, 1992, and was accompanied by an anthem written for the Mongolian horse-head fiddle (*Morin khuuryn süld ayalguu*) a year earlier by the
composers B. Sharav and Ts. Chinzorig. Pegg (*ibid.*, 287) and Santaro
(1999: 144) both mention that President Ochirbat was present at this ceremony, which would make sense given that he decreed the fiddle's creation
and given the symbolic importance of the fiddle to the state government.
But the newspaper *Ardyn erkh* (1992) made no mention of the President's
presence, noting instead that those participating included Vice Premiere
D. Dorligjav, head of the Permanent Committee of the Department of
National Defense, and Ch. Dashdemberel, head of the Presidential Seal.
While an important event, it may not have been considered important
enough for the President to attend. Nor is there any mention that the public was allowed to view this ritual.

Mongolian government officials apparently also devised plans for how
this fiddle, as a new state symbol, would be annually commemorated. The
Ardyn erkh article described that "the *Töriin khan khuur* will be played on
the first day of the *Tsagaan sar* and the State Naadam Holiday, and when
the President or Prime Minister go abroad or when foreign heads of state
make an official state visit" (*Ardyn erkh* 1992: 1). The respected horse-
head fiddle players who were most closely associated with the instrument
were involved in commemorating the *Töriin khan khuur*. An undated photograph (Figure 19), which likely dates to the early 1990s, records what is
apparently a march of famous fiddle players, showing the fiddler G. Jamyan
holding aloft the *Töriin khan khuur*, followed by Ts. Tserendorj and other
fiddler players, holding their fiddles, circling a portion of the central Sükhbaatar Square that is located outside the Government Palace. It is summer
and likely the first day of the State Naadam festival.

Figure 19.   G. Jamyan, Ts. Tserendorj and other horse-head fiddle players convey-ing the *Töriin khan khuur*, outside the Government Palace in Ulaanbaatar (undated photograph, Ts. Tserendorj).

The story of the *Töriin khan khuur* exemplifies two important points about the nature of the modern horse-head fiddle traditions in Mongolia. The first relates to the ways in which symbolic meanings tend to feed back on themselves within the national musical culture. While there is no sub-stantial proof that a horse-head fiddle player named Argasun worked in the court of Chinggis Khan, the narrative about Argasun was promoted by Mongolian scholars and then picked up and popularized in the Mongolian media as actual fact. That this was a "fact" prompted the fiddle player Ts. Tserendorj to suggest the idea of the *Töriin khan khuur* to the Mongolian President, who subsequently decreed its creation, which then feeds back to support the story's factual legitimacy. This situation is not unlike the use of the horse-head fiddle in the opening ceremony of the State Naadam. Both are an imagined representation of an event or situation in the deep past that is continually reaffirmed as "true" through the recurring nature of the event, or in this case, the display of the instrument itself.

The second point relates to the imagined nature of this modern tradition. It is telling that the fiddle maker Ulambayar would turn to a late twentieth century painting of an "old" or pre-Revolutionary fiddle to use as a model for the *Töriin khan khuur*. However accurate that painting may have been, Ulambayar's method suggests the degree to which the modern or *ardyn* musical traditions had separated from older, *ugsaatny* traditions. It also reaffirms the point that the national musical traditions were themselves constructed out of selected *ugsaatny* traditions, which were considered to be rooted in particular cultural contexts. The national musical tradition was meant to represent the "objective properties" of the nation's diverse ethnic groups, often in symbolic ways. It is ironic that Ulambayar should turn to a similar process, one rooted in the Socialist period and practiced throughout the Soviet world, to create a symbol of Mongolian cultural independence.

THE STATE HORSE-HEAD FIDDLE ENSEMBLE

In the same year that the Mongolian government installed the *Töriin khan khuur*, 1992, it allocated the funds for the establishment of the *Ulsyn morin khuuryn chuulga* or State Horse-head Fiddle Ensemble. The Mongolian Parliament passed the resolution that created the Ensemble on July 9, just a few days prior to that year's summer Naadam festival. The resolution described its establishment as honoring "the horse-head fiddle's valued cultural heritage that was created by the Mongolian people" (Otgonsüren 1997: 1).

The Ensemble is a large group officially consisting of twenty-eight people, twenty-six of whom are performers (aside from the director and composer) of whom thirteen are horse-head fiddle players. The Ensemble also employs two *dund khuurs* (mid-sized fiddles, about the size of European violoncellos) and two *ikh khuurs* (large fiddles, resembling European contrabasses). While the *ikh khuurs* were created in the 1950s and 1960s for the *Ikh Chuulga* ensemble, a part of the Folksong & Dance Ensemble, the *dund khuurs* were developed specifically for the Horse-head Fiddle Ensemble in 1992. The Ensemble organizers needed a stringed instrument that had the capabilities and musical timbre or color of a European violoncello, but they did not want to use this specific instrument given its association with European classical music. The Fiddle makers Ulambayar and Baigaljaw thus fashioned a hybrid fiddle that was half horse-head fiddle and half violoncello. The *dund khuur* even features a crown with the head of a tiger, instead of a horse. Other instruments accompanying the fiddles include a *yoochin* (similar to a hammer dulcimer), three *yatga* (plucked zithers), a percussionist, and two singers. The exact make-up of the group tends to vary from concert to concert.

The ensemble performs in a wide variety of contexts, from official state concerts, such as on special holidays or to honor visiting dignitaries, to classical and popular music concerts. Likewise, its repertoire ranges from serious extended compositions to popular songs. The Ensemble's own description of its repertoire suggests a cosmopolitan mix of the national and international, consisting "of more than 500 choice works by contemporary international and Mongolian composers, including N. Jantsannorow, Z. Khangal, B. Sharav, Ts. Chinzorig, State Honored Performer G.

Altankhuyag, D. Battömör, as well as G. Bizet, G. Puccini, P. Tchaikovsky and C. Saint-Saens" (*ibid.*, 3). In fact, in 1999 the Ensemble received a grant from the Soros ("Open Society") Foundation in Mongolia that allowed it to produce a performance of the entire opera "Carmen," by George Bizet, transcribed and arranged for singers and an ensemble of horse-head fiddles.

The idea of creating such an ensemble had been floating about for some time in Mongolia since at least the 1980s. The ensemble's director, Ts. Batchuluun, says that he had the idea in the early 1980s. A small group of well-known fiddlers did establish a horse-head fiddle quartet in this period. But the real push to create a large fiddle ensemble came at the end of that decade with the visit of the fiddlers from Inner Mongolian (see Chapter Four).

Jantsannorow says that when he and Jamyan saw the horse-head fiddle ensemble that Chi. Bulag had established in Höhhot, Inner Mongolia, in 1989 (or 1988), he felt distressed. The Inner Mongolian ensemble, he says, "did not have the real horse-head fiddle sound" and thus he determined that it must be up to the Mongolians themselves to establish their own fiddle ensemble (Jantsannorow 1999.10.09). This concern for the development of a uniquely national musical style or sound extended to the 1989 Horse-head Fiddle Naadam. When asked why no Inner Mongolians other than Chi. Bulag were allowed to participate in it, Ulambayar said that its organizers wanted to include only domestic horse-head fiddle players. "We wanted to work out our own style. We're in something of a competition with them" (Ulambayar 1998.07.17).

Over the years, the State Horse-head Fiddle Ensemble has become an important cultural ambassador for the Mongolian state. It has toured in China, Korea, Japan, and the Buriat province of southern Russia, and has made repeated trips to South Korea and Japan. The association with Japan is particularly close given the relationships that Batchuluun and Jantsannorow have cultivated with benefactors and cultural institutions there, but also given the amazing popularity of the horse-head fiddle with Japanese audiences.

The Horse-head Fiddle Ensemble's touring activities have promoted widespread interest among Mongolia's Asian neighbors in the horse-head fiddle and Mongolian cultural heritage. The Ensemble, for instance, has held a number of high-profile joint concerts with Buriat folk musicians and popular singers, both in Ulaanbaatar and Buriatia, which has generated reviews and commentaries in the Buriat press about the horse-head fiddle and the Buriat's own national identity (Otgonsüren 1997: 3). Seemingly in response, an Inner Mongolian horse-head fiddle ensemble traveled to Buriatia in summer 1999 to tour and perform. The ancient ties between the Buriats and Mongolians were largely suppressed throughout the nineteenth and twentieth centuries by first Tsarist and then Soviet cultural policies. The dueling tours to the region might be the beginnings of a cultural tussle between Inner Mongolian and Mongolian cultural officials over whose version of Mongol cultural identity should have influence in contemporary Buriatia. It is interesting that the horse-head fiddle is at the core of this debate.

The Horse-head Fiddle Ensemble released its first CD recording, *Let the Mount Burkhan Khaldun Bless You!* (1998), which contained selections of works that Jantsannorow wrote for the horse-head fiddle between 1989 and 1996. Jantsannorow speaks about this recording as being a touchstone for all the Mongolian people. He says that a key goal of this project was to create music that sonically represented a national essence, a musical sound which for him embodies what it is to be a Mongolian.

> This [recording] is the result of my twenty-odd year search for the expression of the characteristics of national art, and the best of my compositions for the horse-head fiddle ensemble. I included the best eleven of the more than thirty compositions I wrote for the horse-head fiddle ensemble. When one listens to these compositions, one will gain the understanding that the horse-head fiddle has no pair in its ability to reveal, in a highly refined way, a person's inner feelings just by the rubbing of string on string. It is my hope that when a Mongolian has listened to this music and then goes to sleep or travels far away, it will be impossible for him to become separated from little Mongolia, something which is so valuable to him, which is located in the heart of Asia (Oyuunbileg 1998: 5)

It is perhaps not at all surprising that Jantsannorow would turn to the horse-head fiddle in his search to express what is "so valuable" to a Mongolian. The horse-head fiddle in his compositions is meant to stand as a symbol that encapsulates all that is true and valuable in the Mongolian nation. The symbol is especially dynamic given that the horse-head fiddle has the power to create sounds that "move" people's hearts. But it is still a symbol that has been removed from its specific local contexts and made to stand for the experience and history of all of the people of Mongolia.

Also evident in Jantsannorow's rhetoric is an attempt to objectify not only the Mongolian but also the non-Mongolian Other, which for him includes all those who could threaten the survival of a distinct Mongolian national identity. In the early 1980s, the Other was certainly Russification. But with the appearance of Chi. Bulag and revelations about the progress the Inner Mongolians had made in developing the horse-head fiddle, the Other then became the "Chinese" (Inner Mongolians). In the late 1990s, the Other might well have been Western popular culture, which many feared would overwhelm the national culture. His discourse helps to both objectify these "Others" and to reify their status as "not one of us."

In this light we can better understand Ulambayar's comment, "We need to find our own way," regarding why the Inner Mongolians were not invited to the Jantsannorow's Horse-head Fiddle Naadam in 1989. The surprise that Mongolians felt upon seeing the degree of mastery that the

Inner Mongolians had achieved on the horse-head fiddle touched deeper chords of fear about Chinese civilization. In reiterating the horse-head fiddle's indigenous origins among the Mongolian people, while also showing how they were "perfecting" it to international standards, Ulambayar was pointing to a collective response among Mongolian fiddle makers to the threat that was posed by the "Chinese," even if they were actually ethnic Mongolians. The Mongolians wanted to preempt any effort by the Inner Mongolians to claim the instrument as their own.

This process of identifying those elements that mark Mongolian national identity as distinct from all others, be they rhetorical, aural, or visual, is useful not only for artists like Jantsannorow, but also for politicians and nationalists. On one level, Jantsannorow's CD *Let the Mount Burkhan Khaldan Bless You!* is a pleasant recording of modern national music. But on another level, it is a political statement about contemporary Mongolian identity as expressed through music—a declaration of Jantsannarov's idea about who is in and who is out in the new Mongolia. For Jantsannarov and other cosmopolitan nationalists, the horse-head fiddle is something of a flag that they can "wave" through performances, recordings, and media interviews when they wish to assert a uniquely modern national musical identity.

These developments at the national level, however, do not encompass all of the meanings of the contemporary horse-head fiddle traditions in Mongolia. Despite the tendency of cosmopolitan nationalists, following the universalizing logic of modernism, to assume that the national cultural traditions represents and speaks to all Mongolians, the reality is that alternative, and even decidedly non-modern, fiddle traditions continue to be maintained and even expanded, especially in the nation's rural regions. The relative decline in the ability of the central national institutions to maintain artistic and ideological control over rural cultural institutions in the past decade has created space for clearly alternative narratives about the history and meaning of the horse-head fiddle. As we will see in the final chapter, these narratives are beginning to rise to the surface again, particularly on the nation's peripheries, and to challenge those of the nation's center.

6 The Persistence of Alternative Music Histories

As we saw in the last chapter, the central institutions play a significant role in maintaining and disseminating the modernist narratives about the horse-head fiddle. But other historical constructs regarding this instrument persist in Mongolia, primarily at the local and regional levels. As we have seen, the collapse of the centralized, single-party rule in Mongolia led to the relative decline in the past decade in the ability of the centralized institutions to maintain artistic and ideological control over the actions of the more rural institutions. Many of these rural institutions and even performers and scholars have in turn begun to promote alternative histories of the fiddle that provide a useful new perspective from which to view the modernized and urban national musical traditions. These traditions are "alternative" in the sense that they may not be governed by the same logic of progress and internationalism that shapes the cosmopolitan traditions. Many of these traditions represent older, pre-Revolutionary cultural practices and values that people have managed to maintain in parallel to the modern and urban-based national traditions.

The syncretic or "Europeanized" nature of the modern horse-head fiddle traditions are not universally appreciated either in Ulaanbaatar or the countryside. There are many Mongolians who argue that the nation's cultural institutions conceive of folk music in a much too narrow and constrictive a fashion. They do not feel as though the modernized traditions reflect their or their community's own particular history or identity. In this chapter we will hear the voices of some of these Mongolians, and see how many of them seek to de-emphasize the goals of "Western" modernity in search of the roots of their own local or regional musical styles. This may be the beginning of a new renaissance of folk music in the countryside.

S. BADRAL, ULAANBAATAR

Throughout the 1990s, a number of Mongolians have strongly criticized the standardization and Europeanization of the horse-head fiddle's appearance and sound. While these changes may make the fiddle capable of performing

Western classical music, they argue, they also distance the instrument from its *ugsaatny* or traditional roots. An article by S. Badral[1] on this theme appeared in the Ulaanbaatar-based newspaper *Il Towchoo*. Badral recounts a story of how as a youth in the countryside he enjoyed hearing the fiddle playing of the "local old man Yanjin," who played on "an old instrument with soft strings." The sound of this traditional fiddle, he says, "was deeply saturated with the love, good-hearted emotion and warm character of the Mongolian people," qualities of sound, he says, that are being lost in search for a "Western" sound (Badral 1998: 7).

> Across Mongolian there are many famous and talented horse-head fiddle players and many fiddle groups. But from their melodies can be heard the sad and boring sound of the Western violin. And if we do not pay attention to this, we may one day find that there is no difference between the horse-head fiddle and the Western violin (*ibid.*).

He finds fault with the way fiddles are being constructed, mourning the passing of the days when "all Mongolians" owned a horse-head fiddle, or at least a stick with a carved horse's head, which they respectfully hung on the walls of their *ger*.

> But now a skillfully carved head and nicely decorated horse-head fiddle is hard to find. We can see it only in some museum exhibits. The Folk Song and Dance Ensemble and other ensembles are using horse-head fiddles that were produced wholesale, with ugly forms and bad sounds. Particularly since 1970, the skillfully crafted head of a horse, which is its spirit or soul, seems to have become the form of an *azarga* [stallion] or an *asman* horse [a wild horse, or a horse of poor breeding], or, still further, the head of a bulldog. This is because the people who make the horse-head fiddle these days are not truly skilled, and because of the force of Western culture. Such things are causing the traditional carved form and detailed methods of making fiddles to become lost and forgotten (*ibid.*).

He ends his article with his opinion that the horse-head fiddle traditions need to find their way back to their roots.

> We need to understand that today's horse-head fiddle must reflect the traditional skillful art of our ancestors in the old times and should make the real horse-head fiddle sound. We must have pride in the works left by our twentieth century great artists, like Sharaw, Lodoi Lama, Ü. Yadamsüren, and S. Dondog, who in different forms left their own works of the shape of the horse-head fiddle (*ibid.*).

It is not uncommon to read calls by Mongolians for the return of certain traditions or customs, but it is unusual to read such criticism of the national musical institutions. Badral criticizes nearly every aspect of the professionalization of the horse-head fiddle and suggests that it has separated the fiddle traditions from those of the "old times." From his point of view, modern institutions like the Folksong & Dance Ensemble and urban fiddle-making workshops have strayed from their roots and thus no longer represent what is unique to the Mongolian national identity.

BALJIR KHUURCH, ULAANBAATAR

The horse-head fiddle performer and teacher, Ya. Baljir, had a career that extended from the 1940s to the 1990s. Though a part of the national musical culture almost from its beginning, Baljir was highly critical of the effects of nationalization on the Mongolian musical culture. "People can sing folk songs these days," he says, "but almost no one can sing any very well. Most of the great singers were killed [by the Mongolian People's Revolutionary Party] in the 1930s and 1940s, which caused all the musical traditions to decline. Even today woman do not sing lullabies to their infants. They merely play recordings" (Baljir 1997.05.31).

Like Badral, Baljir was critical of contemporary fiddle playing. "These modern fiddle players are all very good, very professional, but they cannot play a note without musical notation in front of their face. The real Mongolian musicians can play the fiddle just by hearing the music. But the most important thing is that the modern fiddle sound is very modern; it has a modern character." When asked him to explain what he meant by this, he gave an example: "When people hear the traditional horse-head fiddle sound, they feel joy and cry. But when modern artists perform the fiddle, nobody cries, nobody smiles" (*ibid.*). Baljir pins the blame for the loss of these traditional music-making abilities on the MPRP. It played a key role in destroying the traditions of the pre-Revolutionary Mongolian society, he says, first with great force and ruthlessness in the 1930s and 1940s and then more slowly and deliberately from then on.

Baljir was a student of G. Jamyan at the Music & Dance College in Ulaanbaatar. In his prime, from the mid-1950s to the early 1980s, he was a respected performer in Mongolia and was sent on many trips abroad to give concerts and participate in international music festivals and competitions. He mastered the standard national and classical musical repertoire as professional horse-head fiddle players were (and still are) expected to do. Baljir was clearly proud of the advancement and professionalism that he and other fiddle players of his generation had achieved in the socialist period with the support of the Party and Soviet cultural officials. At the same time, however, it was just as clear that he could not accept the necessity the Party felt for the destruction of the traditional forms of music.

But Baljir hoped to change this situation. He devised plans to build a school for horse-head fiddle players and long song singers. The renewal of these traditions, he said, must begin in the countryside instead of Ulaan-baatar or any other urban place.

> People want to redevelop the long song genre in the cities and towns. But this is all wrong. It must begin in the countryside with the families. People in the countryside have the original Mongolian character. This is because they do not listen to modern pop-rock music, as do those in the rural centers, towns and cities (*ibid.*).

He said that he had long tried to enlist the support of officials in the Ministry of Enlightenment (now the Ministry of Culture) in this project, but added that they showed little interest. He was determined to make this project happen, warning that time was running out. Soon, he says, all of the old performers will die, taking these traditions with them. Baljir *khuurch* himself died in early 1998.

He was a man driven by his ideal and passion for the Khalkha traditional musical arts. He was also a cosmopolitan nationalist. The Party brought him to Ulaanbaatar from the countryside as a young man and he learned how to fit into the cosmopolitan musical world of modern Mongolia. He traveled the world and performed the great works of music throughout his long career. But his ideas about the role of tradition in a modern society, his belief that the older traditions of music could exist side-by-side with the developed or modern traditions, did not correspond with those of the Party and mainstream musical institutions. Baljir held that traditional music could complement modern musical practices so long as it remained rooted in the practices of the communities and peoples from which it arose. The changes of 1990 allowed him to reimagine a different musical world in Mongolian that he could help to shape. But it appeared as though no one was listening.

ARKHANGAI THEATER[2] PERFORMERS

Nearly eight years after the 1990 Revolution, leading performers of the Music & Drama Theater, in Tsetserleg, Arkhangai aimag, reflected on what the period around 1990 was like for them. Sitting in his office, theater director Ch. Gankhuyag, who has held the post since the late 1980s, recounted the sudden change in people's attitude towards traditional customs and practices.

> The early 1990s was a time when our society was beginning to change and develop an ultra-nationalist ideology [*ündserkheg üzel*]. The old society was governed by a single party's ideology. In that time, people who worked in offices had to wear suits and dresses. But in this period [around 1990] things really changed. Mongolian national pride

was awakened throughout the nation and old Mongolian traditions were being awakened again. Everybody started to wear the traditional clothes and men wanted to wear their hair long and carry a real Mongolian knife. Everybody began to try to become a real Mongolian. Everything seemed so weird, interesting and strange in that time. You know, it happened suddenly, and it seemed to me that we suddenly had become a different people (Gankhuyag et. al, 1998.11.13).

One of the theaters singers, Sh. Chogsomjaw, joined the conversation when asked how things had changed in the Theater after 1990:

Gankhuyag: Before the 1990, the theater did everything that the Party told us to do.
Chogsomjaw: It was the people of the Council of Ideology who controlled everything here. They always told us what concerts we had to play. But after then, such things disappeared and we became free.
Gankhuyag: Yes, in this new period, we began to produce our works freely.

We started to speak with our own voices, and we also began to criticize the old society and the Party's ideology. In that short period, the people began to become interested in the Theater again, because we began this criticism. The theater's concert performances began to become interesting again. We were finally able to put on comic performances and perform shows that were critical of the Party, something that wasn't allowed before then. Soon after 1990, I was really brave, as a director, and organized a performance about Danzin Rabjai, who was a Mongolian enlightened person [of the nineteenth century]. I was worried that I would be stopped, but I was not (*ibid.*).

However, this renewed community interest in their ensemble's folk music, songs and dances soon faded. This was partly due to the worsening economic situation in the aimag in the years after 1990. The lead horse-head fiddle player in the Theater's folksong & dance ensemble, I. Amartüwshin, a young man with thick black hair that reached almost to his waist, characterized the effect of the situation on the community.

[Since 1990,] there has been a serious economic problem everywhere in the countryside, and there is always the expense of the tickets—of whether or not people have the money in their pockets to buy them. We have to deal with such questions here [in Tsetserleg]. Our tickets only cost 500T [about $.50US]. There is a big difference between the costs of concerts in the city and in the countryside. In Ulaanbaatar, concerts cost much more. But in the countryside, life is often difficult because people don't always receive their salaries in time. If they have 500T, they often have to decide whether to see a concert or buy a loaf of bread. If the concert is free, there is nobody who won't want to see it (*ibid.*).

The salary for the performers, as it was for most other salaried workers throughout the nation, has also not risen in line with inflation throughout this period. Most of the performers found it difficult to earn a living with a base salary of 25,000T a month (about $25.00US).

> This is a really small amount in the countryside, not just in the City [Ulaanbaatar]. With this amount we can buy just 25kg of flour and then we'd have a bit left over. Unlike our friends from the City, we usually have no pocket money, and so can't buy things from the market. The only reason we can live with such a small salary is because our parents help us. We can get some milk or meat from them. It seems like we usually take a tax from our parents! But we don't have it as bad as others. There are so many families with many children where only one person works (Ganbold 1998.11.13).

Theater director Gankhuyag said that this situation has taken its toll on the performers. Some of the Theater's best performers have gone to Ulaanbaatar to find better work, while others have left to enter other lines of work. The folk music repertoire has also suffered, he said: "All of our folk art has been made into 'classical' folk art which is now being left behind." He was referring to the professional folk music traditions, like those performed by the State Folksong & Dance Ensemble, that the performers were trained to perform during the socialist period.

While acknowledging that this modern folklore was an example of the "strong" development of the Mongolian arts during the modern era, Gankhuyag complained that this art had became so complicated and technical that no one but professionals could perform it. With the overall abilities of his performers declining in the face of the economic situation, and little help from the cultural institutions in Ulaanbaatar, they could no longer perform these professional styles of art. Adding to the problem, he said, was that fewer people from the community were attending these performances:

> Not everyone is interested in the traditional arts today. The young people are more interested in the modern [i.e., pop-rock] styles than in the traditional arts, so the traditional things are being left behind. It's just professional people who are interested in these things now. Our traditional art is just something to show to foreigners. In our homeland, which is part of the central Khalkha, our people [traditionally] performed long songs, short songs, fiddle melodies and *biyelgee* [dances]. [Since the socialist period] the modern Mongolian art has been developing quickly, but the traditional things are being left in a place which not every person can reach[3] (Gankhuyag, et al, 1998.11.13).

In saying that the traditional arts of Arkhangai are now "being left in a place which not every person can reach," Gankhuyag is expressing a sense of disconnection that he and those in his community are experiencing. As described above (cf. Chapter Two), the Party worked to professionalize and modernize the musical traditions in the cultural centers of Arkhangai. The original Club had been upgraded to a Cultural Palace, and finally to a Music & Drama Theater. In the process, Party institutions, such as the Department of Ideology, and probably also the Mongolian Composers Union, among others, began to closely supervise and control the content and form of the performances. The amateur musicians, those who specialized in local musical traditions were replaced with professional musicians, many of whom were trained in cultural institutions in Ulaanbaatar. This emphasis on modernized and nationalized musical traditions and the exclusion of local ones led to the disconnection that these community cultural leaders said that they were experiencing in the 1990s.

There is little evidence that these local *ugsaatny* traditions continued to be maintained in other contexts, such as in the homes of the people of the community. The fiddle player Amartüwshin described how in recent years the herding people of the countryside were once again interested in placing a horse-head fiddle on the walls of their *ger*s. They ask him to find them fiddles, saying that they were even willing to accept broken ones. Few people actually perform the traditional fiddle music or dances in their homes, he says. For them, it is more important to have the instrument in their home.

The decline in traditional music making in the Tsetserleg community, Amartüwshin said, is due to changes in its socio-economic situation.

> There is no longer a nomadic lifestyle in our aimag; everything is now so centralized. And the people of these places no longer receive the traditional arts well. The new styles that come from the Western nations are now spreading and increasing throughout the community (Amartuvshin 1998.09.30).

Gankhuyag agrees with Amartüwshin, adding that people are now used to experiencing many different kinds and types of music.

> Today the people are so curious, they do not want to eat just one kind of food, they want to try many different kinds of food. It's the same thing here [in the Theater]; they do not want to listen to the traditional arts only, but also to new styles, the Western styles. But I think it will happen that the traditional arts will become more valuable. I think in the future that traditional music will come together with the other kinds of music, and the research into traditional music will increase. You know, we can't play foreign music well. The traditional art is our Mongolian art; we can play it better than the foreigners. Traditional art is in the people's blood. It goes without question that the young

people of today will know the value of the traditional arts when they get older. They will once again be interested in it (*ibid.*).

Like Baljir, Gankhuyag and these theater performers believe that the traditional or *ugsaatny* musical arts should play a vital role in the musical life of their community, even if it is but one of many musical traditions the members have to choose from. Gankhuyag emphasizes how these arts are an important part of expressing the Mongolian, or at least the central Khalkha, cultural identity. The Theater has had some success with their experimental *kholimog* (mixed) ensemble, which brings together folk instruments like the horse-head fiddle and *yatga*, and "modern" instruments like the Yamaha electric keyboard and a drum set. This ensemble's repertoire consists mostly of arrangements of folk and folk-inspired music. Amartüwshin says that this group draws a relatively larger and younger audience from the community than do their folk music concerts. The group does point to ways in which the Theater is reworking musical traditions to make them more relevant to their community.

Despite such optimism, however, these theater performers also feel isolated from their community. On the one hand, the professional folk music, song, and dance has become increasingly difficult to maintain, given the flight of talented performers to other places or lines of work. On the other hand, given the decades-old break in the maintenance of local traditional arts, there are few people around who still remember the old forms of music, song, and dance, and could bring them back to the Theater stage. This raises the question for these performers of just what "folk" or "traditional" music they should be performing in their local theater.

In hopes of reinvigorating community interest in local Arkhangai musical traditions, Gankhuyag says that they have devised the unusual plan of bringing some of the traditions from the western aimags to their own.

> Our plan is this: we will appoint two of our dancers and one fiddle player to go to Uws aimag,[4] where they will study for two months. They will study the traditional arts there, especially the traditional dances, like the *biyelgee*, and fiddle music. This will happen at the beginning of next year [1999]. Our goal is also to have them learn that aimag's traditional arts and then bring them to Arkhangai. [We will do this] because Western Mongolia has the majority of the heritage of the traditional art in Mongolia. Our theater's goal is to study the arts of Western Mongolia (*ibid.*).

The most senior performer in the Theater, P. Laugüi, added, "We have to make detailed studies of the fiddle's *tatlaga* [a traditional genre of fiddle music]" (*ibid.*). These performers would then train other performers in the Theater, thereby helping to re-establish the performance of "traditional" music in Arkhangai.

The Theater performers hope to transplant or graft traditions from one music culture, the Oirat's, into or onto their own central Khalkha music culture, despite the stylistic differences that have long defined the two. For those in Arkhangai, however, the fact that the Oirat traditions represent examples of a living tradition is more important than the differences between them. Rather than looking to Ulaanbaatar as a source of "authentic" traditions, they are turning instead to the west, the peripheries of the national musical culture. This emphasizes the reality that the modernizing initiatives of the twentieth century played a much greater role in the center than in the peripheral regions. Now those in the center need to look outside, to the periphery, to locate what for them is the authentic.

N. SENGEDORJ, KHOWD AIMAG

As happened throughout the nation, independence from the Soviet Union in the 1990s brought with it a contraction in the size and number of activities that could be supported by the cultural centers in Khowd aimag, in the far west. N. Sengedorj is one of the senior performers in the organization, having worked for decades as an actor, singer, musicians and administrator. In his mid-50s, he is one of the most respected performers in Mongolia as well as director of the aimag's Music and Drama Theater. He likes to portray himself as different from professional Mongolian performers of music or theater because he had no formal arts training. He says he learned how to act, sing and perform from studying with local teachers and from his own ideas. He says, defiantly, that to this day he cannot read musical notation, which is one of the hallmarks of a professional education in twentieth century Mongolia. But Sengedorj's lack of a formal education has not kept him from a long career in the Theater's major theatrical and musical productions. In the socialist period, he says, they were able to mount a large-scale production, such as a Shakespeare play or major concert, about every two months. Since 1990, however, he says the Theater can manage only one dramatic production and one large-scale concert a year. A decade on from 1990, the Khowd Theater employs only thirty full-time performers, down from more than eighty during the 1980s.

As in Arkhangai, lack of money has become a major problem for the Theater. With the significant reduction in the amount of support from the central government, the Theater has had to rely upon support from the aimag administration and ticket sales. But with the difficult economic situation in the aimag, neither the administration nor the local people have much money to buy tickets. In addition, Sengedorj says, the younger generations in Khowd are living more urban-oriented forms of life. They grow up watching television, listening to their radios, and watching movies. Their life is far from what it was like for him as a youth in the countryside, where they had to rely upon their own resources to entertain themselves.

I enjoyed the times when guests would come to visit our *ail* as a child. These people would come to stay and talk with my parents and recite epics [*tuuli*] about heroes and big battles. I would often imagine what they were like. That is the way I was brought up. Even if I did not see the heroes in reality, I saw them in my mind, and so I think my imagination is better than that of today's young people. Today's young people just use calculators, watch television and films, and play computer games (Sengedorj 2000.06.27).

Thus, he says, the situation for the traditional and folk arts in Khowd is getting worse in the past decade. The older masters of these traditions are dying and not passing on their skills to the younger generations, who, he says, are either too busy to learn or not at all interested.

But Sengedorj is realistic about the situation and supports a proposal for the government to combine several aimag theaters into one large regional theater.

It is no longer possible to keep a big theater like ours in each aimag. Each aimag has around 50,000 people, and since many of these are children, that leaves only around 25,000 people who could [potentially] come to our theater. It is not necessary to have one large theater for only 25,000 people. We should combine the efforts of three to five aimags into a single regional theater. Such large theaters would have the resources to make possible large theater productions and concerts. That way we could both keep our traditions and perform the great classical works. If we can develop our local artists, then we could also perform foreign operas or dramas (*ibid.*).

Sengedorj sees a role for the professional artists and musicians of these socialist period institutions in maintaining local and regional traditions, but at the same time he emphasizes the need to rethink the nature of these traditions. In summer 2000, Sengedorj, who considers himself to be primarily an actor, was devising plans to develop what he called a *Mongol dram* or "Mongolian drama." He says that this was to be a distinctly national (*ündesnii*) form of theater that has the aim of reimagining the genre in non-Russian ways.

You see, drama began in Mongolia with the Russians after the People's Revolution of 1921. We had no native teachers, they all came from Russia, and therefore our drama tradition became very Russian. Later, people went to Russian and trained in Russian theater and then brought back what they had learned. So, of course, they brought back Russian influence. In Ulaanbaatar, a drama school was set up, but still all the teachers were Russian or those trained in Russia. So how can the theater we have not be Russian? We had the experience that if someone

tried to make a uniquely Mongolian form of theater, others would joke
about it and think it was funny (*ibid.*).

Sengedorj is touching upon the question of not only the content in the theater traditions, but more importantly, their form. Sengedorj feels that the
national musical culture bears overt Russian influence. He instead wants
to promote a form of theater that can reflect the unique ways in which the
Mongolians interact with the world, and traditional music will play an
important part in this.

> Now I want to set up a 'Mongolian drama.' I think that the Mongo-
> lian theater should reflect the Mongolian ways of seeing. Mongolians
> on stage, for instance, should sit and talk the way Mongolians sit and
> talk. I will start work on this project later this year, and I hope to show
> the first drama by June 2001. In this first *ündesnii dram* [national or
> root drama], I am planning to use traditional musical instruments, such
> as the *ikel* ['fiddle], *tsuur* ['flute'], *towshuur* [plucked 'lute'], and a *khul-*
> *son khuur* [a wooden 'jew's-harp'], which is a musical instrument of the
> Khalkha tribe. We'll also use a *khuuguur*, which is an instrument that
> when it is spun and it produces sounds. And we're even thinking about
> how we can make music with stones. This was one of our traditional
> instruments—one beats stones to produce certain pitches. All of these
> instruments will play real traditional Mongolian melodies. At the same
> time, we won't use any professional instruments in the drama, like the
> *khuuchir*, *yoochin*, or *shanz*, all of which sound like Chinese instru-
> ments and were originated from China. I don't consider these to be real
> Mongolian instruments. We also need technical things for our drama, to
> make it more alive, such as a small dung fire on stage. Everything should
> be Mongolian—the smell, tastes, sounds, visuals; we should show the
> ways in which our people greet each other, sit and talk. Maybe in the
> beginning our audiences won't accept this bravely, but we should none-
> theless continue to carry on the Mongolian traditions (*ibid.*).

In his desire to make a "more alive" Mongolian drama, he would turn the
subject of Mongolian theater back towards an idealized form of the Mongolians themselves, and particularly the Mongolians of the west. Sengedorj
would also avoid the use of the Mongolian "professional" instruments (his
term), in favor of those that the Party long ago dismissed as unsuitable for
a modern and professional music culture.

He is especially adamant about the re-introduction of the *ikel* into his
theater performances. It was decided in the Communist era not to include
this two-stringed folk fiddle into the theater ensembles because it was not
suited to the needs of the new performance contexts, such as the large
concert halls and new instrumental ensembles. "The *ikel* does not have a
strong sound," he says, "and it also easily goes out of tune as the weather

changes. So when this instrument is included in an ensemble, it doesn't fit in well with the other instruments. The *ikel* is not a professional instrument" (*ibid.*). But Sengedorj does not share the opinion of others that because of this it therefore must be kept out of the theater or left behind as a relic of the past.

> The *ikel* is not in the theater. It is still only played in the countryside, among the families. It is a bad thing that there is no *ikel* in the theater. In the old days, people said that we are making a new culture, so we need new things, and so they annihilated the *ikel*. We should not destroy our own traditions; there should be a policy about this (*ibid.*).

Instead, he sees a way in which even this tiny instrument could be incorporated into the musical life of his theater. And in doing so, he acknowledges the continued relevance of the older, pre-modern traditions in the cultural life of his community.

It is as if Sengedorj, the Arkhangai theater performers and the other people quoted in this chapter represent voices warning against the effects of what they see as an incessant encroachment of modern cultural ideals into their local communities. While not against these ideals, per se, they advocate the need for greater resources to protect and develop local cultural diversity. Rather than replacing the existing music culture with something from the distant past, they seek to develop new syncretic forms of musical tradition that reflect contemporary society but that also maintain a clear continuity with local pre-modern musical practice. This involves the possibility of reimagining local traditions that follow very different aesthetic ideals than is typical in the nation's modern folk music culture.

The odds, however, appear stacked against such efforts given the broader forces acting on rural populations in Mongolia today. The decades-long economic stagnation that has gripped rural areas and the subsequent migration of families, and especially young people, from rural to urban areas are draining many rural communities of people and resources. Efforts to reorganize the nation's provinces to better reflect distinct subcultural or regional identities, of which the creation of regional cultural centers would be a part, could be an important component in broader economic and political developments in the countryside. Drawing in the remnants of local pre-modern musical traditions, for example, such as in the way Sengedorj hopes to draw in the ancient *ikel* fiddle into his theatrical productions, could be an important way for local communities to rebuild their local identities. But until any such efforts are undertaken, the trend appears to be moving toward the increasing influence of the cosmopolitan and national musical traditions on local musical scenes and the continued loss of the rich cultural diversity that has marked Mongolian instrumental music for centuries.

List of Interviews

Amartüvshin, I., September 30, 1998 (Ulaanbaatar)
Baljir, Ya., May 31, 1997 (Ulaanbaatar)
Bulag, Chi., January 7, 2004 (Ulaanbaatar)
Enebish, Jambalyn, July 8, 1997 (Ulaanbaatar)
Enebish, Jambalyn, October 25, 1998 (Ulaanbaatar)
Enebish, Jambalyn, November 22, 1998 (Ulaanbaatar)
Enkhjargal, December 05, 1998 (Ulaanbaatar)
Erdenechimeg, L., July 9, 1997 (Ulaanbaatar)
Erdenechimeg, L., October 3, 1999 (Ulaanbaatar)
Ganbold, Ch., November 13, 1998 (Tsetserleg)
Jamyan, G., October 12, 1999 (Ulaanbaatar)
Gankhuyag, Ch., I. Amartüvshin, P. Laugüi, and Sh. Chogsomjav, November 13, 1998 (Tsetserleg)
Jantsannorov, N., October 9, 1999 (Ulaanbaatar)
Jantsannorov, N., October 13, 1999 (Ulaanbaatar)
Jargalsaikhan, D., September 25, 1998 (Ulaanbaatar)
Luvsan, D., September 19, 1997 (Ulaanbaatar)
Sengedorj, N., June 27, 2000 (Khowd)
Sündet, S., August 1, 1997 (Ulaanbaatar)
Tserenpil, D., June 15, 2001 (Ulaanbaatar)
Ulambayar, D., July 17, 1998 (Ulaanbaatar)

Notes

NOTES TO THE INTRODUCTION

1. Cf., Aalto (1962), Bawden (1963), Berlinskii (1933), Desjacques (1986, 1990), Emsheimer (1943/197, 1991a, 1991b), Hamayon (1980), Jenkins (1960), Kara (1970), Nixon (1985), Pegg (1991, 1992a, 1992b, 1995, 2001), Poppe (1979), Santaro (1999), Serruys (1985), Smirnov (1963, 1971, 1975), Stumpf (1887/1975), Vargyas (1968), Walcott (1974).
2. To her credit, however, she did managed to go to Mongolia in 1974 where she traveled to many different parts of the country and made field recordings that remain some of the most historically valuable available today (TSCD909 Topic Records 1994).
3. It should be noted here that Chinese cosmopolitans looked as much to Japan for notions of cultural modernity as to Europe, further complicating the concept of the "West" in China (Kraus 1989: 27).

NOTES TO CHAPTER 1

1. *qumiz* in Turkic, or *airag* in modern Mongolian. This is fermented mare's milk, a popular late-summer drink among the Mongols and many other nomadic peoples of Central and Inner Asia.
2. Another common adjective for a stringed instrument with a rounded body is "bowl-shaped." As we will see below, the Mongols of later centuries commonly used the phrases "spoon-shaped" or "ladle-shaped."
3. The Mongol khanate established in the western part of the Mongol Empire after the Mongol invasion of Russia in the 1240s.
4. Also a type of *cithara*.
5. Classical Mongolian is a form of Mongolian that is somewhere between Middle Mongolian (written in the twelfth to fourteenth centuries) and Modern Mongolian.
6. The term "four-eared" refers to the number of tuning pegs.
7. There remain a number of accounts by travelers, missionaries and explorers to this region, particularly from the eighteenth century on, that await examination for musical descriptions.
8. In fact, Haslund-Christensen purchased and brought back to Denmark nearly all of the instruments that appear in the photographs in his work. Most of these instruments, photographs, and recordings are housed in the National Museum of Denmark.
9. These are modern Khalkha Mongol terms for these components.

10. Though popularly known today as a 'crocodile,' this meaning of the word (Sanskrit *makāra* > Uighur > Mongolian *matar*) is fairly recent, likely influenced in the Communist period by the Soviet-inspired satirical weekly newspaper, *Gümbaraa matar* (The Crocodile).
11. Tigers are traditionally associated with power, serpents with the lords of the underworld, dragons with the sky or "heaven," and horses with the land.
12. *Khil khuur* has since become the common name for the European violin.
13. These are sub-ethnic groups in Inner Mongolia.
14. Other scholars have developed this idea further than Berlinskii (Emsheimer 1971: 86, Grama and Tsuge 1972: 64–65).
15. Dance traditionally was common among the Oirats, but largely absent among the Khalkha Mongols.
16. 108 is the number of beads on a Buddhist rosary.
17. *ülgerchid*, plural, or *ülgerch*, singular; after the Mongolian word for story, *ülger*.
18. Boris Vladimirtsov traveled to western Mongolia in 1911 and again in 1913–1915 (Vladimirtsov 1983: 57).
19. *tuulič* (singular), *tuuličid* (plural)
20. The human skull, like the conch shell (*labia*) (above), were both powerful Buddhist symbols.

NOTES TO CHAPTER 2

1. The name of the capital city changed to Ulaanbaatar in 1924.
2. A Mongolian folk flute
3. It would be interesting to compare this campaign with the "Great Leap Forward" ("that massive utopian experiment") launched by Chairman Mao in the PRC a year earlier (Meisner 1985: 284–285).
4. Chuluunbat provides somewhat different numbers: "Today in Mongolia [1972] there are 14 amateur art theaters, 192 amateur art ensembles and around 2,000 working clubs" (Chuluunbat 1972: 12).
5. Cultural Palaces were considered larger and better equipped than clubs, red gers, or red corners.
6. Party Secretary Tsedenbal reports that 150,000 radios were sold in Mongolia between 1960 and 1965, resulting in a radio ownership ratio of 1.4 radios per 10 people (Tsedenbal 1966: 76, 73). As radios were generally shared within families, this number was likely much higher.
7. In Mongolian: the "Elder brother-Younger brother" relationship (*akh-duugiin khariltsaa*) and the "Eternal friendship" (*mönkhiin nökhörlöl*). The cultural implications of these ideas will be discussed in Chapter Three.
8. This ensemble has been recently renamed to the Great National Orchestra of Mongolia (*Ündesnii ikh nairal khögjim*).
9. This comment, published in the late 1980s, does not acknowledge that *negdels*, or agricultural collectives, did not yet exist when Mördorj was writing this work.
10. Faces were traditionally made out of processed hide (goat, sheep, or camel), but there is evidence that the southern and Khalkha Mongols traditionally made fiddles using wood (Emsheimer 1943/1971, Enebish 1997.07.08).
11. Enebish (1997.07.08) insists that the addition of the *f*-shaped sound holes was not done on the order of Yarovoi but was instead an idea of his Mongolian pupils.
12. The pupils P. Yagdai and S. Goshii may or may not have been involved with this group.

13. The rising sun is also an important Soviet symbol for Communism.

NOTES TO CHAPTER 3

1. The Mongolian Peoples Republic officially became a member organization in the United Nations in 1960.
2. This literature includes translations of works by "Tolstoy, Jules Verne, Robert Louis Stevenson, Jack London, and others" (Rupen 1956: 396, n. 34).
3. He is quoted as warning his colleagues: "No heed should be taken of the anger and protests of some of our people . . . Foreign interference is not dangerous. Much more dangerous is the discrepancy within the Party . . . Do not relax revolutionary zeal!" (*Mongolia* n.d.: 29).
4. It is not clear that Shirendew ever officially graduated from the institute in which he was studying until then, given the outbreak of World War II.

NOTES TO CHAPTER 4

1. Mandukhai Khatun was a fifteenth century Khalkha queen and last living descendent of Kubilai Khan. She is credited with helping to maintain the unity of the Mongol people in the wars against the western Oriats.
2. Compare this to the statement by the popular music singer D. Jargalsaikhan. He told me that he wrote his now famous song "Chinggis Khan," which portrayed the Great Khan as a flawed by still holy figure, in 1979. He sought to premiere the song that year, something that certainly would have landed him in a great deal of trouble. But he was told by "a lama at the Gandan monastery" to not perform the song. Jargalsaikhan says that the lama told him that "the time was not yet right for this" (Jargalsaikhan 1998.09.25).
3. This "fish of peace" is a decades old interpretation of the "yin-yang" symbol given by Rinchen. See also the discussion about *arga-bileg* in Chapter 5.
4. *üzüülelt*, or "indicator," is the same word used by economists to measure economic progress.

NOTES TO CHAPTER 5

1. A number of Mongolian fiddle makers and musicians interviewed for this project cited her dissertation in interviews and conversations.
2. Other narratives with similar sets of ideas about the origins and development of the horse-head fiddle can also be found in: Jambaldorj 1996: 104–105; Mongolian Free Democratic Journalists' Association (MFDJA) 1997: 16; MIAT 1999: 12; and in the exhibit notes for the horse-head fiddle at the Mongolian State Museum of Natural History in Ulaanbaatar (as seen in 1998).
3. All are quotes from Mongolians contacted during the course of this research. Such statements are also commonly told by Inner Mongolians, who share many of these ideas about the history and meaning of the horse-head fiddle in Mongol history and culture. The relationship between the Inner Mongolians and this fiddle is another very important story that has yet to be told.
4. The Nine White Standards are a set of nine tall wooden poles topped with rings of long black horsetail hairs. They were used by Chinggis Khan and his armies during their military campaigns.

5. Recent *Tsagaan sar*s have instead featured a highly produced video, pre-recording in a studio, featuring a young and talented fiddle player, wearing thirteenth century regalia, performing this "Anthem."
6. A ceremonial silk scarf used to show respect.
7. The lotus flower symbol was also the pedestal for the Mongolian soyombo symbol, which was on the Mongolian flag of 1921–1940.

NOTES TO CHAPTER 6

1. Badral, S, "Owog deedees owlogdson morin khuur minu" (My horse-head fiddle, which was inherited from the ancestors), *Il Towcho* 31/303 (1998): 7.
2. A provincial theater located in the town of Tsetserleg, in central Mongolia.
3. *Khün bolgon tisheegee orch chadakhgui baina.*
4. A province in the far western edge of the country where, many believe, ancient musical traditions have been able to survive to the present in degrees that those provinces nearer to the center have not.

Bibliography

Aalto, Pentti 1962. "The Music of the Mongols: An Introduction." In *Aspects of Altaic Civilization*, ed. Denis Sinor. Bloomington: Indiana University Press, pp. 59–65.

Abrahams, Roger D. 1993. 'Phantoms of Romantic Nationalism in Folkloristics,' *Journal of American Folklore* 106 (419): 3–37.

Anderson, Benedict 1991. *Imagined Communities*. London: Verso.

Akim, G. 1991. "Khos chawkhdasny uchir" (Why the two strings?), *Il Towchoo* (July 11–20) 16 (18): 6.

Ardyn Erkh 1992. "Töriin khan khuur zalaw" (The State Fiddle is Installed), *Ardyn Erkh* (People's Right) 47 (351): 1.

Badraa, Jamtsyn 1998a. "Mongol ardyn khögjmiin zemseg, dan khögjliin tüükhiin sudlakh uchir" (Research into the history of the origin and development of Mongolian folk music instrumental art). In *Mongol Ardyn Khögjim* (Mongolian Folk Music). Ulaanbaatar: T&U Printing Company, 86–95.

———— 1998b. "Mongol ardyn urtyn duu" (Mongolian Folk Long Song). In *Mongol Ardyn Khögjim* (Mongolian Folk Music). Ulaanbaatar: T&U Printing Company, 103–106.

———— 1998c. "Khögmdökhiin ur züi" [Musical talent]. In *Mongol Ardyn Khögjim* (Mongolian Folk Music). Ulaanbaatar: T&U Printing Company, 114–119.

———— 1998d. "Mongol ardyn khögjmiin zemseg" [Mongolian Folk Music Instruments]. In *Mongol Ardyn Khögjim* (Mongolian Folk Music). Ulaanbaatar: T&U Printing Company, 96–102.

———— 1998e. "Mongol ardyn khögjmiin zemcgiin züils" (Types of Mongolian Folk Music Instruments). In *Mongol Ardyn Khögjim* (Mongolian Folk Music). Ulaanbaatar: T&U Printing Company, 133–168.

Badrakh, G. 1960 [1937]. *Mongol khögjmiin tüükhees* (From the History of Mongolian Music). Ulaanbaatar: State Publishing House.

Badral, S 1998. "Owog deedees owlogdson morin khuur minu" (My horse-head fiddle, which was inherited from the ancestors), *Il Towcho* 31/303: 7.

Batzengel 1980. "Urtyn Duu, Xöömij, and Morin Xuur." In *Musical Voices of Asia: Report of the Asian Traditional Performing Arts, 1978*. Tokyo: Heibonsha Ltd.

Bawden, Charles R. 1989. *The Modern History of Mongolia*. London: Kegan Paul International.

———— 1963. "'The Mongol Conversation Song.'" In *Aspects of Altaic Civilization*, Volume 23, ed. Denis Sinor. Bloomington: Indiana University Press, pp. 75–86.

Bazarragchaa, B. 1995. "Bi khuuraa bas khuur namaig khöglödög" (I Play My Fiddle and My Fiddle Plays Me), *Ardyn erkh* (July 10) 136 (1095): 8.

Becker, Seymour 1991. "Russia Between East and West: The Intelligentsia, Russian National Identity and the Asian Borderlands," *Central Asian Survey* 10 (4): 47–64.

———— 1986a. "Introduction: Elites and the Transmission of Nationality and Identity," *Central Asian Survey* 5 (3–4): 5–24.

———— 1986b. "The Muslim East in Nineteenth-Century Russian Popular Historiography," *Central Asian Survey* 5 (3–4): 25–47.

Berlinskii, P. 1933. *Mongol'skii pevets i muzykant Ul'dzui Lubsan-Khurchi. Opyt analiza mongol'skogo ustnogo muzykal'no-poeticheskogo tvorchestva* (Mongolian singer and musician Uldzui Lubsan-Khurchi: An attempt at analysis of Mongolian oral musical and poetic artistry). Moscow: Muzgiz.

Bertkov, K., G. Blagodotov, E. Yazovitskaya 1963. *Atlas muzykal'nykh instrumentov narodov SSSR* (Atlas of Folk Music Instruments, USSR). Moscow: State Music Publishing.

Boldbaatar, Jigjid 1999. "The Eight-hundredth Anniversary of Chinggis Khan: The Revival and Suppression of Mongolian National Consciousness." In *Mongolia in the Twentieth Century: Landlocked Cosmopolitan*, edited by Stephen Kotkin and Bruce A. Elleman. Armonk (NY): M.E. Sharpe, 237–246.

———— 1996. "Bodol chiwchirgen, üg tuniu minii nökhör." In *Mongolyn khögjmiin arwankhoyor khörög (Sonatyn allegro)* (Twelve Portraits of Mongolian Music [Sonata allegro]). Ulaanbaatar, 149–158.

Börön 1982. "Morin quyur un egüsül kögjil jiči uralig- un šinji toyimu" (A concise account of the horse-head fiddle's origin, development and artistic character), *Tawun Suwud* (Five Jewels) 1 (no pagination).

Bromley, Julian, and Viktor Kozlov 1989. "The Theory of Ethnos and Ethnic Processes in Soviet Social Sciences," *Comparative Study of Society and History* 31: 425–438.

Bulag, Uradyn E. 1998. *Nationalism and Hybridity in Mongolia*. New York: Oxford University Press.

Chagnaa, J. 1987. "'Minii ekh oron' simfoni" (The 'My Motherland' Symphony), *Duu khögjim* 7: 57.

Chatterjee, Partha 1986. *Nationalist Thought and the Colonial World: A Derivative Discourse?* London: Zed Books, Ltd.

Chuluunbat, Ts. 1972. *Sain duryn uran saikhanchdad tuslamj* (Help for Amateur Artists). Ulaanbaatar: State Publishing House.

Clark, Katerina 2000. *The Soviet Novel: History as Ritual*. Third edition. Bloomington: Indiana University Press.

Comaroff, Jean, and John Comaroff, editors 1993. *Modernity and Its Malcontents: Ritual and Power in Postcolonial Africa*. Chicago: University of Chicago Press.

Damdinsüren, Tsendiin 2001. "Ardiin ülgerch, khuurch, yeröölch nar" (Folk Storytellers, Fiddle Players, and Blessing Song Singers). In *Büren zokhiol*. Third volume. Edited by D. Tsedew. Ulaanbaatar: Interpress, 49–52.

———— 1959. "Argasun quyurčin iin domog" (The Legend of Argasun Khuurch). In *Mongyol uran jokiyal-un degeji jayun bilig orusibai* (Collection of 100 Wisdoms from the Masterpieces of Mongolian Literature). Ulaanbaatar.

Dashdondog, S. 1965. "Basic Questions of Arts and Culture," *Translations on Mongolia*, 63 (January 12): 25–30.

Dashdorj, D. and S. Tsoodol 1971. *Ardyn duu khögjmiin suu bilegtnüüd* (The geniuses of folk song and music). Ulaanbaatar: State Publishing House.

Dashpürew, D., and S. K. Soni 1992. *Reign of Terror in Mongolia, 1920–1990*. New Delhi: Absecon Highlands.

Dawson, Christopher, ed. 1980. *The Mission to Asia: Narratives and Letters of the Franciscan Missionaries in Mongolia and China in the Thirteenth and*

Fourteenth Centuries. Translated by a Nun of Stanbrook Abbey. London: Sheed and Ward.

Desjacques, Alain 1990. "La dimension orphique de la musique Mongole," *Cahiers de Musiques Traditionnelles* 3: 97–107.

—— 1986. *Notes to Mongolie: musique et chants de l'atltaï*. Orstom-Selaf CETO 811.

Doerfer, Gerhard 1963. *Türkische und mongolische Elemente im Neupersischen: Unter Besonderer berücksichtigung älterer neupersischer Geschichtsquellen, vor allem der Mongolen-und Timuridenzeit*. Band I: Mongolische Elemente im Neupersischen. Wiesbaben: Franz Steiner Verlag GMBH.

Dulam, Sh. 1987. "Conte, chant et instruments de musique: Quelques légends d'origine mongoles" (Stories, song and musical instruments: some origin legends of the Mongols), *Études mongoles* 18: 33–47.

Dulmaa, Sh. 1989. "Morin khuuryn urlag" (The Art of the Horse-head Fiddle), *Zaluu üye* (Youth) 6: 14–15.

Emsheimer, Ernst 1991a. "Earliest reports about the music of the Mongols." In *Studia ethnomusicologica eurasiatica (Festschrift to Ernst Emsheimer on the occasion of his 80th birthday)*, Volume II. Stockholm: Musikhistoriska museet, pp. 227–239.

—— 1991b. "Peter Simon Pallas's Organological and Ethnomusicological Observations among the Kalmyks in the Year 1769—an Ethno-Historical Study." In *Studia ethnomusicologica eurasiatica (Festschrift to Ernst Emsheimer on the occasion of his 80th birthday)*, Volume II. Stockholm: Musikhistoriska museet, pp. 241–262.

—— 1971 [1943]. "Preliminary remarks on Mongolian music and instruments." In *The music of the Mongols, Part I: Eastern Mongolia*, by Henning Haslund-Christensen. New York: Da Capo Press, 69–95.

Enebish, Jambalyn 1991. "Morin khuur" (The Horse-head Fiddle). In *Khögjmiin ulamjlal shinechleliin asuudald* (Problems of the Renewal of the Study of Music). Ulaanbaatar: State Publishing House, 77–85.

—— 1982. "Mongolyn khögjim" (Mongolian Music), *Soyol* 1: 28–32.

Enkhee, L. 1968. "Shine morin khuur" (New Horse-head Fiddle), *Orchin üyeiin Mongol uls* (Contemporary Mongolia) 4 (123): 6–7.

Erdenechimeg, Luwsannorowyn 1994. *Khuuryn tatlaga* (The Fiddle's Tatlaga). Ulaanbaatar.

—— 1993. *Morin khuuryn awiag arga bilgiin onolyn üügnees sudlakh n'* (A study of the sound of the horse-head fiddle from the perspective of the theory of 'arga-bileg'), Ph.D. dissertation. Department of Culture and Art, Mongolian National University of the Arts.

Forsyth, James 1996. *A History of the Peoples of Siberia: Russia's North Asian Colongy 1581–1990*. Cambridge: Cambridge University Press.

Geertz, Clifford 1973. "After the Revolution: The Fate of Nationalism in the New States." In *The Interpretation of Cultures: Selected Essays*. New York: Basic Books, 234–254.

Gilmour, James 1970. *Among the Mongols*. New York: Praeger Publishers.

Ginsburg, Tom 1999. "Nationalism, Elites, and Mongolia's Rapid Transformation." In *Mongolia in the Twentieth Century: Landlocked Cosmopolitan*, edited by Stephen Kotkin and Bruce A. Elleman. Armonk, NY: M.E. Sharpe, 247–276.

Gonchigsümlaa, S. 1961. "Ulaan-baataryn Tukhai Duu (Val's)" (A Song About Ulaanbaatar [Waltz]). Musical notation. Ulaanbaatar.

Grame, Theodore C., and Gen'ichi Tsuge 1972. "Steed Symbolism on Eurasian String Instruments," *The Musical Quarterly* (58 (1): 57–66.

Grant, Bruce 1995. *In the Soviet House of Culture: A Century of Perestroikas.* Princeton: Princeton University Press.

Hamayon, Roberte 1980. "Mongol Music." In *The Grove Dictionary of Music and Musicians*, edited by Stanley Sadie. London: MacMillan Publishers Ltd., 482–485.

Haslund-Christensen, Henning 1971 [1943]. "On the Trail of Ancient Mongol Tunes." *The Music of the Mongols, Part I: Eastern Mongolia.* New York: Da Capo Press, pp. 13–38.

Hasumi, Haruo 1997. "Field Notes: Living on the Steppes." Liner notes for *Mongolia: Living Music of the Steppes, Instrumental Music and Song of Mongolia*, Music of the Earth MCM 3001.

Hobsbawm, Eric 1983. "Introduction: Inventing Traditions." In *The Invention of Tradition.* Cambridge: Cambridge University Press, pp. 1–14.

Hobsbawm, Eric, and Terence Ranger, ed. 1983 *The Invention of Tradition.* Cambridge: Cambridge University Press.

Huc, Évariste Régis, and Joseph Gabet 1928. *Travels in Tartary, Thibet and China, 1844–1846.* Volume One. Translated by William Hazlitt. New York: Harper & Brothers.

Humphrey, Caroline 1992. "The Moral Authority of the Past in Post-Socialist Mongolia," *Religion, State and Society* 20 (3–4): 375–389.

Jackson, Peter 1990. *The Mission of Friar William of Rubruck: His journey to the court of the Great Khan Möngke, 1253–1255.* London: Hakluyt Society.

Jambaldorj, Sumiyagiin 1996. "Morin Khuur" (The Horse-head Fiddle). In *Morin Erdene* (Horse Jewel). Ulaanbaatar: The Mongolian Horse Society, 104–105.

Jamyan, G. 1978. "Atryn öglöö" (Pristine Morning). Musical notation. Ulaanbaatar.

———— *Morin khuuryn surakh garyn awlaga* (The Horse-head Fiddle Study Handbook). Ulaanbaatar: State Publishing House.

Jantsannorow, Natsagiin 1998. Liner notes to *Let the Mount Burkhan Khaldun Bless You!* Admon, Co.

———— 1996. *Mongolyn khögjmiin arwankhoyor khorog (sonatyn allegro)* [Twelve Portraits of Mongolian Music: Sonata's Allegro]. Ulaanbaatar: [No publisher listed].

———— 1989. "Orchin üye khögjmiin urlag" (The Contemporary Musical Arts). In *Mongol Khögjmiin Sudlal* (Mongolian Music Research), Vol. I. Ulaanbaatar, 5–23.

Jenkins, Jean Lynn 1960. "The Morienhur: A Mongolian Fiddle," *Man* 60: 129–130.

Jusdanis, Gregory 2001. *The Necessary Nation.* Princeton: Princeton University Press.

Kara, György 1970. *Chants d'un Barde Mongol.* Budapest: Akadémiai Kiadó.

———— 1967. "Huit Chants Tchakhars," *Acta Orientalia Hungaria* 20 (1): 76–100.

Karpat. Kemal H. 1986. "Introduction: Elites and the Transmission of Nationality and Identity," *Central Asian Survey* 5 (3–4): 5–24.

Khüükhenbaatar, D., and D. Tömörtogoo 1968. *Mongolyn soyol* (Mongolian Culture). Ulaanbaatar: Academy of Sciences.

Kler, Joseph 1947. "The Horse in the Life of the Ordos Mongols," *Primitive Man* 20 (182): 15–25.

Kozlov, Viktor 1988. *The Peoples of the Soviet Union.* Translated by Pauline M. Tiffen. Bloomington: Indiana University Press.

Kraus, Richard Curt 1989. *Pianos and Politics in China: Middle-Class Ambitions and the Struggle over Western Music.* New York: Oxford University Press.

Levin, Theodore 1996. *The Hundred Thousand Fools of God: Musical Travels in Central Asia (and Queens, New York)*. Bloomington: Indiana University Press.

Levin, Theodore and Valentina Suzukei 2006. *Where Rivers And Mountains Sing: Sound, Music, And Nomadism in Tuva And Beyond*. Bloomington: Indiana University Press.

Magban, Sh. 1964. "Cultural Leap-Forward," *Translations on Mongolia* 64 (December 22): 43–48.

Meisner, Maurice 1985. "Iconoclasm and Cultural Revolution in China and Russia." In *Bolshevik Culture*, ed. Abbott Gleason, Peter Kenez, and Richard Stites. Bloomington: Indiana University Press, 279–293.

MFDJA (Mongolian Free Democratic Journalists' Association) 1997. "Morin khuur" (Horse-head Fiddle), *Glimpse at Mongol Culture* 1: 16.

MIAT 1999. "The Horse Fiddle," *Sky Land* (in flight magazine of MIAT Mongolian Airlines) (September-October): 12–13.

——— n.d. "The Tale of an Instrument," *Sky Land* (in flight magazine of MIAT Mongolian Airlines): 9.

——— n.d. *Mongolia: Yesterday and To-Day*. Tientsin: Tientsin Press Print.

——— 1986. *Modern 'Mongol Zurag' Style Painting*. Ulaanbaatar: State Publishing House.

Mongolian People's Revolutionary Party (MPRP) 1971. *Bügd nairamdakh Mongol ard uls 50 jil* (50 Years of the Mongolian People's Republic). Ulaanbaatar.

——— 1966. "Resolution of the 15th Congress of the Mongolian People's Revolutionary Party on the Report of the Central Committee of the MPRP." In *15th Congress of the Mongolian People's Revolutionary Party: Speeches, Reports, Resolutions (June 7–11, 1966)*. Ulaanbaatar: Political Literature Publishing House, 181–209.

Nansalmaa, D. 1987 "Ardyn khögjim" (Folk Music). In *Khalkha ugsaatny züi (XIX-XX zuuny zaag üye)* (Ethnography of the Khalkha, 19th-20th century), Vol. I, edited by S. Badamkhatan. Ulaanbaatar: State Publishing House, 334–357.

Natsagdorj, D. 1989 "My Native Land." In *Modern Mongolian Poetry (1921–1986)*, edited by D. Tsedew. Ulaanbaatar: State Publishing House, 13–14.

——— 1989. "Spring," "Summer," "Autumn," "Winter." In *Modern Mongolian Poetry (1921–1986)*, edited by D. Tsedew. Ulaanbaatar: State Publishing House, 20–23.

——— 1974. "Son of the Old World." In *Mongolian Short Stories*, edited by Henry G. Schwarz. Bellingham: Western Washington State College, 1–3.

Natsagdorj, Ts. 1989. "Simfoniin büteel, önöögiin shaardlaga" (Symphonic works, today's conditions). In *Mongol Khögjmiin Sudlal* (Mongolian Music Research), Vol. I. Ulaanbaatar, 35–41.

Natsagdorj, Sh. 1981. *BNMAU-yn Soyolyn Tüükh (1921–1940)* [Cultural History of the MPR (1921–1940)], Vol. I. Ulaanbaatar: State Publishing House.

Nixon, Andrea 1985. "Historical aspects of Mongolian music." Paper presented at the 7th Asian Music Congress, Ulaanbaatar.

Noll, William 1993. "Music Institutions and National Consciousness among Polish and Ukrainian Peasants." In *Ethnomusicology and Modern Music History*, ed. By Stephen Blum, Philip V. Bohlman, and Daniel M. Neuman. Chicago: University of Illinois Press, 139–158.

Ortner, Sherry B. 1973. "On Key Symbols," *American Anthropologist* 75: 1338–1346.

Otgonsüren D. 1997. "Taniltsuulga: Mongol ulsyn morin khuuri'n chuulga" (An Introduction to the Mongolian State Horse-head Fiddle Ensemble). Ulaanbaatar: Railroad Printing Company.

Oyuunbileg, T. 1998. "N. Jantsannorow: Mongoli'n ikh urlagiin, ikh khögjmiin ankhni' CD gej itgeltei khelj chadna" (N. Jantsannorow: [We] can say with confidence that [this] is Mongolia's first CD of great art and great music), *Zasgiin Gazryn Medee* 173/1125 (August 28): 5.

Pegg, Carole 2001. *Mongolian Music, Dance, & Oral Narrative*. Seattle: University of Washington Press.

———— 1995. "Ritual, religion and magic in West Mongolian (Oirad) heroic epic performance," *British Journal of Ethnomusicology* 4: 77–99.

———— 1992a. "The Epic is Dead, Long-Live the Ülger?." In *Asiatische Forschungen* 120, Fragen der mongolischen Heldendichtung 5, ed. Walther Heissig. Wiesbaden: Harrassowitz Verlag, pp. 194–205.

———— 1992b. "Mongolian conceptualizations of overtone singing (xöömii), *British Journal of Ethnomusicology* 1: 31–54.

———— 1991. "The Revival of Ethnic and Cultural Identity in West Mongolia: The Altai Uriangkhai Tsuur, the Tuvan Shuur and the Kazak Sybyzgy," *Jounal of the Anglo-Mongolian Survey* 12 (1–2): 71–84.

Phillips, E.D. 1969. *The Mongols*. London: Thames and Hudson.

Polo, Marco 1958. *The Travels of Marco Polo*. Translated by Ronald Latham. London: Penguin Books.

Poppe, Nicholas 1979. *The Heroic Epic of the Khalkha Mongols*. Second edition. Bloomington, Indiana: The Mongolia Society, Inc.

Regsüren, D. 1973. *Arkhangai aimgiin tüükh*. Tsetserleg: Arkhangain Ünen.

Revin, V. 1988. "Days of Soviet Culture in Mongolia," *Far Eastern Affairs* 1: 104–113.

Rupen, Robert A. 1964. *Mongols of the Twentieth Century, Part I*. Bloomington: Indiana University Press.

———— 1956. "Cyben Žamcaranovič Žamcarano (1880-?1940)," *Harvard Journal of Asian Studies* 19: 126–145.

———— 1958. "The Buriat Intelligentsia," *Far Eastern Quarterly* 15: 383–398.

Sandag, Shagdariin, and Harry H. Kendall 2000 *Poisoned Arrows: The Stalin-Choibalsan Mongolian Massacres, 1921–1941*. Boulder: Westview Press.

Sanders, Alan J.K. 1996. *Historical Dictionary of Mongolia*. Asian Historical Dictionaries, No. 19. London: The Scarecrow Press, Inc.

———— 1989. "Afterward." In *The Modern History of Mongolia*. London: Kegan Paul International, 425–437.

Santaro, Mikhail 1999. *Morin khuur—Khyalgasny ezerkhigch* (The Horse-head Fiddle—An Oppressor of Strings). Ulaanbaatar: Admon.

Schmidt, Isaac Jacob 1829. *Geschichte der Ost-Mongolen und ihres Fürstenhauses, verfasst von Ssanang Ssetsen, chungtaidschi der Ordus*. St. Petersburg: Gedruckt bei N. Gretsch.

Serruys, Henry 1985. "Music and Song for Animals," *Études mongoles* 16: 61–67.

Shanin, Teodor 1989. "Ethnicity in the Soviet Union: Analytical Perceptions and Political Strategies," *Comparative Study of Society and History* 31: 409–416.

Shirendew, Bazaryn 1997. *Through the Ocean Waves: The Autobiography of Bazaryn Shirendew*. Translated by Temujin Onon. Bellingham, WA: Western Washington University.

Slobin, Mark 1969. *Kirgiz Instrumental Music*. New York: Society for Asian Music.

Smith, Anthony D. 1997. "The 'Golden Age' and National Renewal."' In *Myths and Nationhood*, edited by Geoffrey Hosking and George Schöpflin. New York: Routledge, 36–59.

———— 1984. "National Identity and Myths of Ethnic Descent," *Research in Social Movements, Conflict and Change* 7: 95–130.

Smirnov, B. F. 1975. *Muzika narodnoi mongolii*. Moscow: Muzika.

————1971. *Mongol'skaya Narodnaya Muzika*. Moscow: "Soviet Composer."

—— 1963. *Muzikal'naya kul'tura mongolii.* Moscow: Gosudarstvennoe muzykal'noe izdatel'stvo

—— 1982. "Soyol urlagiin araw khonog" (Ten Days of Culture and Art), *Soyol* 4: 13.

Sterner, G. 1961. "Bloc Coverage of Chinese and Mongolian Celebrations Compared." *Radio Free Europe Evaluation and Analysis Department report 104-4-99* (July 13, 1961). From the Open Society Archives, <http://osaarchivum.org/files/holdings/300/8/3/text/104–4-99.shtml>. Accessed December 20, 2007.

Stump, Carl 1887/1975. "Mongolische Gesänge." In *Sammelbände für vergleichende Musikwissenschaft herausgegeben von Carl Stumpf und Erich Moritz von Hornbostel.* New York: Georg Olms Verlag, pp. 105–112.

Sükhbaatar, Günjiin 1980. *Mongolchuudyn ertnii öwög: Khünnü naryn aj akhui niigmiin baiguulal, soyol, ugsaa garwal (meo IV-me II zuun)* (The Mongolian's ancient ancestors: Khünnü people's economy, social structure, culture and ethnic origins [4th century BC-2nd century AD]). Edited by N. Ser-Odjaw. Ulaanbaatar: Academy of Sciences.

Szynkiewicz, Slawoj 1990. "Mythologized representations in Soviet thinking on the nationalities problem," *Anthropology Today* 6 (2): 2–5.

Tishkov, Valery A. 1992. "Inventions and Manifestations of Ethno-Nationalism in and after the Soviet Union." In *Ethnicity and Conflict in a Post-Communist World: The Soviet Union, Eastern Europe and China,* edited by Kumar Rupesinghe, Peter King, and Olga Vorkunova. New York: St. Martin's Press, pp. 41–64.

Tsedenbal, Yu. 1966. "Report of the Central Committee of the Mongolian People's Revolutionary Party to the *15th Congress of the MPRP.*" In *15th Congress of the Mongolian People's Revolutionary Party: Speeches, Reports, Resolutions (June 7–11, 1966).* Ulaanbaatar: Political Literature Publishing House, 11–114.

Tsend, D. 2000. "'Argasun khorch' (Khuurch)-iin Domog," ('Argasun khorch': a fiddle player's legend) *'Studia litterarum' Tsuwral* 7 (24): 16–20.

Tsendorj, G. 1983. *BNMAU-yn mergejliin khögjmiin khamtlaguud üüsej khögjsön n'* (The origins and development of the Mongolian Peoples Republic's professional music ensembles). Ulaanbaatar: State Publishing House.

Tüdew, L., editor 1983. *Khüükhed-zaluuchuudyn newterkhii toli I* (Children-Youth Encyclopedia I). Ulaanbaatar: State Publishing House.

—— 1986. *Khüükhed-zaluuchuudyn newterkhii toli II* (Children-Youth Encyclopedia II). Ulaanbaatar: State Publishing House.

Tuohy, Sue 1988. *Imagining the Chinese Tradition: The Case of Hua'er Songs, Festivals, and Scholarship.* Ph.D. Dissertation. Indiana University.

Turino, Thomas 2000. *Nationalists, Cosmopolitans, and Popular Music in Zimbabwe.* Chicago: University of Chicago Press.

van Staden, Maya Matthea 1999. Liner notes to *Naaryts biilye (Let's Dance), Mongolyn khuuryn tatlaga.* Ensemble Altai-Hangai. PAN 2061CD.

Vargyas, Lajos 1968. "Performing Styles of Mongolian Chant," *Journal of the International Folk Music Council* 20: 70–72

Vietze, Hans-Peter 1992. *Altan Tobci: eine mongolische Chronik des XVII. Jahrhunderts von blo bzan bstan 'jin.* Tokyo: Institute for the Study of Languages and Cultures of Asia and Africa.

Vladimirtsov, B.Ya. 1983. "The Oirat-Mongolian Heroic Epic," *Mongolia Studies: Journal of the Mongolia Society* 8: 5–58.

Vyzgo, T.S. 1980. *Muzykal'nye instrumenty sredney Azii, Istoricheskie ocherki* (Musical instruments of Central Asia). Moscow: Izdatel'stva 'Muzyka'

Walcott, Ronald 1974. "The Chöömij of Mongolia: A Spectral Analysis of Overtone Singing," *Selected Reports in Ethnomusicology* 2 (1): 54–59

Index

A

Akim, G., 130–133
Altan namar (Golden Autumn), 106, 115
Altan quyur (Golden Fiddle), 128–129
Altan tobch (Golden Summary), 21, 128
Amartüwshin, I., 150–153
Arga-bileg, 130–133, 163n3
Argasun, 123–124, 128–130, 133, 137, 141
Anderson, Benedict, 13–14

B

Badraa, Jamtsyn, 19, 26, 28, 64, 97–99, 100, 103, 106, 126–128
Badrakh, G., 126
Badral, S., 146–148
Baljir, Ya., 148–149
Batchuluun, Ts., 112, 116, 143
Batu Khan, 18
Bawden, Charles, 50, 110
Berlinskii, P., 28, 29, 32, 33, 44, 45, 162n14
biiwaa. See pipa
bowed lutes, 1, 16, 17, 19, 20, 22–24, 27, 39, 62, 65, 70, 78, 93, 124, 125, 130–133, 147; construction of, 25–30, 162nn10–11; cultural attributes of, 30–39; and revolution, 42, 43, 44, 45, 46; *shana-gan khuur* (ladle fiddle), 26, 28, 123–124, 125–126, 128, 133, 161n2; *ikel*, 28, 29, 156–157
Brezhnev, Leonid, 97, 100, 108
Bulag, Chi., 111–115, *116*, 119, 143, 144
Bulag, Uradyn, 111, 114
Buuran, D., 67, 68, 69, 101

C

Carpini, John of Plano, 18
China, 22, 24, 38, 42, 82, 84, 87, 95, 96, 99, 100, 124, 126–128, 143, 156; Chinese cosmopolitanism, 8–9, 161n3; Chinese in Mongolia, 20–21, 29, 32, 39–40, 42, 43, 59, 79, 80, 84, 110; Mongolian fear of, 80, 84,110–111, 112–115, 144–145; Manchu Qing Dynasty, 20–21, 46, 80; Chinese Dynastic histories, 19, 124, 127
Chinggis Khan, 2, 16, 17, 18, 19, 21, 44, 46, 47, 80, 87, 104, 111, 112, 122–123, 124, 128–129, 133, 134, 135, 137, 138, 141; contemporary revival of, 122, 163n2; Chinggis Khan Incident, 94–97; Chinggis Khan Mausoleum, 1–2
Choibalsang, Marshall Kh., 44, 47, 62, 75, 90, 91
Choidog, E., 60, 76, 108
Comaroff, Jean and John, 11
cosmopolitanism, 1, 7–12, 15, 62, 69, 71, 78, 79, 80, 81, 86, 96–97, 132, 134, 142, 146, 157; cosmopolitan nationalists, 12, 13, 15, 69, 74, 79, 89, 96, 99, 100, 105, 120, 145, 149
cultural centers, 13, 14, 48–50, 51–52, 53, 54, 59, 63, 65, 162n5; in Töw province, 66; in Arkhangai province, 149–154, 164n2; in Khowd province, 154–157

D

Damdinsüren, B., 60, 62
Damdinsüren, Ts., 93–94, 96, 98, 106, 128–130

Danzinrabjai, Noyon Khutagt, 130–
    131, 150
Dulam, Sh., 35, 36
Dulmaa, Sh., 117–120

E
Emsheimer, Ernst, 4, 5, 22, 25, 26, 28, 29
Enebish, Jambalyn, 3, 26, 28–29, 34,
    35, 45, 66, 69, 94, 125, 130
Enkhjargal, 35, 69
Erdenechimeg, L., 19, 111, 112, 132,
    133
ethnos, theory of, 77, 78

G
Gaadamba, Sh., 129
Gabet, Joseph, 23
Gankhuyag, Ch., 149–154
Geertz, Clifford, 10, 74, 82
Gilmour, James, 23–24, 25, 28, 29, 30
Ginsburg, Tom, 7–8, 9, 74, 78–79, 92,
    99
Gonchigsümlaa, S., 60, 70, 108

H
Hamayon, Roberte, 5
Haslund-Christensen, Henny, 4, 25, 26,
    28, 29, 39, 40–44, 85–86, 161n8
Hasumi, Haruo, 28
Hobsbawn, Eric, and Terence Ranger,
    11–12
Hsiung-nu. *See* Xiongnu
Huc, Évariste Régis, 23
Humphrey, Caroline, 2, 122, 135

I
invented or imagined traditions, 5,
    6–7, 12–14, 15, 29–30, 70, 99,
    120, 135, 138, 141–142, 149,
    155–157

J
Jamyan, G., 3, 55–57, 62, 66–67, 68,
    70–71, 101, 112, 114, 115, 116,
    120, 137, 140, 141, 143, 148
Jantsannorov, N., 15, 99, 100–120,
    122, 137, 142, 143–145
Japan, 8, 20, 28, 40, 42, 44, 84, 112,
    123, 127, 143, 161n3
Jenkins, Jean Lynn, 4–5, 161n2
Jigmed, 45

K
Kara, Gyorgy, 37, 59, 129–130

Khangal, Z., 107, 109, 142
Khökhöö Namjil, 36–37, 137
Khrushchev, Nikita, 97, 100
Khünnü. *See* Xiongnu
kobys (Kirgiz horse-hair fiddle), 22,
    127–128
Kler, Joseph, 30–31
Kozlov, Viktor, 73–74
Kraus, Richard, 8–9
Kubilai Khan, 19

L
Levin, Ted, 6, 7, 13, 38
Lunar New Year, 2, 23, 32, 35, 121,
    131, 136–137, 140, 164n5
Luwsan, 28, 29, 32–33, 44, 45, 93,
    123, 124

M
Mongol Empire, 16, 17–20, 87, 94,
    122, 124, 129, 135
Mongols:
    Buriat Mongols, 28, 79–83,
    143–144; Kalmyk Mongols,
    21–23, 24, 29; Khalkha Mongo-
    lians, 17, 20–21, 24–25, 26, 29,
    30, 31, 34, 35, 37, 81, 87–88,
    113, 114–115, 124, 134, 149,
    151, 153, 154, 156; Oirat (or
    western) Mongolians, 17, 20–21,
    22, 24, 25, 26, 28, 29, 31, 32,
    33, 34, 35, 37, 38, 126, 153–
    157, 161n3; Inner (or southern)
    Mongolians, 19, 20, 24, 25, 26,
    28, 29, 30, 40–44, 47, 84, 85,
    110–115, 116, 129, 143–145
Mongolian Academy of Sciences, 69,
    82, 94–95, 110–111, 130
Mongolian musical composition,
    60–63, 93, 103, 105–109, 115
Mongolian musical genres:
    ardyn ("modern folk") music,
    14–15, 47–69, 146, 151–152,
    156, 157; *ugsaatny* ("tradi-
    tional") music, 10, 14, 16–46,
    78, 92–93, 98, 117–118, 130–
    132, 136, 139–140, 141–142,
    147–150, 151–154, 155–157;
    songodog (classical) music, 3, 14,
    54, 56, 57–59, 60, 62, 64, 66,
    68–70, 106–109, 142–143, 147
Mongolian musical instruments:
    ewer büree (bull's horn), 58, 64;
    khuuchir (two- or four-stringed

bowed lute), 22, 23, 24, 29, 38, 43, 49, 58, 62, 64, 66, 68, 124, 156, 161n6; *limbe* (flute), 55, 58, 62; *shanz* (plucked lute), 58, 107, 156; *towshuur* (plucked lute), 26, 34, 126, 156; *tsuur* (vertical flute), 20, 28, 35, 156; *yatga* (plucked zither), 20, 22, 58, 66, 68, 107, 142, 153; *yoochin* (hammer dulcimer), 58, 66, 142, 156

Mongolian national musical culture, 2, 3, 6, 14–15, 46, 68–69, 101, 104–105, 106–107, 109, 132, 134, 141–142, 144–145, 157; building of, 47–65, 66

Mongolian national musical institutions: Mongolian Composer's Union, 62–63, 106–107, 116, 152; State Folksong & Dance Ensemble, 2, 57–58, 59, 63, 64, 74, 102, 121, 135, 136, 142, 147–148, 151; State Academic Theater, 57, 58; State Music & Dance College, 54–55, 56, 65, 67, 101, 109, 112, 148; State Musical Instrument Factory, 65, 69, 116–119, 138; State Opera and Dance Theater, 57, 61

Mongolian Peoples Revolutionary Party, 4, 5–6, 7, 8, 9, 15, 44, 45, 47, 48, 49, 50, 51, 52, 53, 54, 55, 59, 62, 63, 65, 66, 68–69, 72, 73, 74, 75, 78, 79, 82, 83–86, 87, 89–92, 93, 94–99, 100–101, 102–106, 108, 110, 115–116, 117, 121, 122, 136, 148, 149, 150, 152, 156

Peoples Revolution of 1921, 1, 3, 5, 15, 17, 24, 44, 45, 47, 48, 57, 62, 72, 73, 74, 75, 79, 82, 83, 84, 85, 86, 88, 89, 91, 92, 93, 95, 100, 104, 106, 120, 122, 124, 155; Mongolian revolutionaries, 46, 74–75; anti-revolutionaries, 44–45, 47, 79, 81–83, 86, 91, 96, 112; pre-Revolutionary society, 1, 9, 12, 14–15, 16–46, 50, 59, 61–62, 77, 93, 98, 121, 123–133, 134, 136, 141, 148

Peoples Revolution of 1990, 1, 2, 3, 5, 6, 72, 104, 106, 121–122, 134, 136, 137, 149–150, 154

Mongolian print, electronic, and broadcast media, 13, 45, 51, 52–53, 57, 98, 102, 119, 121, 123–126, 141, 145, 154, 162n6

Mongolian song, 19, 21, 22, 25, 30, 31, 32, 35, 36, 41, 42, 43, 45, 52, 55, 60, 62, 63, 64, 66, 70, 92, 93, 94, 107, 127, 132, 134, 142, 150, 153; Revolutionary songs, 43, 45, 48, 46, 60, 62, 93; *bogino duu* (short song), 119, 151; *niitiin duu* (common song), 52, 53, 62, 101; *tuuli* (epic song), 23, 32–34, 36, 42, 44, 45, 155, 162n19; *urtyn duu* (long song), 98, 119, 134, 148–149, 151; *zokhiolyn duu* (composed song), 52, 53, 101, 106

Mongolian State Government Palace, 1, 2, 121, 135, 136, 140, 141

Mongolian State Naadam, 2–3, 32, 62, 121, 131, 134–135, 140, 141, 142

Mongolian State Ritual Palace, 137, 140

morin khuur (horse-head fiddle), 1, 2–3, 4–5, 7, 15, 16, 28, 30, 35, 36, 37, 38, 46, 48, 55–57, 58, 64, 66–72, 74, 78, 99, 101, 102, 104, 107, 109, 111–120, 121–145, 146–148, 151, 152, 153; as national symbol, 1, 2, 3, 7, 9, 15, 58, 66, 69–75, 77–78, 87, 109, 115, 119–120, 121, 122, 132, 133, 134, 135, 137, 138, 140–142, 144; modeled after violoncello, 3, 55–56, 58, 67, 142; timbre (or sound color) of, 28–29, 36, 37–38, 56, 64, 123, 142, 147; and sound mimesis, 38–39, 42–43, 162n20; *tatlaga* genre, 31, 153; as a "Great Tradition," 6–7, 13, 14–15, 120; *ikh khuur* (great horse-head fiddle), 58, 64, 118, 142; *dund khuur* (mid-sized horse-head fiddle), 142; *Töriin khan khuur* (or State Sovereign Fiddle), 2, 121, 137–142; Horse-head Fiddle Naadam, 115–120, 122, 137, 143, 144; Horse-head Fiddle Center, 114, 115, 119, 137; Horse-head Fiddle Anthem, 136–137, 140; State Horse-head

Fiddle Ensemble, 2, 102, 114, 121, 142–145
Möngke Khan, 18
Mördorj, L., 58, 60, 62, 108, 162n9

N

Nansalmaa, D., 124–125, 130
Natsagdorj, D., 86–89, 131–132
Noll, William, 13

O

Ochirbat, P., 121, 137, 138, 140

P

Pallas, Peter Simon, 21–22
Parchen, 33, 44
Parliament Building. *See* State Government Palace
Pegg, Carole, 2, 5, 32, 33–34, 45, 140
Pelliot, Paul, 127–128
pipa, 20, 124, 125, 126
Polo, Marco, 18–19, 135

R

Rinchen, B., 97, 98, 106
Rinchino, Elbekdorzhi R., 79, 81, 83–86
Rubruck, William of, 18
Rupen, Robert A., 81
Russia, 3, 7–8, 9–10, 18, 21, 22, 38, 40, 46, 49, 50, 53, 54, 62, 64, 65, 66, 74, 75–79, 80–81, 82, 83, 87, 88, 90–92, 95, 100, 101, 102–103, 104, 105–106, 108–109, 110, 124, 143, 155–156; Russian racism, 9–10, 80–81; Russification, 10, 79–81, 102, 144

S

Sandag, Shagdaryn, 91
Sangrup, 42–44
Santaro, Mikhail, 140
Schnitscher, Christopher, 22, 29
Secret History of the Mongols, 17, 130
Sengedorj, N., 154–157
shamanism, 33, 37, 87, 121
Sharav, B., 107, 140, 142
Shirendew, B., 86, 89–93, 163n4
Smirnov, Boris, 45
Soviet Union, 1, 4, 6, 7, 8, 13, 53, 64, 65, 67, 71, 73, 74, 76, 79,

83, 84, 85, 90, 91, 96, 97, 98, 99, 100, 106, 109, 110, 122, 154; Soviet influence, 1, 3, 4, 5, 6–7, 8, 9, 10, 11, 12, 13, 15, 44–45, 46, 47, 53–54, 62, 64, 65, 67–68, 71–72, 73–79, 81, 82, 83–84, 85, 86, 89, 90–92, 95–96, 97–99, 100–101, 102, 103, 107, 109, 110, 122, 142, 143, 148, 154; Soviet leadership, 4, 8, 9, 44, 54, 86, 95–97, 98, 99, 100, 102, 104, 108
Sükhbaatar, G., 110, 128

T

"Ten Days of Culture and the Arts" Festival, 65–66
Tishkov, Valery, 6, 7
Tömör-Ochir, D., 94–95, 98
Tsedenbal, Y., 51, 53, 65, 73, 90, 91, 94–96, 98, 103, 108
Tsedenbal-Filatova, Anastasya Ivanovna, 102–103
Tsedendorj, M., 1, 131
Tserendorj, Ts., 116, 137, 140, 141
Tserenpil, D., 69, 111, 130
Tuohy, Sue, 13
Turino, Thomas, 10–11, 12

U

Ulambayar, D., 68, 69, 112–114, 115, 116–117, 137–140, 141–142, 143, 144–145
Uzbekistan, 6–7, 19–20

V

van Staden, Maya Matthea, 29, 30, 31, 38
Vladimirtsov, Boris, 32, 33, 44

X

Xiongnu, 110, 124–128, 132, 133

Y

Yarovoi, Denis Vladimirovich, 67–69, 120, 138
Yadamsüren, Ü., 139, 147

Z

Zhamtsarano, Tsyben Zhamtsaranovich, 79–86, 122, 163n3